LENNON AND MCCARTNEY

Lennon and McCartney: Painting with Sound explores the work of two of the most influential composers of the twentieth century. Five decades after the breakup of The Beatles, the music of John Lennon and Paul McCartney continues to fascinate and inspire. Evidence suggests that their uniquely eclectic approach can be traced back to the Liverpool College of Art. Following that idea, this book explores the creative dialogue between John Lennon and Paul McCartney, both with The Beatles and on their own, that grew out of that early influence. The book is presented in three parts: Part I, Stretching the Canvas, considers the Liverpool College of Art as the backdrop for John and Paul's early collaborations with painter and musician Stuart Sutcliffe. This is followed by discussions of select works created by the band between 1962 and 1969. Part II, Extending the Space, provides an exploration of the long-distance creative dialogue between Lennon and McCartney as demonstrated in their respective solo recordings of the 1970s. Part III, New Colours, considers the final works of the Lennon and McCartney creative dialogue, as well as various McCartney solo projects released in the years that followed Lennon's death in 1980. Here, the focus is on Paul's development as a painter, its effect on his creativity, and his subsequent efforts to establish the Liverpool Institute for Performing Arts as a world-class arts conservatory.

Thomas MacFarlane has written various books and articles on popular music. His research explores connections between music composition, sound recording, and human culture. He taught music composition and arts analysis courses at New York University where he also helped create a programme in popular music studies. Currently, he works as a writer, musician, and composer.

LENNON AND MCCARTNEY

Painting with Sound

Thomas MacFarlane

Routledge
Taylor & Francis Group

LONDON AND NEW YORK

Cover image: © shutterstock

First published 2023
by Routledge
4 Park Square, Milton Park, Abingdon, Oxon OX14 4RN

and by Routledge
605 Third Avenue, New York, NY 10158

Routledge is an imprint of the Taylor & Francis Group, an informa business

British Library Cataloguing-in-Publication Data
A catalogue record for this book is available from the British Library

Library of Congress Cataloging-in-Publication Data
A catalog record has been requested for this book

ISBN: 978-1-032-29139-0 (hbk)
ISBN: 978-1-032-22460-2 (pbk)
ISBN: 978-1-003-30021-2 (ebk)

DOI: 10.4324/9781003300212

Typeset in Bembo
by Newgen Publishing UK

For Mae Orsini and Paul Horan

CONTENTS

ACKNOWLEDGMENTS

I would like to extend my grateful appreciation to the following scholars and friends whose insights and suggestions were essential to the completion of this study: Ken Scott, Olivier Julien, Michael McLuhan, Emily Parsons, Joe Norman, Sheila Eyre, Alex Butler, Eddie Carlson, Paul Horan, Dan Veksler, Patrick Hagan, and Dalton Corr. Also, my very special thanks to Heidi Bishop for her feedback and encouragement during the writing process. Finally, I would like to thank my family and friends for their continued love and support.

EXAMPLES

ACKNOWLEDGMENTS

INTRODUCTION

Painting with Sound

Lennon and McCartney: Painting with Sound explores the work of two of the most influential composers of the twentieth century. Five decades after the breakup of The Beatles, the music of John Lennon and Paul McCartney continues to fascinate and inspire. Their innovative recordings helped to redefine musical practice and became a touchstone for what author Ian MacDonald has described as 'a new "simultaneous" popular art'.[1] Evidence suggests that their uniquely eclectic approach can be traced back to the Liverpool College of Art. Following that idea, this book explores the creative dialogue between John Lennon and Paul McCartney, both with The Beatles and on their own, that grew out of that early influence.

The book is presented in three parts: Part I, Stretching the Canvas, considers the Liverpool College of Art as the backdrop for John and Paul's early collaborations with painter and musician Stuart Sutcliffe. This is followed by discussions of select works created by the band between 1962 and 1969. Part II, Extending the Space, provides an exploration of the long-distance creative dialogue between Lennon and McCartney as demonstrated in their respective solo recordings of the 1970s. Part III, New Colours, considers the final works of the Lennon and McCartney creative dialogue, as well as various McCartney solo projects released in the years that followed Lennon's death in 1980. Here, the focus is on Paul's development as a painter, its effect on his creativity, and his subsequent efforts to establish the Liverpool Institute for Performing Arts as a world-class arts conservatory.

Lennon and McCartney: Painting with Sound employs Songscape analysis, a multi-layered approach designed to engage a recorded work on its own terms. Songscape builds from the notion that a music recording is essentially a hybrid art form comprising traditional musical elements and spatial effects generated by electronic means. Songscape emerged from the desire to find effective ways to explore and discuss a relatively new art form. It is presented here as one possible approach.

DOI: 10.4324/9781003300212-1

Readers are encouraged to modify it as they see fit or to come up with alternate approaches of their own.

Songscape was first developed for my book *The Music of George Harrison* (2019) and consists of three levels of discussion regarding the recorded work. The first level focuses on the song from the perspective of the composer in which the raw materials are considered in terms of how they might be formed into musical structures. This is followed by a consideration of the track itself, derived from relevant accounts of the recording process. Songscape then concludes with an interpretation of the spatial imagery evident on the finished song/track. The process also allows for the consideration of entire albums as virtual galleries of recorded sound.

Songscape is employed here to explore selected songs/tracks from The Beatles catalogue, as well as the respective solo catalogues of John Lennon and Paul McCartney. These were chosen on the basis of how well they represented significant aspects of the creative dialogue carried on between the two artists, both with The Beatles and on their own. This selection is not intended to be definitive and readers are encouraged to consider other candidates that may fit well within the proposed model. Finally, it should be noted that the goal of this study is not to reduce or to explain. Instead, it is hoped that *Lennon and McCartney: Painting with Sound* will help generate new insights into a complex and compelling creative process.

Note

1 Ian MacDonald, *Revolution in the Head: The Beatles' Records and the Sixties* (London: Vintage, 2008), 23.

PART I
Stretching the Canvas

1

ART PROJECTS

Our story begins at the Liverpool College of Art, which was located at 68 Hope Street, directly adjacent to the Liverpool Institute High School for Boys on Mount Street. Although these two buildings originally comprised one institution, they would later be split off into two separate schools.[1,2] In the mid-twentieth century, the curriculum offered at the college was typical of art schools of the time. Students were tutored and judged on such skills as Free Drawing, Colour Schemes, Graining, Stencilling, Painting, Lining, and Lettering. They would also study Drawing from Nature and the Grammar of Heraldry.[3]

In contrast with the free-spirited approach often associated with arts education, the regimen at the college was evidently quite demanding. Rod Murray, who began his studies in September 1956, described the rigours of the weekly schedule:

> The college week was very structured, almost like school, with mornings and afternoons broken down into classes for the basics, life drawing and anatomy, structure in nature (taught by Alfred K. Wiffen), perspective drawing, the basics of sculpture and modelling plus weekly composition exercises in drawing and painting set either in the area close to college or in the local parks and docks. These would be exhibited at the end of the week and a critique given by Arthur Ballard.[4]

Soon, a young man would arrive who would create quite a stir. This new student was clearly talented, but also rebellious and undisciplined. Thus, he must have found the schedule described above to be rather challenging. Nevertheless, he would go on to become one of the most celebrated and successful students in the school's long and illustrious history – and he never even earned a degree ...[5]

DOI: 10.4324/9781003300212-3

John Lennon

John Winston Lennon arrived at the Liverpool College of Art in September 1957.[6] He clearly had a lot to offer, but his unique array of talents and interests seemed to fall between the cracks of the curriculum as it existed in those days. In his *History of Liverpool Regional College of Art, 1825–1970* (1985), author Colin Morris described the disconnect between the stated goals of the curriculum and Lennon's unique talents and abilities:

> Measured against the standards demanded by the course, Lennon's early efforts fell short. Yet [Arthur] Ballard found 'this notebook full of caricatures – of myself, the other tutors, the students – all done with descriptions and verse, and it was the wittiest thing I'd ever seen in my life'. Here was a student with an unusual talent, and there was no way the Ministry of Education could give it the stamp of approval; John Lennon failed his Lettering exam.[7]

The notebook Ballard seems to be referring to here is an instalment of *The Daily Howl*, a work that John self-published regularly for the amusement of his friends and fellow students.[8]

June Furlong, a model at the college for many years, remembered John Lennon well. During a session in which she posed nude for a life-drawing class, John challenged conventional expectations by drawing her wristwatch, and nothing else.[9] She described how their friendship evolved:

> When he came in for a class, he'd pull his chair right up close to me and we'd talk, talk, talk for the whole time – about art, about the colleges where I'd worked in London and all the artists I'd met. And there was something about him you couldn't help but take notice of, even though no one seemed to think his work was much good.[10]

Furlong's feelings about John seem typical of a general view about him among faculty and staff. The sense one gets is that he was considered to be rather special, but in a way that couldn't easily be defined. Thus, it may have been difficult to determine exactly how he might be helped to grow and develop at the College. Soon, however, he would meet a fellow student who would be able to take him to the next creative level.

Stuart Sutcliffe

Students from the art college would regularly meet at Þe Cracke, a pub located at 13 Rice Street just off Hope Street. There, they could drink, let off some steam, and share ideas.[11] Even today, a visitor to the pub is likely to find someone willing to engage in discussions regarding the direction of art, changing political systems, and the economic realities of the modern world. It was there that Bill Harry, an aspiring writer and fellow student at the college, introduced John Lennon to someone who would come to exert a considerable influence on him. That student's name was Stuart Sutcliffe.[12]

Born in Edinburgh on 23 June 1940, Sutcliffe was a gifted artist who had arrived at the college the previous year.[13] He would, in effect, take John under his wing and mentor him not only in the fine arts but in a variety of other subjects as well. As author Philip Norman described it: 'His [Lennon's] friendship with Stuart Sutcliffe amounted to a one-man degree course, even if largely conducted in student flats and smoky bar-parlors'.[14] In spite of its informal nature, John was very receptive to the tutorial provided by Stuart, as Rod Murray pointed out: 'I think John looked up to him as a mentor in art, and also in general knowledge about things. And he admired Stuart's talent as an artist'.[15]

Through his work as a painter, Stuart had a connection to the cultural trends that were driving contemporary art at the time. In an article for the book *Stuart Sutcliffe: A Retrospective* (2008), critic Donald Kuspit outlined Stuart's influences:

> Stuart Sutcliffe's Abstract Expressionism belongs to the wave of post-World War II Expressionism that emerged in Europe in the aftermath of its collapse. Appearing first in Cobra (1948–51), and variously known as *l'art Informal* (intuitive art), *un art autre* (an other art or outsider art), and *tachisme* (the art of spotting, blotting, or staining), it was an assertion of energy and spontaneity.[16]

The connection that Kuspit makes here between Sutcliffe's approach to painting and the Cobra movement is particularly interesting. In fact, it may help to explain the remarkably diverse nature of The Beatles' subsequent creative output. The name 'Cobra' abbreviates and combines the names of the cities of Copenhagen, Brussels, and Amsterdam. The group was formed in 1948 by Asgar Jorn, Karel Appel, Corneille, Jean Atlan, and Pierre Alechinsky.[17] In the book *The Cobra Movement in Postwar Europe: Reanimating Art* (2021), author Karen Kurczynski describes the group's intentions:

> Cobra wanted to animate art as a living force in society, not a 'dead' object in a museum but a site of connection among people – especially those excluded from recognition by the art world ... The Cobra group animated a network of creative actors who brought their experiments into the public sphere in various ways, rethinking not only the object of art, but the exhibition, the film screening, the public lecture, the artist's book, and the journal as creative interventions.[18]

James Paul McCartney

Next door to the art college was the Liverpool Institute and High School for Boys. Paul McCartney had become a student there in September 1953.[19] Seemingly destined for a career as a teacher, Paul was a gifted musician who would soon be writing songs of his own. Moreover, he also showed talent as a graphic artist and would later win a prize for a picture he would paint of St Aidan's church in Liverpool.[20] He didn't really take much interest in his schoolwork, but one teacher did manage to make an impression on him: 'There was nobody until my English teacher [the inspirational Alan Durband] started to show me fun bits of literature and that to me is the whole secret of everything. I've been on that trail ever since'.[21]

As the years progressed, McCartney's reputation as a musician tended to walk ahead of him. On 6 July 1957, he was taken by a mutual friend to see John Lennon who was playing with his band at a church fete in Woolton. Although Lennon's guitar skills were limited, McCartney was impressed with his voice and his stage presence. He was also taken with the way in which John improvised lyrics to 'Come Go with Me' by the Del-Vikings.[22] Following the performance, he was introduced to John and demonstrated his own skills as a singer and guitarist. John was suitably impressed and even though McCartney was a bit younger, he asked him to join the band. Paul soon agreed, and the two became senior partners in a project that would ultimately become known as The Beatles.[23]

McCartney's proximity to the art college made it possible for him and John to regularly develop their skills as performers and pop composers. During Lennon's tenure, the president at the college was William L. Stevenson.[24] Colin Morris describes how he was inadvertently made aware of John and Paul's musical activities:

> William Stevenson's office frequently resounded to the regular thump of guitars and tapping feet in the room upstairs during the lunch breaks as Lennon extended his other talent with a schoolboy called Paul McCartney who used to sneak into the college from the Institute High School next-door.[25]

Paul had also begun working on the Quarrymen line-up, gradually replacing those members who were there, not because of their musical skills but rather because they were friends with John.[26] Since neither he nor Lennon were accomplished enough for the job of lead guitarist, Paul began to lobby for his friend George Harrison to fill the spot. A fellow student at the Institute, George was a talented musician but he was also very young. Despite this, John was gradually won over. Now, with the core members in place, they began the gruelling process of trying to become a professional group.[27]

One of the lingering problems for the band involved the question of who was going to be the steady bassist. As confirmed six-string guitarists, Lennon, McCartney, and Harrison had all resisted taking on the role. Then, in 1959, Sutcliffe submitted one of his works for The John Moores Liverpool Exhibition 2. Entitled *Summer Painting*, it was among those subsequently chosen to be featured at the Walker Art Gallery.[28] John Moores himself was so impressed by the painting that he purchased it for the sum of £65. Of course, this was all seen as a blessing by the members of the band since it would now enable Sutcliffe to purchase a bass guitar. At the urging of John, Paul, and George, he promptly did so, began to learn the instrument, and soon joined the band.[29]

The Dissenters

Meanwhile, back at Þe Cracke, another new group was forming. On an evening in June 1960, John Lennon, Stuart Sutcliffe, Bill Harry, and Rod Murray attended a poetry reading that, as it turned out, would help determine their creative paths in the years to come. After the reading, they gathered at the pub to discuss what they'd heard. This event is now commemorated with a plaque at the pub that reads as follows:

> In June 1960 these 4 art students attended a poetry reading by Royston Ellis (The 'Paperback Writer' in Paul McCartney's song 1966); Ellis's work was heavily influenced by Allen Ginsberg and other Americans. Afterwards, the 4 came here to discuss what they'd heard. They were unimpressed and decided to put Liverpool 'on the map' each in their own way as 'The Dissenters'; The rest is ...[30]

The Beatles were continuing to develop as performers and songwriters, and their identity as a creative force on the scene was becoming more widely known. As a result of this growing notoriety, John was asked to pen an article for Bill Harry's new arts paper, *Mersey Beat*. The piece he created was published in 1961 as 'Being A Short Diversion On The Dubious Origins Of Beatles (Translated From The John Lennon)'. There, he answered the question of just how the band got their distinctive and unusual name: 'It came in a vision – a man appeared on a flaming pie and said unto them "From this day on you are Beatles with an 'A'". "Thank you, mister man", they said, thanking him'.[31] In point of fact, it was Sutcliffe and Lennon who came up with the name the previous year.[32]

Hamburg

During the summer of 1960, the band began travelling to Hamburg, Germany for a series of club engagements. As a result of these demanding gigs, they would deepen their musical skills just to survive the rigours of this new environment. In addition to advancing the band musically, the Hamburg experience also extended their education in the fine arts. In *Many Years from Now* (1998), Barry Miles points out that upon their arrival in Hamburg, 'two members of The Beatles were still technically at Liverpool College of Art'.[33] This was quickly recognized by Astrid Kirchherr and Klaus Voormann, two members of the Hamburg arts community, who came to embrace The Beatles as colleagues and friends.[34]

Stuart Sutcliffe seemed to benefit the most from this new environment. He was still the bass player, but his work as a painter really seemed to blossom and mature within the context of the vibrant European arts scene. Donald Kuspit describes how the new cultural environment seemed to feed the young artist's work:

> Germany was where the action was – where the contradictions of life, the simultaneity of disintegration and reintegration, the aura of violence and

hope, were at their most intense. It was this intensity that Sutcliffe captured in his own relentlessly intense art.[35]

Ultimately, Sutcliffe decided to remain in Germany and continue his art studies there. This made sense because although he loved the band, it was generally understood that his real passion was for painting. He began studying with Eduardo Paolozzi at the Hamburg School of Art and also became seriously involved with Astrid Kirchherr with whom he was planning to start a new life. Sadly, this was not to be. Following a period of ill health, Stuart died from a seizure at the age of twenty-one.[36] In *The Making of a Modern University: Liverpool John Moores University* (2017), authors Roger Webster and Shonagh Wilkie provide an overview of Sutcliffe's accomplishments as an artist and the importance of his influence:

> He left behind a 600-piece body of work – an extensive portfolio by any standards – and was recognised as one of the pioneers in the new concept of pop art. He was both a highly regarded painter and a precocious stylist with his 'James Dean' image, quite radical in the traditional duffle-coated art school circles.[37]

Naturally, the loss of their friend was devastating for The Beatles. Lennon, in particular, was inconsolable.[38] The group carried on, but it must have been clear in the wake of Sutcliffe's death that his sensibility and influence had been a critical factor in their development as a band. Soon, however, they would receive news that would ultimately validate their friend's belief in their talent and potential. Their manager, Brian Epstein, contacted them to let them know that he had secured an audition for the group at EMI Studios. They were expected to report there on 6 June 1962 to meet with George Martin.[39]

Abbey Road

As one approaches 3 Abbey Road, one notices that the surrounding area has become one of London's most popular landmarks. On a warm summer's day, one can encounter tourists from all over the planet queuing up to be photographed in the simple act of crossing the street. Passing motorists wait patiently as they do so. Gradually, one begins to realize that these are fans who are attempting to recreate the cover of an album that was released in 1969.[40] Behind them is the building in which that album was recorded: Abbey Road Studios.

One is immediately struck by the subtle charm of the building itself. Nestled in the heart of a sedate residential neighbourhood in St John's Wood, this most famous of recording studios is decidedly humble in appearance. As Brian Southall pointed out, this was evidently the intention from the start.

> The work to convert a detached London residence into a recording studio took two years to complete and involved the development not just of 3

Abbey Road but adjoining land as well ... In just under two years 3 Abbey Road was transformed into the world's largest building devoted exclusively to gramophone recording – without the average passer-by even noticing the difference.[41]

The modest exterior veils a remarkable history concerning the diverse artists who have worked there since the studio first opened its doors in 1931.[42] That list includes Sir Edward Elgar, Noël Coward, Fats Waller, Arturo Toscanini, Glenn Miller, Gracie Fields, Peter Sellers, The Goons, and Beyond the Fringe, to name a few.[43]

The Beatles arrived at Abbey Road, then called EMI Studios, in 1962. By then, they had become seasoned performers and had already worked with some very big names. This, however, was different. During an interview with author Mark Lewisohn in 1988, Paul McCartney shared his impressions of the remarkable environment:

> I loved it. I loved the variety of artists that went there. These days you go to a recording studio and you tend to see other groups, other musicians, because that's where the industry is now, that's where the money is. But then you'd see Sir Tyrone Guthrie, Barenboim ... You'd see classical sessions going on in number one – we were always being asked to turn down because a classical piano was being recorded in number one and they could hear us.[44]

During their audition, The Beatles had initially impressed producer George Martin with their personalities as much as their music.[45] As a result, he agreed to sign them up. Together, he and the band produced a promising single released later that year to moderate success. Their next project involved recording a full-length album to capitalize on the success of their second single, 'Please Please Me'. This turned out to be the breakthrough that The Beatles and Martin had been waiting for. The second side of the LP opened with the song that had been their first single.

'Love Me Do'

The Beatles' first musical offering was a near-skiffle song entitled 'Love Me Do'. The opening section employs the kind of relationship between melody and bass that Paul had used in his first composition, 'I Lost My Little Girl'.[46] This new song, however, contains a much longer musical line. The effect is enhanced by the vocal harmonies of John and Paul. Together, their voices create curious geometric patterns that seem to hang in space like a mobile as the song unfolds. Another important factor is the way John and Paul simultaneously hit strong notes in their respective ranges during the song's climactic moment. Finally, there is the harmonica played by John that suggests the influence of 'Hey! Baby' by Bruce Channel.[47]

'Love Me Do' was recorded in EMI Studio Two on 4 and 11 September 1962. The musicians on the track were John Lennon (vocals, harmonica); Paul McCartney (vocals, bass); George Harrison (guitar); Ringo Starr (drums, tambourine); and Andy

White (drums). The reason two drummers are listed here is that George Martin was not confident in Ringo's abilities during the initial session on 4 September and decided to hire a professional studio drummer for the remake recorded on 11 September.[48] Early pressings of the single feature Ringo, while the version that appears on the *Please Please Me* LP has Andy White on drums and Ringo on tambourine.[49] There was also another last-minute change to the song's arrangement that was due to the limitations of the recording process as it existed in 1962.

In live performance, John would sing the song's climactic hook line, but would abruptly cut it short in order to play the song's distinctive harmonica riff. On hearing this effect, George Martin was not amused and suggested that Paul sing the line so that the melody could overlap with the harmonica riff. McCartney later described how intimidating this particular experience was for him: 'We were doing it live, there was no real overdubbing, so I was suddenly given this massive moment, on our first record, no backing, where everything stopped, the spotlight was on me ... I was terrified'.[50]

'Love Me Do' suggests the beginnings of an eclectic approach to composition. As already mentioned, the song seemed influenced by skiffle, a unique brand of folk music that was popular in Great Britain in the 1950s. The acoustic guitars and harmonica certainly suggest a folk band playing enthusiastically at a local club. There are also elements of American country music in the two-part harmony vocals. Together, these qualities suggest an international cultural space in which elements from diverse sources can be blended together to great effect.

'Please Please Me'

Side one of The Beatles' first LP closed with the song that had been their second single. In fact, as previously mentioned, the song's commercial success was the impetus behind the entire LP project. Originally conceived by Lennon as a tender balled in the style of Roy Orbison, the song had been reworked, at producer George Martin's request, into an energetic pop-rock song. It effectively recycled elements from 'Love Me Do' such as the striking vocal harmonies and the signature harmonica line, but these were now nested within a structure that indicated a new ease with musical form. The song's chord structure was also adventurous in a manner that suggested where the band would be going on their next LP, *With The Beatles* (1963).

'Please Please Me' was recorded in EMI Studio Two during an evening session on 26 November 1962. The musicians on the track were John Lennon (vocals, guitar, harmonica); Paul McCartney (vocals, bass); George Harrison (guitar); and Ringo Starr (drums). Unlike 'Love Me Do', Lennon's harmonica line was recorded separately as an overdub, giving greater flexibility and control over the final sound. Also, Ringo had now become firmly established as The Beatles' drummer, so there was no need for a session player.[51]

The space created for 'Please Please Me' suggests that The Beatles were becoming more and more comfortable at EMI Studios. Their first single, although impressive, seemed somewhat tentative in its approach to the studio space. Here, the band seems completely at ease. As a result, their work begins to take on a new dimension. Throughout the track, they seem to be painting the space with musical sound.

'There's a Place'

The penultimate track on The Beatles' first LP was another Lennon–McCartney original. Inspired by a lyric from the Leonard Bernstein/Stephen Sondheim musical *West Side Story*, the new song was called 'There's a Place'. The song was among those that created an interesting contrast with 'Love Me Do' in that the guitars heard on the track are electric rather than acoustic. There is also an intriguing ambiguity concerning the identity of the melodic line, as McCartney later pointed out: 'We both sang it. I took the high harmony, John took the lower harmony or melody. This was a nice thing because we didn't actually have to decide where the melody was till later'.[52]

'There's a Place' was the first song recorded during The Beatles' marathon session to complete their first LP on 11 February 1963. Evidently realizing that they might be creating a lasting document of their work thus far, The Beatles opted to skip their lunch break and continue rehearsing. That afternoon, just as they had done on 'Please Please Me', they added a harmonica overdub to 'There's a Place'. The difference in audio quality is striking. The harmonica seems to be resonating within a much larger space, and this greatly enhances the effect of the take they had recorded earlier that day.[53]

As compared with 'Love Me Do', the space created for 'There's a Place' suggests a new maturity. While the earlier track could be said to feature a child's view of the world, this time we get a grittier sense of things as seen by a young man coming of age. The song narrates his struggle to maintain a connection with the youthful interior space that is the source of his creativity. The now-primitive timbre of the electric guitars seems to suggest the murky waters of a busy shipping lane. A young man growing up in such an environment might well wonder what his prospects could be.

Studio Two

The room that would come to seem like The Beatles' own private workshop at EMI was called Studio Two. Like the building's exterior, the space has a disarmingly humble quality. The walls are painted white and feature cloth bags hung at intervals around the room to enhance the sound. These were originally filled with eel grass, until that was later deemed a fire hazard and replaced. Fluorescent lighting can give the room a harsh, business-like quality. However, when lit softly, it takes on a cosy quality that recalls the comforts of a quiet evening at home.[54]

One of the most interesting qualities of Studio Two is how the space seems to radiate the ambience of an art studio. Spatially, it seems reminiscent of the painting studios at the Liverpool College of Art.[55] One might not be surprised to see a group of students walk into the room and set up their easels to paint. A model, perhaps June Furlong herself, would soon follow and the class/session would begin. The difference, of course, is that while a painting studio is built to maximize the presence of natural light, a recording studio must focus on sound.

Sitting and listening in Studio Two, one notices that the soundspace seems soft. Music that is created here seems gently cushioned by the room's architectural design. The recordings that immediately come to mind are those created by artists such as Ray Noble and Al Bowlly in the 1930s. The dreamlike quality of those sounds would be right at home. Their gentle, dance-like gestures would sit very comfortably within the space of Studio Two.[56]

During their recording career, The Beatles inhabited this studio. In a sense, the room seemed to become a second home for them. It allowed them to evolve their musical ideas while at the same time connecting with the memories of the various artists mentioned earlier who had worked there throughout the years. In *The Poetics of Space* (1958), Gaston Bachelard described the connections between our stored memories and the spaces we inhabit:

> Not only our memories, but the things we have forgotten are 'housed'. Our soul is an abode. And by remembering 'houses' and 'rooms', we learn to 'abide' within ourselves. Now everything becomes clear, the house images move in both directions: they are in us as much as we are in them.[57]

'It Won't Be Long'

The opening cut of The Beatles' next LP sounds more like a 45-rpm single than an album track, and with the benefit of hindsight, one can see why. By now, the band was becoming very adept with the techniques that can be used to generate interest in a pop song. Previously, this was observed in relation to the two-part melody line of 'There's a Place'. They were also becoming skilled in the art of using a listener's expectations as a guide for how they might better craft their musical structures. 'It Won't Be Long' finds The Beatles creating another compelling ambiguity, this time regarding the identity of the various sections of the song.

The Beatles choose to open the song with what seems like a chorus, but which has here been repurposed to function as a kind of fanfare introduction to get the listener's attention. When we next hear this idea, it is as a contrast to the song's primary section, which features a uniquely crafted harmonic progression that is rather unusual for pop songs of that era. The song also features a third contrasting section that is very chromatic and seems related to the song's lyrical coda. Each of these sections can seem too well balanced in that they are each distinctive enough to become the song's primary focus. This may be the reason 'It Won't Be Long' was not ultimately chosen as a single; the song lacks the necessary hierarchy that can create a contour between the various sections within a piece.

'It Won't Be Long' was recorded in EMI Studio Two on 30 July 1963. The Beatles completed ten takes of the song between 10:00 am and 1:30 pm. They returned to the song later that day and completed various takes and edit pieces, from which the final version of the song would be assembled. The day turned out to be extraordinarily productive. In addition to 'It Won't Be Long', The Beatles recorded five additional album tracks.[58]

In keeping with the feelings described in the lyrics, the space of 'It Won't Be Long' is decidedly compressed. The singer's sense of urgency is palpable as the band urges him on to continue with his tale of impending reunion with his loved one. The pressure is lifted briefly during one of the song's contrasting sections, but this relief is short-lived. We quickly find ourselves back in the high-pressured landscape of desire as the singer continues to tell his tale. The scene ultimately resolves in a descending coda in which it seems clear that the love he has been missing will soon be restored.

'All My Loving'

The third track on side one of *With The Beatles* was a McCartney song called 'All My Loving'. Here, Paul had produced what is arguably the band's most accomplished example of musical alchemy to date. 'All My Loving' consists of two main sections, plus a solo interlude for the guitar that is built on standard blues changes. Rhythmically, 'All My Loving' combines elements of big band jazz and country swing, which is deftly blended to create something that is decidedly new. It also serves to release the tense longing of Lennon's character that had driven the narrative of 'It Won't Be Long'.

People tend to forget how important it was for groups like The Beatles to gain approval from the previous generation. This applies to how listeners might respond to the group's musical ideas. It also connects at the professional level in which established artists may or may not give their seal of approval. In the case of 'All My Loving', listeners responded to the band's custom musical blend with enthusiasm. As it turns out, the professional approval of the song was subtle, but no less enthusiastic.

In 1964, Herb Alpert & The Tijuana Brass released the LP *South of the Border*. One of the tracks featured was an instrumental cover of 'All My Loving'.[59] During the intro, the arrangement pointed out something very interesting regarding the musical pedigree of The Beatles' song. Herb Alpert began with a short melodic fragment derived from McCartney's opening vocal line. He then followed this with a brief melodic quote from Frank Sinatra's 1954 recording of Cole Porter's 'I Get a Kick Out of You'.[60] This quote seems to be pointing listeners to The Beatles' own evident reference to Sinatra's recording. In the process, Alpert seems to suggest that Tin Pan Alley, Frank Sinatra, and American jazz are all important antecedents to The Beatles.

'All My Loving' was the final track recorded on 30 July 1963 in EMI Studio Two. It was completed immediately following the session for 'It Won't Be Long'.[61] The players on the track were Paul McCartney on bass and double-tracked vocals; John Lennon on rhythm guitar and backing vocals; George Harrison on lead guitar and backing vocals; and Ringo Starr on drums.[62] Evidently, the long day of recording

(10:00 am to 11:00 pm) had warmed up the band considerably. Their fluid performance on 'All My Loving' is among their very best.

The space of 'All My Loving' sounds compressed in a manner similar to 'It Won't Be Long'. Like that song/track, the opening phrase emerges suddenly, followed by the full band bursting through. The difference here seems to be rooted in the rhythm. For all its tension, the underlying swing pattern iterated prominently by McCartney's bass line and Lennon's dynamic rhythm guitar effectively releases this tension as the song unfolds. In that sense, the open space in which the electric guitar plays a solo seem like a proper respite or reward.

'Not a Second Time'

Lennon's new track 'Not a Second Time' seems a perfect blend of songwriting and studio craft. His primary section features a truncated version of an early rock and roll progression under a vocal line that dances melodically throughout. The contrasting section seems to separate form and function with a progression that shouldn't work, but does. The sheer intensity of the vocal delivery is the key attraction here. As the song unfolds, Lennon's double-tracked vocal line seems less like a musical element and more like a force of nature.

'Not a Second Time' was recorded in EMI Studio Two during an all-day session on 11 September 1963. Recorded during the evening session (7:00–10:15 pm), the track was completed in a relatively straightforward manner.[63] The musicians on the basic track were John Lennon on vocals and acoustic guitar; Paul McCartney on bass; George Harrison on acoustic guitar; Ringo Starr on drums; and George Martin on piano.[64] As mentioned above, Lennon's double-tracked vocal is truly remarkable. It creates a unique effect that would be further explored and developed during the following year.

The space of 'Not a Second Time' suggests an interesting balance between the modern and the primitive. The song's musical materials are so basic and timeless that they could work in a variety of different contexts. At the same time, the recording technique used to develop these materials was state-of-the-art for its time. Thus, the space of 'Not a Second Time' involves both the past and the present. In the process, it engenders a near-universal charm that allows listeners to access it from various directions.

In the earlier description of Songscape, it was asserted that this approach also allows for the considerations of entire LPs as virtual galleries of recorded sound. With regard to The Beatles' first two albums, we will have to make a slight adjustment. The reason is that *Please Please Me* and *With The Beatles* are half-galleries at best. The modern term is EP (extended play) rather than LP. This is understandable since The Beatles were still trying to find their feet in terms of song quantity. Thus, the first two Beatle albums rely on a balance of original songs from the band and cover versions derived from their stage repertoire. In that regard, it might be useful to consider the two together as a single LP.

Discounting the four songs derived from singles that were added to *Please Please Me*, we have a total of twelve original tracks. Listening to these chronologically, in the order in which they were originally presented on their respective albums, one notices a move from performance mode towards something that more closely resembles a painter's stance. Brushstrokes are added to existing recordings and the auditory space is expanded accordingly. In effect, The Beatles and their collaborators were beginning to paint with sound.

In His Own Write

Over the next few months, The Beatles would bounce across contemporary culture at a dizzying pace. They would soon embark on a series of promotional appearances in America that would increase their visibility and boost their appeal. After that, the band would return to Britain to begin making their first feature-length film. Naturally, they were expected to compose music for the project, and they happily obliged. First, however, one of the composing Beatles would embark on a new career as a published author.

Actually, Lennon's new career wasn't quite so new. As previously mentioned, he had been self-publishing his own works since the mid-1950s. This, however, had basically been a hobby through which he would amuse himself, his friends, and his bandmates.[65] Now, he drew on some of that material to create a delightful collection of poems, stories, and caricatures called In His Own Write. His literary voice suggested a wide variety of influences from Lewis Carroll to Edward Lear to James Joyce. Actually, in a curious twist, it turns out that Lennon had never read Joyce, as he himself pointed out: 'so the first thing I do is buy Finnegans Wake and read a chapter and it's great, you know, and I dug it and I felt as though, "Here's an old friend"'.[66]

No one really expected The Beatles' first film to be anything more than a jolly jukebox musical. Instead, they surprised everyone by producing what may be one of the most important films of the early 1960s. Director Richard Lester and playwright Alun Owen had crafted a world that was perfectly suited to The Beatles' unique comic sensibilities. Throughout, they employed surrealistic touches that challenge the logic of linear narrative while also highlighting the band's natural anarchic wit. It is interesting to consider how the film's dialogue suggests the tone of In His Own Write.

In one memorable scene, John encounters a young woman in the hall of a television studio. The woman is delightfully played by Anna Quayle. She recognizes him but can't seem to determine exactly who he is. John continually denies that he is the person she believes him to be. Gradually, we come to understand that Anna seems to have mistaken John Lennon for himself!

'Things We Said Today'

As mentioned, The Beatles had agreed to compose music for their first film. They would now seize the opportunity to create an entire album of songs composed by John Lennon and Paul McCartney. Gauging by who was singing lead vocal on a given track, John Lennon dominates the collection with nine tracks, plus one written for George in the style of 'Do You Want to Know a Secret?'. Paul sings lead on three exceptional songs that continue to expand on the notion of what might be possible on a pop record. One of these was a haunting piece called 'Things We Said Today'.

Here, McCartney effectively sets up his easel and begins to work. 'Things We Said Today' presents a portrait of a rainy day. In this portrait, however, cloudy skies can quickly be transformed into revitalizing sunlight through moves to the relative major and parallel major keys. In this regard, the song seems somewhat experimental for its time. Ultimately, however, it could be seen as an antecedent for works such as 'Bus Stop' by The Hollies and 'No Milk Today' by Herman's Hermits.

The recording of 'Things We Said Today' was completed in EMI Studio Two on 2 June 1964. The session during which the song was recorded took place between 2:30 and 5:30 pm.[67] The musicians on the track were Paul McCartney (vocals, bass); John Lennon (acoustic guitar, piano); George Harrison (lead guitar); and Ringo Starr (drums, percussion). According to Mark Lewisohn, the piano played by Lennon was ultimately omitted from the mix. However, some of its sounds were picked up by other microphones, so it is still audible on the final version of the track.[68]

As previously mentioned, the song seems to create a rendering of a rainy day. The acoustic guitar part suggests intermittent thunder and reinforces the notion that the weather is changeable and often threatening. In the foreground are two melancholy lovers who seem to be thinking philosophically about the nature of their relationship. Gradually, one can perceive a blurred distinction between foreground (lovers) and background (weather). Ultimately, both are seen as one, existing together within an essential cycle.

'Can't Buy Me Love'

One of the most memorable sequences in *A Hard Day's Night* depicts the band frolicking in a field outside the TV studio where the film is set. The score for this sequence was a new song from McCartney called 'Can't Buy Me Love'. Based largely around blues changes in C major, the song creates an infectious drive that seems part folk and part country swing. As on 'It Won't Be Long', the contrasting section is repurposed here as an introduction to great effect. Building on 'All My Loving', McCartney continues to develop his skills as a composer and performer.

The recording of 'Can't Buy Me Love' took place at EMI Path & Marconi Studios in Paris. The session took place on 29 January 1964 and was booked primarily to record German-language versions of 'I Want to Hold Your Hand' and 'She Loves You'. However, during the session, the band also quickly dashed off a very efficient recording of 'Can't Buy Me Love'.[69] The players were Paul McCartney on vocals and bass; John Lennon on acoustic guitar; George Harrison on lead guitar, and Ringo Starr on drums.[70] Additional mixes of the song were created at EMI Studios on 26 February 1964.[71]

Although 'Can't Buy Me Love' draws on blues, folk, and country sources, the space created on the recording seems most closely connected with the kind of folk music popular in the early 1960s. The acoustic guitar, bass, and light drums drive the action throughout. Harrison punctuates on electric guitar but seems very careful in his articulations so as not to disturb the overall sound. McCartney's vocal, the most clear-cut pop element at work here, glides over the top of the soundscape with ease. Along the way, he supplies painterly melodic brushstrokes that suggest elements of the various musical sources mentioned above.

'A Hard Day's Night'

Author Ian MacDonald pointed out that Ringo Starr was the source of the title of The Beatles' first film. Ringo reportedly used the phrase to describe an especially taxing day on the film set. MacDonald also mentions that the phrase appears (in slightly altered form) in John's book *In His Own Write*, published a few days after.[72] In 'Sad Michael', one finds the line, 'He'd had a hard days night that day'.[73] Whatever the provenance of the phrase, it had now become the name of the film. Thus, Lennon and McCartney were promptly asked to write a title song. The piece they created, although made on demand, remains one of the most memorable in their catalogue.

'A Hard Day's Night' featured John and Paul in contrasting sections. Lennon's section was blues-based with subtle alterations suggesting a modern influence on the form. McCartney's was more folk derived and featured secondary chords throughout. Both sections are activated by the rhythmic intensity of the performance. There is also a strikingly original opening chord cluster – but more on that later.

'A Hard Day's Night' was recorded in EMI Studio Two on 16 April 1964. The song was completed during a session that took place between 10:00 am and 1:00 pm.[74] Track 1 featured the entire band. John and Paul's vocals were simultaneously added to Track 2. The lead vocals were then doubled on Track 3 with a cowbell played by Ringo Starr and bongos played by engineer Norman Smith. George Martin (piano) and George Harrison (guitar) then recorded a half-speed solo onto the remaining track (Track 4), along with additional flourishes by each that were added to the song's intro (Martin) and coda (Harrison).[75]

The key to understanding the spatial imagery of 'A Hard Day's Night' seems to be the harmonic cluster that introduces the song/track, album, and film. This unique chord seems to transcend tonal function in order to foreground the qualities of sound itself. In the process, it manages to simultaneously exist across multiple media formats: song, album, and film. The end result is a kind of mixed-media gallery. The use of the chord at the very beginning of the film is particularly intriguing.

The opening image of *A Hard Day's Night* is monochromatic, suggesting that we may be watching newsreel footage. The image appears a fraction of a second before the chord cluster is heard. The pole of a street lamp divides the image just to the right of centre. On the left, we see George Harrison and John Lennon running along the sidewalk towards the viewer. Behind them is a group of girls who are also running and seem determined to catch them.

To the right of the street lamp is a line of cars parked at the curb. Beyond the parked cars are more people running and seemingly trying to join in with those chasing John and George. Until now, we have only heard the chord cluster resonating through the space of the recording and the image. Now, as Lennon's vocal signals the beginning of the song, the running figure of Ringo Starr emerges from behind and between Lennon and Harrison. As he runs, he accidentally trips Harrison and the two tumble down to the pavement.

As mentioned, the image appears first and is followed quickly by the chord. Thus, our eyes seem to tell us that the chord we hear has somehow been generated by the image. However, we also know that in keeping with the differing speeds of light and sound, the chord may well be the source of the image but is naturally heard later. This playful juxtaposition of sight and sound generates a remarkable amount of energy. As a result, one begins to wonder if the entire film that follows may well be rooted in this dance of the senses.

Earlier, it was asserted that the opening chord of the song/track, album, and film seemed to transcend tonal function. How, then, should one regard this unique cluster? Perhaps it could be viewed as a brushstroke bridging multiple forms. This may be why it was necessary to liberate the chord from a purely tonal context. It needed to move freely through the various art forms on offer, while also subtly partaking of each. In the process, it unifies song/track, album, and film in one bold and sweeping gesture.

Notes

1 Paul Du Noyer, *Conversations with McCartney* (New York: The Overlook Press, 2016), 52.
2 C.W. Hale, *A Short History of the Origins of Art and Design Further Education in Liverpool* (pamphlet) 1977 (courtesy of the archives of John Moores University).
3 *The National Painters' And Decorators' Joint Education Committee of England and Wales, 1954 Examinations And Competition, Results & Examiners' Reports*, 40 Kings Street West, Manchester 3 (courtesy of the archives of John Moores University).
4 Matthew H. Clough and Colin Fallows (eds.), *Stuart Sutcliffe: A Retrospective* (Liverpool: Victoria Gallery & Museum, Liverpool University Press, 2008), 16.
5 Philip Norman, *John Lennon: The Life* (Toronto: Anchor Canada, 2009), 190.
6 Mark Lewisohn, *Tune In: The Beatles All These Years, Volume 1* (New York: Crown Archetype, 2013), 142.
7 Colin Morris, *History of Liverpool Regional College of Art, 1825–1970* (1985. MPhil thesis. Housed in Special Collection), 158 (courtesy of the archives of John Moores University).
8 Mark Lewisohn, *Tune In: The Beatles All These Years, Volume 1* (New York: Crown Archetype, 2013), 69.
9 Roger Webster and Shonagh Wilkie, *The Making of a Modern University: Liverpool John Moores University* (London: Third Millennium Publishing, 2017), 38 (courtesy of the archives of John Moores University).
10 Philip Norman, *John Lennon: The Life* (Toronto: Anchor Canada, 2009), 130.

11 Mark Lewisohn, *Tune In: The Beatles All These Years, Volume 1* (New York: Crown Archetype, 2013), 189.

12 Philip Norman, *John Lennon: The Life* (Toronto: Anchor Canada, 2009), 135.

13 Mark Lewisohn, *Tune In: The Beatles All These Years, Volume 1* (New York: Crown Archetype, 2013), 276.

14 Philip Norman, *John Lennon: The Life* (Toronto: Anchor Canada, 2009), 133.

15 Mark Lewisohn, *Tune In: The Beatles All These Years, Volume 1* (New York: Crown Archetype, 2013), 190.

16 Matthew H. Clough and Colin Fallows (eds.), *Stuart Sutcliffe: A Retrospective* (Liverpool: Victoria Gallery & Museum, Liverpool University Press, 2008), 8.

17 Harold Osborne (ed.), *The Oxford Companion to Twentieth-Century Art* (New York: Oxford University Press, 1981), 116.

18 Karen Kurczynski, *The Cobra Movement in Postwar Europe: Reanimating Art* (New York and London: Routledge, 2021), 3.

19 Mark Lewisohn, *Tune In: The Beatles All These Years, Volume 1* (New York: Crown Archetype, 2013), 63.

20 Brian Clarke, *Paul McCartney: Paintings* (Boston, MA: Bulfinch Press, 2000), 29.

21 Paul Du Noyer, *Conversations with McCartney* (New York: The Overlook Press, 2016), 23.

22 Mark Lewisohn, *Tune In: The Beatles All These Years, Volume 1* (New York: Crown Archetype, 2013), 128–129.

23 Philip Norman, *John Lennon: The Life* (Toronto: Anchor Canada, 2009), 107–109.

24 C.W. Hale, *A Short History of the Origins of Art and Design Further Education in Liverpool* (pamphlet) 1977 (courtesy of the archives of John Moores University).

25 Colin Morris, *History of Liverpool Regional College of Art, 1825–1970* (1985. MPhil thesis. Housed in Special Collection), 185 (courtesy of the archives of John Moores University).

26 Philip Norman, *John Lennon: The Life* (Toronto: Anchor Canada, 2009), 138–139.

27 Philip Norman, *John Lennon: The Life* (Toronto: Anchor Canada, 2009), 136–137.

28 Mark Lewisohn, *Tune In: The Beatles All These Years, Volume 1* (New York: Crown Archetype, 2013), 237–238.

29 Philip Norman, *John Lennon: The Life* (Toronto: Anchor Canada, 2009), 168.

30 Author's notes from a visit to Þe Cracke (21 January 2020).

31 Mark Lewisohn, *Tune In: The Beatles All These Years, Volume 1* (New York: Crown Archetype, 2013), 422–424.

32 Mark Lewisohn, *Tune In: The Beatles All These Years, Volume 1* (New York: Crown Archetype, 2013), 291–292.

33 Barry Miles and Paul McCartney, *Many Years from Now* (New York: H. Holt, 1997), 13–14.

34 Philip Norman, *John Lennon: The Life* (Toronto: Anchor Canada, 2009), 210–212.

35 Matthew H. Clough and Colin Fallows (eds.), *Stuart Sutcliffe: A Retrospective* (Liverpool: Victoria Gallery & Museum, Liverpool University Press, 2008), 9.

36 Philip Norman, *John Lennon: The Life* (Toronto: Anchor Canada, 2009), 262.

37 Roger Webster and Shonagh Wilkie, *The Making of a Modern University: Liverpool John Moores University* (London: Third Millennium Publishing, 2017), 42 (courtesy of the archives of John Moores University).

38 Philip Norman, *John Lennon: The Life* (Toronto: Anchor Canada, 2009), 266.

39 Philip Norman, *John Lennon: The Life* (Toronto: Anchor Canada, 2009), 268.

40 'The Abbey Road Crossing – Has It Moved?', Beatles in London, 20 August 2021, https://beatlesinlondon.com/the-abbey-road-crossing-has-it-moved.

41 Brian Southall, *Abbey Road: The Story of the World's Most Famous Recording Studios* (Cambridge: P. Stephens, 1982), 17.

42 Mark Lewisohn, *The Beatles Recording Sessions* (New York: Harmony Books, 1988), 4.

43 Author's notes from The Abbey Road Lectures 2018 (3 August 2018).

44 Mark Lewisohn, *The Beatles Recording Sessions* (New York: Harmony Books, 1988), 8.

45 Mark Lewisohn, *The Beatles Recording Sessions* (New York: Harmony Books, 1988), 17.

46 'South Bank Show Originals Paul McCartney'. YouTube. Junio Estevez, 11 July 2014. https://youtu.be/rZDq6LSx5vA?t=301.

47 Ian MacDonald, *Revolution in the Head: The Beatles' Records and the Sixties* (London: Vintage, 2008), 58.

48 Mark Lewisohn, *The Beatles Recording Sessions* (New York: Harmony Books, 1988), 20.

49 Ian MacDonald, *Revolution in the Head: The Beatles' Records and the Sixties* (London: Vintage, 2008), 59.

50 Mark Lewisohn, *The Beatles Recording Sessions* (New York: Harmony Books, 1988), 6.

51 Ian MacDonald, *Revolution in the Head: The Beatles' Records and the Sixties* (London: Vintage, 2008), 62.

52 Barry Miles and Paul McCartney, *Many Years from Now* (New York: H. Holt, 1997), 95.

53 Mark Lewisohn, *The Beatles Recording Sessions* (New York: Harmony Books, 1988), 24.

54 Author's notes from The Abbey Road Lectures 2018 (3 August 2018).

55 Author's notes from a visit to the Liverpool Institute for Performing Arts (LIPA) (20 January 2020).

56 Author's notes from The Abbey Road Lectures 2018 (3 August 2018).

57 Gaston Bachelard, *The Poetics of Space* (Boston, MA: Beacon Press, 1994), xxxvii.

58 Mark Lewisohn, *The Beatles Recording Sessions* (New York: Harmony Books, 1988), 34.

59 'South of the Border – Herb Alpert, Herb Alpert & the Tijuana Brass: Songs, Reviews, Credits'. AllMusic, 31 December 1969. www.allmusic.com/album/mw0000198338.

60 'Songs for Young Lovers'. Accessed 19 March 2022. www.loc.gov/static/programs/natio nal-recording-preservation-board/documents/SongsForYoungLovers.pdf.

61 Mark Lewisohn, *The Beatles Recording Sessions* (New York: Harmony Books, 1988), 34.

62 Ian MacDonald, *Revolution in the Head: The Beatles' Records and the Sixties* (London: Vintage, 2008), 95.

63 Mark Lewisohn, *The Beatles Recording Sessions* (New York: Harmony Books, 1988), 35.

64 Ian MacDonald, *Revolution in the Head: The Beatles' Records and the Sixties* (London: Vintage, 2008), 97.

65 Mark Lewisohn, *Tune In: The Beatles All These Years, Volume 1* (New York: Crown Archetype, 2013), 69.

66 'John Lennon – Full Interview, 6/6/1968 – [Remastered, HD]'. YouTube. fshoaps, 15 August 2021. https://youtu.be/A8UXCAKVZT8?t=339.

67 Mark Lewisohn, *The Beatles Recording Sessions* (New York: Harmony Books, 1988), 44.

68 Ian MacDonald, *Revolution in the Head: The Beatles' Records and the Sixties* (London: Vintage, 2008), 120.

69 Mark Lewisohn, *The Beatles Recording Sessions* (New York: Harmony Books, 1988), 38.

70 Ian MacDonald, *Revolution in the Head: The Beatles' Records and the Sixties* (London: Vintage, 2008), 104.

71 Mark Lewisohn, *The Beatles Recording Sessions* (New York: Harmony Books, 1988), 40.

72 Ian MacDonald, *Revolution in the Head: The Beatles' Records and the Sixties* (London: Vintage, 2008), 115.

73 John Lennon, *In His Own Write* (London: Jonathan Cape, 1964), 35.

74 Mark Lewisohn, *The Beatles Recording Sessions* (New York: Harmony Books, 1988), 43.

75 Kevin Ryan and Brian Kehew, *Recording The Beatles: The Studio Equipment and Techniques Used to Create Their Classic Albums* (Houston, TX: Curvebender Publishers, 2006), 381.

2

CREATIVE SPACES

1964 was turning out to be a banner year for The Beatles. Their fame was continuing to grow and they were in the process of becoming a truly global phenomenon. Along the way, they deepened their cultural presence through a variety of media forms: records (albums and singles); radio broadcasts; television appearances (*The Ed Sullivan Show*); books (*In His Own Write*); and cinema (*A Hard Day's Night*). Success in any one of these fields would have been impressive enough, but by the middle of 1964, The Beatles seemed to have conquered them all.

Throughout, they had kept up a busy schedule of live performances. In addition to their appearances in North America earlier in the year, they now embarked on a five-country tour that coincided with the release of *A Hard Day's Night* and its accompanying LP.[1] This, of course, did not leave much time for composing new material. However, as per their custom, they planned to record a new LP for the coming holiday season.[2] The collection they offered was the somewhat sarcastically titled *Beatles for Sale*.

In addition to the various career milestones mentioned above, the soundtrack album for *A Hard Day's Night* had been a first in that it had consisted entirely of original songs by John Lennon and Paul McCartney. Now, with new songs in limited supply, they returned to the format of their first two albums by including a mixture of new, original tracks along with cover songs derived from their onstage repertoire. In a further response to the daunting time constraints, the band now began to turn EMI Studios into a creative workshop, as Ringo Starr describes:

> We did it all in there: rehearsing, recording and finishing songs ... The ideas were there for the first verse, or a chorus, but it could be changed by the writers as we were doing it, or if anyone had a good idea. The first form in which I'd hear a newly written tune would be on the guitar or piano. It's

DOI: 10.4324/9781003300212-4

great to hear the progression through takes of various songs. They'd change dramatically.[3]

Beatles for Sale laid down a series of creative threads that the band would continue to explore over the next two years. One of these was the artwork featured on the album's foldout cover and inner-sleeve design. There, the band was photographed in front of a collage of famous British and American screen actors. This idea would be developed further on the elaborate sleeve design for *Sgt. Pepper's Lonely Hearts Club Band* (1967). So, although it may initially seem like a necessary holding action, *Beatles for Sale* is an important step towards the progressive Beatles LPs that would follow.

'No Reply'

Beatles for Sale opens with the distinctive voice of John Lennon. Unlike the openings of *Please Please Me*, *With The Beatles*, and *A Hard Day's Night*, this one is noteworthy for its delicate touch. In support of Lennon's vocal is a gently strummed acoustic guitar. Such sounds had certainly featured on earlier Beatle tracks. Now, however, they seem an increasingly important part of the band's musical fabric. As the delicacy gives way to a sense of urgency, it becomes clear that The Beatles are now in the process of blending their trademark power-pop approach with an emerging folk-rock aesthetic.

Continuing the move towards structural variety last heard on key tracks from *A Hard Day's Night*, the opening track of *Beatles for Sale* also features a varied and interesting approach to musical form. Following on the technique employed on 'I'll Be Back', the song features two contrasting sections to the main idea. In the book *Many Years from Now* (1998), McCartney describes the song's collaborative origins as well as his and Lennon's approach to the creation of contrasting sections:

> We wrote 'No Reply' together but from a strong original idea of his. I think he pretty much had that one, but as usual, if he didn't have the third verse and the middle eight, then he'd play it to me pretty much formed, then we would shove a bit in the middle or I'd throw in an idea.[4]

'No Reply' was recorded in EMI Studio Two on 30 September 1964. In keeping with the band's tight schedule, the song was finished in just one session. Understandably, the effort to produce top-notch performances under pressure was taking its toll, as Mark Lewisohn points out: 'John's voice was beginning to wilt after the long day in the studios, so Paul was left to do the high register harmonies behind John's lead vocal'.[5] McCartney's vocal is of particular interest here. In each contrasting section of 'No Reply', his voice often attains a siren-like effect that emphasizes the emotional urgency experienced by the main character. Another more obscure source for this effect might be its uncanny similarity to the sound of a jet engine, a feature of the high-powered world in which The Beatles now moved.

Another interesting aspect of 'No Reply' is how it highlights The Beatles' increasing awareness regarding the power of dramatic space. The text of the song focuses on the anxieties of the main character who sees his lover in an intimate embrace with someone else. The subtle harmonic inflections of the chord progression do much to effectively convey the sorrow inherent in this situation. In addition, one also gets the sense that through the recorded performance of the song, the drama described in the text is being staged withing the space of EMI Studio Two. This quality was enhanced at the remix stage when a liberal amount of echo was added to the lead vocal.[6]

'I'll Follow the Sun'

Before The Beatles had become a serious professional project, Paul McCartney had been writing songs for several years on his own. One of the earliest of these was 'I'll Follow the Sun', a gentle folk ballad in a standard form that nevertheless features some remarkable compositional brushstrokes. In an interview with author Mark Lewisohn, Paul described the song's origin: 'Yes, I wrote that in my front parlour in Forthlin Road. I was about 16 … I remember standing in the parlour, with my guitar, looking out through the lace curtains of the window, and writing that one'.[7]

'I'll Follow the Sun' establishes its tonal centre with a quick move from the tonic to the subdominant chord, and back again. The main section then commences with a melodic line that ascends in fourths over a bass line that begins its descent from scale degree five. As it continues to unfold, the melody unexpectedly finds a note from the blues scale. This surprise lends the progression a distinctive tonal colour. In the process, the relationship between the melody and bass creates a fascinating geometric pattern that seems to play with the listener's expectation of balance and symmetry.

The recording of 'I'll Follow the Sun' was begun in EMI Studio Two on 18 October 1964.[8] The instrumentation for the track is another step forward in that the recording process itself suggested new sounds and new arrangements. As previously noted, the band was now moving increasingly towards the use of non-amplified instrumentation. This trend seems consistent with the kind of varied approach to sound that was very much on their minds in 1964, as McCartney points out: 'We didn't want to fall into the Supremes trap where they all sounded rather similar, so to that end, we were always keen on having varied instrumentation'.[9]

The spatial imagery created for 'I'll Follow the Sun' seems consistent with the ambience and mood of a painter's studio. The personal reflection conveyed through the lyric suggests a painter's preoccupation with natural light and the movement of the sun. Despite the melancholy outlook of the singer's current relationship, he knows that his art is rooted in nature and thus will always sustain him. In Chapter 1, it was asserted that McCartney had effectively set up his easel with 'Things We Said Today'. Here, he continues to develop his studio as a space that is connected to the natural world.

Peter and Dudley

In a thread that tracks back to *In His Own Write* and *A Hard Day's Night*, Lennon was asked to appear as a special guest on a new television show starring Peter Cook and Dudley Moore, one half of the legendary comedy troupe, Beyond the Fringe. Their new programme, called *Not Only... But Also*, had its premiere on BBC 2 on 9 January 1965.[10] During the broadcast, John recited excerpts from his book and also appeared in a filmed dramatization of his poem, 'Deaf Ted, Danoota, and Me'. While Dudley Moore narrates the poem in voiceover, Lennon, Norman Rossington, and Moore frolic merrily in a pastoral setting. When viewed over fifty years later, this short film still manages to raise a laugh.

In 1965, The Beatles attempted to repeat the threefold strategy of the previous year with the publication of Lennon's second book, the release of a new Beatles film, and a collection of songs for the accompanying soundtrack LP. Each of these elements were very successful in their own right, but the project did not achieve the balance and unity evident in *A Hard Day's Night*. As previously noted, the language of Lennon's first book had informed the world of *A Hard Day's Night* (1964). This was not the case with Lennon's new book (*A Spaniard in the Works*), in which the author largely had to begin anew with fresh material:

> The second book was more disciplined because it was started from scratch. They said, 'You've got so many months to write a book in'. I wrote *In His Own Write* – at least some of it – while I was still at school, and it came spontaneously. But once it became: 'We want another book from you, Mr. Lennon', I could only loosen up to it with a bottle of Johnnie Walker, all I thought, 'If it takes a bottle every night to get me to write ...'[11]

The Beatles' second film was a humorous spoof in the style of James Bond. Directed again by Richard Lester, *Help!* revels in the frenzied mood and imagery of 1960s pop culture. The band members, as always, are charismatic as four eccentric rock musicians, but they often seem strangely disconnected from the fantasy-driven narrative.

Unlike the film, the soundtrack album for *Help!* appears to have been firmly under The Beatles' control. Here, they manage to build effectively on the creative momentum generated by their previous LPs. Apart from two cover songs, one retrieved from the band's stage act and the other a current favourite of Ringo's, the album consists of twelve Beatle originals including two songs by George Harrison, who was just beginning to emerge as a composer in his own right. As on *Beatles for Sale*, the acoustic guitar continues to emerge as an important part of The Beatles' sound. In that regard, two new works by Lennon and McCartney are of particular interest.

'You've Got to Hide Your Love Away'

The move the band was making towards the acoustic sounds of folk music was at least partly attributable to the influence of Bob Dylan. The band had met Dylan the previous year and he is credited with having introduced them to the sub-stance that had made the filming of *Help!* such a hazy, somewhat lazy experience. More importantly, Dylan's approach to the quality of his lyrics had already been expanding the scope of The Beatles' songwriting, as McCartney himself says: 'We were great great admirers of Dylan. We loved him and had done since his first album which I'd had in Liverpool. John had listened to his stuff and been very influenced'.[12]

'You've Got to Hide Your Love Away' employs a folk-song model that The Beatles proceed to colour with a somewhat unusual harmonic choice for the style. Specifically, this involves the use of a chord built on the flat seventh during the song's opening section. This section alternates with another that consists entirely of primary chords. The presence of the flat seventh chord during the main section generates a curious momentum, and, as a result, no further sections are required. Instead, The Beatles opt to repurpose the opening section as a coda with a new melodic line played on alto and tenor flutes. The colours created here, combined with the chord choice described above, adds enough weight to carry the song for-ward towards a very convincing and satisfying conclusion.

Recording for 'You've Got to Hide Your Love Away' commenced in EMI Studio Two on 18 February 1965. The instrumentation follows the approach taken for 'I'll Follow the Sun' in that the accent is on acoustic guitars and Lennon's lead vocals. On that track, Ringo had simply tapped his knees; here, he plays brushes (presum-ably on his drum kit) and tambourine as well. 'You've Got to Hide Your Love Away' also features musician Johnnie Scott on the alto and tenor flutes featured during the song's coda. Remarkably, this was the first time an outside musician had appeared on a Beatles recording since Andy White had filled in for Ringo Starr during the sessions for 'Love Me Do' and 'P.S. I Love You' in 1962.[13]

The space created on 'You've Got to Hide Your Love Away' neatly combines exterior and interior settings. At the outset, the singer turns his face to a wall, but we are not exactly clear on whether he is inside or outside. The tone, however, suggests an interior in which he seems to have learned a truth he did not want to know. Then, he shouts like a folk singer or town crier to get our attention, suggesting that he is now outside and being counselled on private matters in a public space. Thus, over the course of the song/track we seem to be moving from interior to exterior space and back again.

'Yesterday'

Paul McCartney's most famous contribution to the *Help!* sessions began as a melody that came to him in a dream. He later described how he then began trying to work out chord changes along with a suitable lyric. Initially, he was unable to come up with either words or title, so he settled on the humorous, improvised fragment, 'Scrambled eggs, oh, my baby, how I love your legs'. Concerned that he might be unconsciously transcribing an existing work, he played the song for various friends and colleagues. He was assured by all that the tune was good, sounded like him, and thus was probably okay.[14]

In the book *Many Years from Now* (1998), McCartney's colleague and co-author Barry Miles commented on the song's provenance by making an interesting observation regarding the relationship between dreams and the creative process:

> Freud suggests that dream formation is determined in part by the previous day's activities and it would be interesting to know what Paul had been listening to the night before. The melody of 'Yesterday' may be a dream-work transformation of something completely unlikely, from a television theme song to a classical piece; or, more probably, a musical idea he had already been playing with but which emerged from the dream state so different that it was unrecognisable.[15]

Building on Barry Miles' astute observations, we can now reasonably speculate on the origins of what was to become Paul's best-known song.

'Yesterday' may fit the definition of what has come to be known as a contrafact; that is, a composition based on, or derived from, a pre-existing musical work. It applies particularly well to the jazz process in which a soloist will create a set of improvisations over a set of existing chord changes. These can then become the foundation for a new composition, such as Charlie Parker's 'Ornithology', which is based on the chord progression from 'How High the Moon'. The term 'contrafact' was introduced by jazz scholars in the late twentieth century. However, it has yet to gain widespread acceptance by jazz practitioners.[16]

In terms of its underlying chord progression, 'Yesterday' suggests possible connections with 'Confirmation', a song composed by Charlie Parker in 1945, but not officially recorded by the artist until 1953.[17] Parker's tune takes an unembellished approach to the relative minor key in that it uses a proper chord progression to move there from the original tonic chord. Paul seems to have adapted this harmonic motion to the idiom of the acoustic folk guitar and thus provided a more rustic quality to the overall sound. Curiously, Parker's 'Confirmation' may itself be a contrafact based on the song 'Twilight Time' released by The Three Suns in 1944.[18] In addition, prior to its presumed influence on 'Yesterday', the song had already been employed by John Coltrane as the basis for '26–2', recorded in 1960.[19]

'Yesterday' presents an evident imbalance in its musical structure in that it contains a seven-measure opening section that then appears four times over the course of the song. Considered in relation to the eight-measure contrasting section that appears twice, the missing measures tease the listener's expectations for symmetry and balance.[20] Ultimately, the expected balance is achieved, and was, in fact, already happening as the song unfolded. In the introduction to 'Yesterday', we hear two measures of McCartney strumming a tonic chord on his acoustic guitar. If we then fast forward to the coda, we notice that it also contains two measures, which outline a graceful descent into a plagal cadence. Taken together, the introduction and coda comprise all of the missing measures for each appearance of the opening section.

The most unique musical feature of 'Yesterday' is the instrumental backing track behind McCartney and his acoustic guitar. Building on the previous innovation of using flutes to colour the coda of 'You've Got to Hide Your Love Away', George Martin here created a detailed score for string quartet. 'Yesterday' was recorded in EMI Studio Two on 14 June 1965. During that session, which lasted from the afternoon into the evening, McCartney performed three songs in markedly different styles. First, he led the band through the irresistible 'I've Just Seen a Face'. This was then followed by 'I'm Down', a raucous rocker in garage-band style. Finally, with just his acoustic guitar for accompaniment, McCartney recorded 'Yesterday'.[21]

Building on the idea of the power of dramatic space in a sound recording, the staging of 'Yesterday' is remarkably effective. McCartney's lyric describes the mysterious loss of a loved one in which there is no clear explanation as to why that person had to leave. The imbalances in the musical setting suggest the sense of emptiness created by the loss. The singer contemplates this emptiness as he tells us the story. Lest the mood become too tragic, there is also a clear sense that balance can be restored via the missing elements (measures) embedded in the experience itself.

'In My Life'

In the autumn of 1965, The Beatles were at it again. Following the release of *Help!*, they had embarked on another tour of America, this one far more extensive than the last. Thus, once again, there was not much time available to produce new material. However, as had been the case the previous year, they were obliged to record another new album in time for the holiday season. Thus, on 12 October 1965, they met at EMI Studios to begin work on the album that was to be called *Rubber Soul*.

The new album would complete a technological journey begun with *Please Please Me* (1963) in which the band, with George Martin, had attempted to recreate the performance space of a ballroom or theatre. *With The Beatles* (1963) then continued with the presentation of high-powered performances, this time compressed so that the music seems to be taking place much closer to the listener. *A Hard Day's Night* (1964) and *Beatles for Sale* (1964) further explored the idea of intimacy through the expanded use of acoustic guitars. *Help!* (1965) also added acoustic guitars into the mix, and further expanded the palette by employing orchestral instruments that were well beyond the scope of then-contemporary rock and roll. Now, with *Rubber Soul*, they would present listeners with a gallery of intimate spaces that also managed to preserve the sense of urgency evident in their previous works.

The creative distance that The Beatles had travelled since 1963 was truly remarkable. Naturally, this development was not lost on their contemporaries in popular music. Brian Wilson of The Beach Boys took special note of the significance of *Rubber Soul*:

> It's a whole album of Beatles folk songs, a whole album where everything flows together and everything works .... It wasn't just the lyrics and the

melodies but the production and their harmonies … They were great poets about simple things, but that also made it easier to hear the song. And they never did anything clumsy. It was like perfect pitch but for entire songs.[22]

Rubber Soul features two songs/tracks that especially stand out with regard to the overall theme of this book: 'Michelle', which recreates the hip, casual elegance of an art school party, and 'In My Life', which constitutes The Beatles' first conscious exploration into the peculiar power of memory.

Since its initial release, the actual songwriting credit for 'In My Life' has been somewhat unclear. In later interviews, John Lennon took much of the credit.[23] For his part, however, Paul McCartney claims that the piece was largely a collaboration between the two that took place during a songwriting session at Lennon's home:

I said, 'Well, you haven't got a tune, let me just go and work on it'. And I went down to the half-landing, where John had a Mellotron, and I sat there and put together a tune based in my mind on Smokey Robinson and the Miracles …You refer back to something you've loved and try and take the spirit of that and write something new. So I recall writing the whole melody. And it actually does sound very like me, if you analyse it. I was obviously working to lyrics. The melody's structure is very me.[24]

The melody does, in fact, seem more typical of McCartney's approach. There is also the rather unconventional use of a tonic chord with the flat seventh in the bass. It is interesting to consider how this cluster contains elements of the altered subtonic chord that was a distinctive feature in the chorus of 'Ticket to Ride', another song often attributed more to John, but which Paul asserts was written together from Lennon's initial inspiration. In the book *The Beatles: A Musical Evolution* (1983), Terence J. O'Grady describes how the climactic harmony from 'Ticket to Ride' generates a remarkably poignant effect, since none of the tones featured in the melody are featured in the underlying chord.[25] Here, the effect is similar, but more along the lines of a question about the nature of memory.

The narrative regarding the authorship of 'In My Life' was further complicated in 2018 by research conducted by Jason Brown in a presentation entitled, 'Assessing Authorship of Beatles Songs from Musical Content: Bayesian Classification Modeling from Bags-of-Words Representations'. During the 11 August 2018 broadcast of NPR's Weekend Edition Saturday, Stanford mathematics professor Keith Devlin summarized Jason Brown's findings regarding the authorship of 'In My Life':

Cutting to the chase, it turns out Lennon wrote the whole thing. When you do the math by counting the little bits that are unique to the people, the probability that McCartney wrote it was .018 – that's essentially zero. In other words, this is pretty well definitive. Lennon wrote the music. And in situations like this, you'd better believe the math because it's much more reliable than people's recollections.[26]

The arrangement of 'In My Life' is rather unusual by Beatles standards. One may be led to wonder if the band is somehow reaching for a more complete instrumentation than they were yet able to achieve. However, it is also worth pointing out that they seem to be playing their electric instruments with an acoustic sensibility. This is particularly evident in the delicate placement of each part that tends to emphasize the space between the sounds. Thus, it seems that with this song/track The Beatles are envisioning a hybrid form that blends elements of their original musical approach with the acoustic sounds they were now exploring.

'In My Life' was begun in EMI Studio Two on 18 October 1965.[27] During the session, the basic elements of the arrangement were recorded. What then remained was the question of a suitable instrumental solo. On 22 October 1965, The Beatles returned to the track and resolved the question. Author Mark Lewisohn describes how this was achieved:

> First task of the day was to superimpose an instrumental break onto the previously recorded 'In My Life'. But using which instrument? One of the keyboard types certainly, with George Martin playing. The tape box reveals that he originally tried a Hammond organ. Not right. Then he decided on a piano, though there was a problem in playing the type of solo he wanted, baroque style, at the right tempo. The solution was to play at half the speed and then play back the tape at double-speed.[28]

The resulting solo is remarkable in that the studio techniques employed for the session ultimately suggested the intended sound of a Baroque keyboard. George Martin's solo refines the musical effect generated by the unusual chord choice described earlier. He then follows the basic outline of the melody but adjusts the counterpoint accordingly. He then closes with a brief quote from J.S. Bach's 'Sheep May Safely Graze', and thereby completes the musical reference.[29]

The space created for/by 'In My Life' suggests a blending of distinct musical eras separated by time. Here, the various elements that characterize the song/track seem to work symbolically: the space between the parts of the arrangement blends electric instruments with an acoustic sensibility; the sound of the Baroque keyboard, realized by the skilful manipulation of recording technology, exists in the present but conjures up images of the past; and finally, the contrapuntal techniques associated with the Baroque era in Western music are seen as a tool for clarifying musical expression in the present. Each of these elements underscores the singer's ambition to use memory to retrieve people, places, and things that have been lost or obscured over time. Taken together, they define a dynamic creative space in which various eras seem to simultaneously resonate. One might say that this space is a zone of hope in which everything that is needed is available, provided you know how to access it.

'Michelle'

Here was another stellar offering from McCartney that further demonstrated The Beatles' precocious musical range. 'Michelle' is a gentle ballad with French overtones that fit perfectly within mid-1960s popular music and its emphasis on diverse styles and approaches. As we'll see, the song was begun years earlier, but was readied for recording with a new contrasting section suggested by Lennon:

> [Paul] and I were staying somewhere, and he walked in and hummed the first few bars, with the words, you know [sings verse of 'Michelle'], and he says, 'Where do I go from here?' I had been listening to [jazz/blues singer] Nina Simone – I think it was 'I Put A Spell On You'. There was a line in it that went [taps his fingers and sings, gruffly]: 'I love you. I love you, I love you'. That's what made me think of the middle eight for 'Michelle'.[30]

'Michelle' completes the band's gradual move towards more varied musical colours and textures through its reliance on acoustic guitars and exquisite vocal harmonies. Mature listeners who may have still held reservations about The Beatles were likely to be won over by this beautiful song/track. The setting of 'Michelle' is considerably more elegant than the one created for 'In My Life', suggesting that The Beatles' compositional skills were growing with remarkable speed. Composed initially on guitar, 'Michelle' nevertheless displayed a pianistic approach to the instrument that would then be echoed in the arrangement used on the full recording. In *Many Years from Now* (1998), Paul described the inspiration for this approach:

> 'Michelle' was a tune that I'd written in Chet Atkins' finger-pickin' style. There is a song he did called 'Trambone' with a repetitive top line, and he played a bass line whilst playing a melody. This was an innovation for us; even though classical guitarists had played it, no rock 'n' roll guitarists had played it … But based on Atkins's 'Trambone', I wanted to write something with a melody and a bass line on it, so I did.[31]

One of the most distinctive musical features of 'Michelle' is its introduction in the parallel minor key. Built on a descending chromatic line on acoustic guitar, the introduction also features a remarkable rising line on bass guitar that reaches towards the instrument's upper register and back again. In the process, it suggests the graceful gesture of a dancer combined with the fluid brushstroke of a painter working on canvas. Here, McCartney seems to be using his bass guitar to explore the expressive possibilities of registral colour. Evidently conceived during the recording session itself, this line turns the introduction into an important recurring section.

'Michelle' was recorded in EMI Studio Two on 3 November 1965. The session was unusually lengthy for The Beatles at this time. Beginning in the afternoon at 2:30 pm, it finally wrapped at 11:30 pm. In *The Beatles Recording Sessions*, Mark Lewisohn describes the details of the recording:

In the afternoon The Beatles concentrated on the rhythm track, using up all four tracks of the tape. First task in the evening (although the day was really one continuous session) was to copy this tape onto another, simultaneously mixing down to three tracks. This was called take two. The Beatles then spent the remainder of the day overdubbing the lovely vocal work and guitars onto the newly vacated track.[32]

At the beginning of this chapter, 'No Reply' was considered in terms of the way it constitutes an exploration of dramatic space to 'stage' the song. 'Michelle' takes this idea a step further. In the book *Many Years from Now* (1998), McCartney described a particular party given by one of John's tutors from the art college: 'I remember sitting around there, and my recollection is of a black turtleneck sweater and sitting very enigmatically in the corner, playing this rather French tune'.[33] The impression one gets is that the young musician was trying to draw attention to himself in the middle of a sophisticated crowd of older artists. 'Michelle' re-paints the party in Vermeer-like fashion so that Paul, with The Beatles firmly behind him, is now the focus of the scene.

Acoustic Galleries

The LP-as-gallery idea seems particularly apt for *Rubber Soul* because of the consistency of the material presented throughout. However, one does encounter an interesting problem with regard to differences between the American and British releases. Although this was common practice for Beatles albums in the early 1960s, it's still controversial in that it tends to distort what the band was trying to achieve. It might be argued, however, that *Rubber Soul* is a curious exception to that rule.

The American release of the *Rubber Soul* LP removed 'Drive My Car', 'Nowhere Man', 'What Goes On', and 'If I Needed Someone' from the original order. To make up the difference, two songs were added. The first was Paul's 'I've Just Seen a Face', a country and western song that was used to open the album and neatly set the tone for the largely acoustic tone that would follow. The second was Lennon's 'It's Only Love', which featured electric lead guitar but was otherwise driven by twelve-string acoustic guitars.[34] Each of these had been previously excluded from the American release of *Help!* (1965).[35]

Using the American release as the model, we can now consider *Rubber Soul* as a virtual gallery of recorded sound. The binary nature of the medium of the vinyl LP means that there are two separate rooms in this gallery. Side one can be seen as a unified gesture initiated by Paul McCartney that begins with 'I've Just Seen a Face' and ends with 'Michelle'. Side two seems to be an adjacent room that belongs more to John Lennon in that it begins with 'It's Only Love' and ends with 'Run for Your Life'. The resulting sense of contrast suggests that this gallery space was structured around the ongoing creative dialogue between John Lennon and Paul McCartney.

'She Said She Said'

In April 1966, The Beatles returned to the studio once again to begin recording tracks for another new album. The collection they produced would ultimately be called *Revolver* and would largely constitute a move away from the acoustic ambience of *Rubber Soul* towards a heavier, more intense sound. The lyrical themes are also more meditative, suggesting a new maturity in the writing. These themes are then explored through an even more sophisticated and expansive approach to arrangement and production. In that regard, two songs/tracks from the album stand out: 'Eleanor Rigby' and 'She Said She Said'.

In 1965, John Lennon had a curious exchange with actor Peter Fonda. At a party where LSD was being used, the actor reportedly told Lennon that he knew what it was like to be dead. John responded simply that he didn't want to know.[36] The experience stayed with him and the following year he used it as the basis for a new song. He opted to make the character a woman rather than a man, and the resulting track was thus called 'She Said She Said'.

'She Said She Said' was recorded in B flat major, an unusual key for The Beatles, and one that may suggest a synaesthetic interest in tonal colour.[37] The song also featured an elaborate game with time that was so striking, it drew the attention of the serious musical establishment. In the television documentary *Inside Pop: The Rock Revolution* (1967), composer and musicologist Leonard Bernstein saw fit to comment on the song's ingenious rhythmic effects:

> You know a remarkable song of theirs called 'She Said, She Said'? Well, in that song which goes nicely along in four, there's again a sneaky switch to 3/4 time only this time it's not just for one bar, but for a whole passage. [plays excerpt] Did you get it? ... Now, the point I want to make is that such oddities as these are not just tricks or show-off devices. In terms of pop music's basic English, so to speak, they are real inventions.[38]

Recording began in EMI Studio Two on 21 June 1966.[39] At the outset, the song had no title, but by the end of the session it was called 'She Said She Said'. Remarkably, even though the sound is clearly identifiable as The Beatles, the exact instrumentation regarding who played what has been somewhat unclear. In *Many Years from Now* (1998), McCartney commented on this question: 'I'm not sure but I think it was one of the only Beatle records I never played on. I think we'd had a barney ... and they said, "Well, we'll do it". I think George played bass'.[40]

The spatial imagery on 'She Said She Said' seems to benefit from McCartney's absence. This is no reflection on the artist or his talent. It may simply be that his presence, particularly on the song's opening section, would likely have caused a decidedly bright approach to the overall arrangement, as evidenced on Lennon-driven songs such as 'Nowhere Man' or 'And Your Bird Can Sing'. Here, however, John seems particularly invested in the remarkable shift created by the move from common time to waltz time and back again. This painterly effect creates a change

in the tone of 'She Said She Said' in which the cloudy ambiguity of adulthood gives
way to the sunny enthusiasm of youth.

'Eleanor Rigby'

When asked by actress Kim Hunter to explain the theme of *A Streetcar Named
Desire*, playwright Tennessee Williams replied that he thought it was 'a plea for the
understanding of the delicate people'.[41] In his most distinctive contribution to
Revolver, Paul McCartney makes a similar plea with his portrait of a lonely spinster
named 'Eleanor Rigby'. The lyric also features a character named Father McKenzie,
who goes through the daily motions of a religious life while realizing that no
one seems to care. In a series of masterful musical brushstrokes, the song paints its
characters with sympathy and great care. The theme is the damage done by a society
obsessed with human progress at the expense of humanity itself.

Composed in the key of E minor, 'Eleanor Rigby' opens with its powerful chorus
hook, now repurposed as an introduction. Here, and throughout, McCartney makes
the most of very minimal material by employing only two basic chords. Additional
variety is generated by a descending chromatic line that connects the chords, and
the instrumental colours of the strings present on the backing track. Producer
George Martin created the score and cited the music of film composer Bernard
Herrmann as his primary inspiration. However, it's also interesting to consider how
the ensemble employs the kind of forceful rhythmic gestures normally associated
with guitar, an instrument that is noticeably absent from the track.[42]

The challenge during the initial session was to capture the string sounds in
a manner that contained the urgent intensity of rock and roll. Engineer Geoff
Emerick described how this was achieved:

> We did one take with the mics fairly close, then on the next take I decided
> to get extreme and move the mics in *really* close – perhaps just an inch
> or so away from each instrument. It was a fine line; I didn't want to
> make the musicians so uncomfortable that they couldn't give their best
> performance.[43]

The recording of 'Eleanor Rigby' began in EMI Studio Two on 28 April 1966.
The vocal parts by Paul McCartney, John Lennon, and George Harrison were all
recorded the following day in EMI Studio Three. McCartney then returned on 6
June to record an additional vocal to complete the track.[44]

'Eleanor Rigby' seems the closest The Beatles had come to blending the effects
of music and painting within the space created by recording technology. The world
presented here seems Dickensian in that it is one in which 'delicate' people are
often discarded by the machinery of the modern age. Eleanor is one of these people.
Abandoned by society, she takes her hopes and dreams with her to her grave. Here,
The Beatles, like Dickens before them, seem to be asking questions about the
ultimate outcome of human progress. They wonder aloud if anyone can be saved in

the modern world. The bold and urgent brushstrokes of the string accompaniment suggest that this is an issue that must be addressed immediately, if not sooner.

Revolving Galleries

In the painting *Untitled (Hamburg Series)*, Stuart Sutcliffe created a fascinating image that might be worth considering in relation to the function of *Revolver* as a gallery of recorded sound. The painting is dominated by shades of grey outlined by geometric figures that emerge in a tactile manner from the surface of the canvas. Just as it begins to seem that the colours of the work are suggesting that there is no hope, subtle reddish-pink curves seem to emerge from below the surface of the canvas. One then notices the masterful qualities of Sutcliffe's brushstrokes that are at once soothing, confident, and searching. The overall effect here is that although a dark outlook may seem to prevail, there is always the sense that humanity will emerge from the chaos and be reborn.[45]

The virtual gallery of *Revolver* connects with ideas evident in Sutcliffe's painting in that the album often seems to be taking place under a clouded sky. As compared with *Rubber Soul*, the mood here is decidedly more serious with lyrics that describe crushing taxes, psychedelic delusions, doctors pushing drugs on their patients, and humanity losing ground in an increasingly mechanized world. Despite the relatively bleak outlook evident in the subject matter, *Revolver*, like Stuart Sutcliffe's painting, offers the possibility of hope. Throughout the LP, bright colours created by surprising temporal shifts, new key areas, and exotic instrumentation repeatedly peek through the gloom. Like the pink curves under the surface of the image on Sutcliffe's canvas, these elements suggest that the troubles of our time are temporary, and that ultimately humanity will prevail.

Earlier in this chapter, it was asserted that the American release of *Rubber Soul* (1965) was actually more consistent with the creative trends evident in The Beatles' catalogue up to that point. The changes made on that version tended to accent the acoustic ambience that seemed to be a key feature of that collection. However, in the case of *Revolver* (1966), the UK version is far superior.[46] The reasons for this are interesting to consider. Although the changes made to the US version of *Revolver* may have tended to make it sound superficially similar to *Rubber Soul*, they also tended to compromise the ways in which the LP worked as a gallery of recorded sound.[47]

Images of a Woman

In the summer of 1966, The Beatles were bravely carrying on with another world tour. At the end of June, they were playing a series of gigs in Tokyo, Japan. Since they were still enduring the effects of Beatlemania and could not easily leave their hotel, they decided to amuse themselves with a project. Together, each taking a corner of the canvas, they created a painting. They called this painting *Images of a Woman*.

Photographer Robert Whitaker was travelling with the band at the time and documented The Beatles' experiences during the tour. On the official website for the project 'Art in a Corner', a link is provided to a webpage that features Whitaker's photos of The Beatles deeply involved in the painting process. In these photos, each Beatle is seen to focus intently on their own corner of the canvas. The page also contains an account of the creation of the painting that is attributed to Whitaker, in which it is asserted that 'it was simple boredom that drove George, John, Paul and Ringo to create the painting together. Worked on over two nights, the photographer said they were listening to their new album, *Revolver*, while they painted, played over and over'.[48]

Live performance had allowed The Beatles to begin the process of experimentation and to explore the potential of rock and roll. Now, however, a creative tension was emerging between live performance and music recording. Specifically, the band was having difficulty reproducing their complex studio-based ideas onstage. They tried, but it was becoming clear that The Beatles now belonged to a different medium. In 1966, they abandoned live performance in order to focus exclusively on transforming the recording studio into a workshop for the creation of musical art.

Notes

1 Mark Lewisohn, *The Beatles Recording Sessions* (New York: Harmony Books, 1988), 45.

2 Mark Lewisohn, *The Beatles Recording Sessions* (New York: Harmony Books, 1988), 47.

3 The Beatles, *Anthology* (San Francisco, CA: Chronicle Books, 2000), 159.

4 Barry Miles and Paul McCartney, *Many Years from Now* (New York: H. Holt, 1997), 176.

5 Mark Lewisohn, *The Beatles Recording Sessions* (New York: Harmony Books, 1988), 49.

6 Ian MacDonald, *Revolution in the Head: The Beatles' Records and the Sixties* (London: Vintage, 2008), 131–132.

7 Mark Lewisohn, *The Beatles Recording Sessions* (New York: Harmony Books, 1988), 12.

8 Ian MacDonald, *Revolution in the Head: The Beatles' Records and the Sixties* (London: Vintage, 2008), 138.

9 Barry Miles and Paul McCartney, *Many Years from Now* (New York: H. Holt, 1997), 38–39.

10 Paul Hamilton, Peter Gordon, and Dan Kieran (eds.), *How Very Interesting: Peter Cook's Universe and All That Surrounds It* (London: Snowbooks, 2006), 85.

11 The Beatles, *Anthology* (San Francisco, CA: Chronicle Books, 2000), 176.

12 Barry Miles and Paul McCartney, *Many Years from Now* (New York: H. Holt, 1997), 187.

13 Mark Lewisohn, *The Beatles Recording Sessions* (New York: Harmony Books, 1988), 55.

14 Barry Miles and Paul McCartney, *Many Years from Now* (New York: H. Holt, 1997), 201–203.

15 Barry Miles and Paul McCartney, *Many Years from Now* (New York: H. Holt, 1997), 203.

16 Henry Martin, *Charlie Parker, Composer* (New York: Oxford University Press, 2020), 18.

17 Henry Martin, *Charlie Parker, Composer* (New York: Oxford University Press, 2020), 94.

18 Henry Martin, *Charlie Parker, Composer* (New York: Oxford University Press, 2020), 18.

19 Ted Gioia, *The Jazz Standards: A Guide to the Repertoire* (New York: Oxford University Press, 2012), 71.

20 Leonard Bernstein, *The Unanswered Question: Six Talks at Harvard* (Cambridge, MA: Harvard University Press, 1976), 86–115.

21 Mark Lewisohn, *The Beatles Recording Sessions* (New York: Harmony Books, 1988), 59.

22 Brian Wilson with Ben Greenman, *I Am Brian Wilson: A Memoir* (Boston, MA: Da Capo Press, 2016), 92.

23 John Lennon, *Lennon Remembers* (London and New York: Verso, 2000), 85.

24 Barry Miles and Paul McCartney, *Many Years from Now* (New York: H. Holt, 1997), 277.

25 Terence J. O'Grady, *The Beatles: A Musical Evolution* (Boston, MA: Twayne Publishers, 1983), 68.

26 Scott Simon and Ned Wharton, 'A Songwriting Mystery Solved: Math Proves John Lennon Wrote "In My Life"'. NPR, 11 August 2018. www.npr.org/2018/08/11/637468 053/a-songwriting-mystery-solved-math-proves-john-lennon-wrote-in-my-life.

27 Ian MacDonald, *Revolution in the Head: The Beatles' Records and the Sixties* (London: Vintage, 2008), 169.

28 Mark Lewisohn, *The Beatles Recording Sessions* (New York: Harmony Books, 1988), 65.

29 This may provide support for Jason Brown's assertion regarding the authorship of the song. McCartney's compositional process seems to be more orderly as compared with Lennon's approach, in which he seems to view the entire process – that is, music and recording – as one unified gesture.

30 David Sheff, *All We Are Saying: The Last Major Interview with John Lennon and Yoko Ono* (New York: St. Martin's Griffin, 2000), 136.

31 Barry Miles and Paul McCartney, *Many Years from Now* (New York: H. Holt, 1997), 273.

32 Mark Lewisohn, *The Beatles Recording Sessions* (New York: Harmony Books, 1988), 67.

33 Barry Miles and Paul McCartney, *Many Years from Now* (New York: H. Holt, 1997), 273.

34 *Rubber Soul*, Capitol, liner notes, 1965.

35 *Help!*, Capitol, liner notes, 1965.

36 Philip Norman, *John Lennon: The Life* (Toronto: Anchor Canada, 2009), 427.

37 Ian MacDonald, *Revolution in the Head: The Beatles' Records and the Sixties* (London: Vintage, 2008), 211.

38 'Inside Pop – The Rock Revolution'. YouTube. drksrfr, 16 March 2012. https://youtu. be/afU76JJcquI?t=412.

39 Mark Lewisohn, *The Beatles Recording Sessions* (New York: Harmony Books, 1988), 84.

40 Barry Miles and Paul McCartney, *Many Years from Now* (New York: H. Holt, 1997), 288.

41 'Changing Stages (BBC/Richard Eyre) – Pt.1 America'. YouTube. Leo Butler, 20 April 2017. https://youtu.be/CGaW6-V0TvM?t=2597.

42 Mark Lewisohn, *The Beatles Recording Sessions* (New York: Harmony Books, 1988), 77.

43 Geoff Emerick and Howard Massey, *Here, There, and Everywhere: My Life Recording the Music of The Beatles* (New York: Gotham Books, 2006), 127.

44 Mark Lewisohn, *The Beatles Recording Sessions* (New York: Harmony Books, 1988), 77.

45 Drawn from notes taken during a viewing of *Untitled (Hamburg Series)* by Stuart Sutcliffe at the Guggenheim, 1071 Fifth Avenue, New York, 15 December 2019.

46 *Revolver*, Parlophone, liner notes, 1966.

47 *Revolver*, Capitol, liner notes, 1966.

48 'Images of a Woman'. Art in a Corner. Accessed 19 March 2022. www.artinacorner. co.uk/images-of-a-woman.

3

'SO IF YOU HEAR A WONDROUS SIGHT'[1]

The final leg of their 1966 world concert tour took The Beatles once again through the heart of America. However, as compared with their experience the year before, the mood was considerably darker. Attendance at many of their shows was down, and it was rather obvious that they had been writing and recording beyond the scope of a standard four-piece rock band.[2] The multi-tracked vocal harmonies and varied instrumentation they'd been using on their sound recordings were not yet practical to reliably reproduce in a live concert setting. It must have been clear to The Beatles themselves that this phase of their career was coming to an end.

Following their final concert at Candlestick Park in San Francisco on 29 August 1966, the band members temporarily went their separate ways: Harrison followed up on his continuing interest in Eastern culture by visiting India to study music and meditation; Ringo took advantage of the break by opting to spend time at home with his family; Paul McCartney tried his hand at film scoring and wrote music for *The Family Way*, a domestic drama produced by The Boulting Brothers; and finally, in an interesting parallel with his partner Paul, John Lennon went on location playing a serious role in a new film.[3]

Lennon was playing a character in a comedy called *How I Won the War*. Directed by Richard Lester, the film explored the experiences of a group of British soldiers stranded behind enemy lines during the Second World War. Lennon received good notices for his performance as Musketeer Gripweed, and thus validated Lester's faith in his innate abilities as an actor. Sadly, *How I Won the War* would mark Lennon's final appearance as a character in a full-length fictional film.[4] However, in musical terms, his time on location in Almería, Spain inspired a new song/track that would become one of his most important contributions to The Beatles' recorded catalogue.[5]

DOI: 10.4324/9781003300212-5

'Strawberry Fields Forever'

The title of the new song was taken from the name of the garden of a Salvation Army home in the neighbourhood where Lennon grew up. This was a refuge where he could explore, play, or just let his mind wander.

> It's a Salvation Army home that was near the house I lived in with my auntie in the suburbs. There were two famous houses there. One was owned by Gladstone, which was a reformatory for boys, which I could see out my window. And Strawberry Fields was just around the corner from that. It was an old Victorian house converted for Salvation Army orphans, and as a kid I used to go to their garden parties with my friends Ivan, Nigel, and Pete … But I just took the name – it had nothing to do with the Salvation Army. As an image – Strawberry Fields for ever.[6]

In *Many Years from Now* (1998), Paul McCartney described his own memory of Strawberry Fields as being 'a secret garden like in *The Lion, the Witch and the Wardrobe* and he thought of it like that … It was an escape for John'.[7]

Lennon had been reminded of Strawberry Fields while in Spain and began composing the song there. He also seems to have been thinking back to his fondness for the works of Lewis Carroll, since he then proceeded to infuse the song with colourful images that suggested a latter-day Wonderland. When The Beatles regrouped at EMI Studios in November 1966, he played the piece for producer George Martin. At that point, it was simply voice accompanied by acoustic guitar. Martin was enchanted by the song's gentle lyricism and began working with the band to create a suitable arrangement.[8]

'Strawberry Fields Forever' primarily consists of two contrasting sections. In keeping with the dreamy, rootless quality of the lyric, these sections create a curious ambiguity as to the song's actual key centre. The shifts in the harmonic progression make it difficult to get one's footing as to the home key. This quality is intensified by the fact that the release version of the song/track is not in concert pitch. Instead, 'Strawberry Fields Forever' seems to float between keys in a manner that suggests that the listener has entered a dream state and embarked on a colourful journey between worlds.

In addition to the two main sections described above, 'Strawberry Fields Forever' also features a curious, extended coda that seems to have been conceived and realized during the recording process. A variety of melodic fragments float in and out of the mix as the song fades away gradually into the distance. Following a fleeting silence, the track fades back in, suggesting that the musicians have circled back towards the listener. The returning sounds are more chaotic, suggesting that some kind of transformation may have occurred during the brief fade-out. Then, a deep voice utters an absurd non sequitur ('Cranberry sauce') before a more conclusive fade-out is achieved.

The first phase in the recording of 'Strawberry Fields Forever' began on 24 November 1966. The initial arrangement evolved by George Martin and the band was delicate and interesting. The introduction was played by McCartney on a mellotron set to emulate the sound of a flute. The other elements on the first take were Lennon on lead vocal; Harrison on guitar; and Ringo on drums. The overdubs that followed consisted of double-tracked vocals, additional three-part harmony vocals, maracas, and slide guitar.[9]

On Sunday 27 November 1966, John took a well-deserved break from the recording of 'Strawberry Fields Forever'. That morning, he would perform in another segment for the comedy programme, *Not Only... But Also*. During his first appearance on the show, he had read selections from *In His Own Write*, and performed with Dudley Moore in a delightful filmed sequence. Now he would work side by side with Peter Cook himself in a sketch where Peter played an American journalist filming a segment on the 'Ad Lav', an exclusive gentlemen's lavatory situated in the heart of London. As Cook tries to enter the establishment, his character is stopped by Lennon who plays the street attendant for the lavatory.[10]

FADE IN:

EXT. CITY STREET. DAY.

VOICEOVER (COOK)
This is London's most fashionable lavatory spot.
Here, film stars rub shoulders with royalty in an
atmosphere of cosmopolitan sophistication.

INTERVIEWER (COOK)
Good evening.

ATTENDANT (LENNON)
Excuse me, sir. Are you a member?

INTERVIEWER
I'm sorry, I'm not. I'm from American television.
I'm doing an interview downstairs.

ATTENDANT
Well, I'm sorry, sir. You must be a member to go in here.

INTERVIEWER
Would it help if I told you that I was the Duke and
Duchess of Windsor?

ATTENDANT
Oh, sorry, sir. I didn't recognize you – madam ...[11]

Lennon handles the surrealistic wordplay of the sequence with ease and, in the process, seems to be accessing his persona from *A Hard Day's Night*. Remarkably, the sketch showed him to be on the same page as Peter Cook, one of the most talented comedy writers of his generation.

Additional takes of 'Strawberry Fields Forever' were begun on 28 November 1966 and completed the following day. Upon listening to the completed version, now called Take 7, John wondered if the song might benefit from additional instrumentation. He conferred with George Martin on how best to proceed. After some consideration, they settled on trumpets and cellos as the best option. Thus began the second phase in the saga of 'Strawberry Fields Forever'.[12]

Recordings of the new rhythm track commenced in EMI Studio Two on 8 December 1966 and continued the following day. Here, The Beatles took the opportunity to further their experimentation with musical colour. They raised the key to C major, increased the tempo, and employed unusual instrumentation such as a swarmandal played by Harrison and drum cymbals recorded with the tape running backwards to create sonic envelopes on the finished track. On 15 December 1966, four trumpets and three cellos were recorded from a score prepared by George Martin. Lennon added his lead vocals, and with that, phase two of the track was completed.[13]

Lennon listened to this new version (Take 26) and told George Martin that he liked the first section of the initial recording, but preferred the second section of version two. He then asked if the two versions could somehow be edited together to feature the best sections of both. Martin and engineer Geoff Emerick then considered how to solve the problem of joining two versions of the same song that were recorded in different tempos and different keys! The solution they arrived at involved an elaborate edit of the two final versions: Take 7 and Take 26. Their strategy to compensate for the problems of different keys and tempos was to increase the speed of the first version slightly while slowing down the speed of the second. This brought the two tracks into alignment regarding tempo and key. The edit occurs at fifty-nine seconds into the released version of the finished track.[14]

Rooted in the original musical materials, as well as the recording process itself, the virtual space created for 'Strawberry Fields Forever' involves access to alternate modes of sensory experience. Here, The Beatles approach a stable aspect of musical language (key area) as something to be expressively moulded towards new perceptual effects. In that regard, the motion of the edit from version one to version two creates a brushstroke of remarkable power. The listener/viewer is invited to ride this gesture through the looking glass into a landscape of sound and colour.

'Penny Lane'

The title of Lennon's recent track had revealed a strategy for The Beatles' upcoming works that involved a kind of excavation of self; that is, a mining of experiences from their childhood as the source material for composition. In keeping with this idea, Paul McCartney now presented 'Penny Lane', a song set on a Liverpool street that he and John frequented in their youth.[15]

The structure of 'Penny Lane' rests on the alternation of two contrasting sections. In earlier works, McCartney had demonstrated his ability to create intriguing geometric patterns using musical elements such as melody, harmony, and meter. Here, he brings the backdrop of tonality itself into the mix and uses two different key areas respectively for each section: B major for the verse and A major for the chorus. The song's concluding passage is a restatement of the chorus now in B major, the key area of the verse.

The recording of 'Penny Lane' began in EMI Studio Two on 29 December 1966. In an approach that would increasingly become the norm over the next few years, Paul began the recording process on his own. He carefully crafted a series of piano tracks in an effort to create a suitably colourful rhythm track.[16] Additional overdubs were added the following day, including a lead vocal by McCartney, backed by Lennon, which was recorded with the tape machine running slow, resulting in the parts sounding slightly over a half-step higher on playback. Overdubs by The Beatles continued as McCartney worked with George Martin to create an arrangement for brass and woodwinds (with double bass added for good measure) that was recorded on 9 and 12 January 1967.[17]

Despite all the fine work done on 'Penny Lane' to date, something was still missing from the final picture. Suddenly, the answer revealed itself. McCartney happened to watch a BBC 2 broadcast of the English Chamber Orchestra from Guildford Cathedral performing J.S. Bach's Brandenburg Concerto Number 2 in F Major. He liked the sound of the piccolo trumpet and wondered if it might fit into his new song/track. Conferring with George Martin, the two came up with an appropriate solo.[18]

In 'Penny Lane', the two distinct key areas seem to correspond with the contrasting mental landscapes described in the text. The first concerns various experiences and images from the past, recalled from memory, which are nevertheless described with remarkable attention to detail; the second provides a colourful rendering of experiences in the present tense that, like 'Strawberry Fields Forever', seems to suggest the influence of Lewis Carroll. Thus, the listener is presented with a virtual landscape that alternately includes elements of both past and present. In the song's remarkable concluding section, the present tense is coloured with the key area of the past and thereby suggests an ultimate unification of the past and the present through the creative process. As author Tyler Shores points out in the essay, '"Memory and Muchness": Alice and the Philosophy of Memory':

> We live in memory, and by memory, but as Alice tells us, we needn't be troubled by the thought that the person we remember being yesterday may be different from the person we are now, or are yet to become.[19]

As can be seen in the preceding discussions, The Beatles were now taking their time in the recording studio. Relieved of the pressure of fitting sessions in between extended tours, they now focused exclusively on the studio as their primary creative workshop. As a result, the band missed their customary Christmas release of new material. Instead, they offered up 'Penny Lane' and 'Strawberry Fields Forever'. On 17 February 1967, the two tracks were released as a double-A-sided 45-rpm single.[20]

The Beatles had previously released two double A-sides: the first, 'We Can Work It Out' and 'Day Tripper', was recorded during the sessions for *Rubber Soul* in 1965; the second, which consisted of 'Yellow Submarine' and 'Eleanor Rigby', was culled from the sessions for *Revolver* and released on 5 August 1966.[21] Although each of these had been brilliant in their own right, their latest record suggested the possibility of a new kind of organic flow and unity between the respective sides of a 45-rpm single. An interesting way of regarding this is to consider the two sides as a single work with two panels; that is, a diptych.

In the book *Gardner's Art Through the Ages: A Global History* (2013), a diptych is defined as 'A two-paneled painting or *altarpiece*'.[22] A twentieth-century example of this form is *Marilyn Diptych* (1962) in which a repeating silkscreen image of Marilyn Monroe appears on two separate, successive panels. The images on the first panel are strikingly colourful, while those on the second panel are in monochrome and suggest faded newsprint. The flow between the two panels generates remarkable emotional power when considered in relation to Monroe's tragic fate. Philosopher and art critic Arthur C. Danto described the work in this way:

> It is like a graphic representation of Marilyn dying, without the smile leaving her face … there is repetition, but it is a transformative repetition, in which the accidentalities of the silk-screen medium are allowed to remain, like the honks and squawks of a saxophone solo, in performances by John Coltrane.[23]

'Strawberry Fields Forever' and 'Penny Lane' achieve a similar kind of flow across the sides/panels of a 45-rpm record. In Lennon's track, the edit created from version one into version two works as an expressive gesture of remarkable power. Through this gesture, we are invited to journey from the present tense into an undetermined landscape of sight and sound. In 'Penny Lane', McCartney uses two key areas to represent each side of this journey. He then shifts the anticipated characteristics for each so that they begin to exhibit qualities that are more commonly associated with the other. In the final moments, the two worlds are brought together, suggesting that past and present can be productively unified within human consciousness and experience.

The Beatles were not the first to incorporate this idea into a musical context. Prominent examples of the diptych form in music include *Medieval Diptych* (1962) by Alan Rawsthorne[24] and *Diptych* for brass quintet and band (1963) by Gunther Schuller.[25] The key difference in The Beatles' approach seems to lie in the medium of sound recording itself. Author and art curator Donna DeSalvo described a similar situation existing in the works of Andy Warhol:

Once he wed that silkscreen with the painting, once photography became embedded within painting in a way it had never been before, he never goes back to using those other techniques again. And this sets up a completely different way for him to operate, and, in a sense, makes evident the source materials that he's been using all along. And this is fundamental. He marries form and content in a way that's inextricable. You cannot pull them apart … And of course, that's the thing that really makes for great art. He pushed the language forward.[26]

As previously mentioned, 'Strawberry Fields Forever' and 'Penny Lane' suggest the two panels of a diptych folded back on one another. Although existing separately on the two sides of a 45-rpm record, they are also intimately joined within the same physical medium. Thus, as in the works of Andy Warhol cited above, the medium becomes a necessary aspect of the artwork, and the result is a deep and lasting marriage of content and form.

Musical Imagery

With the release of their double-A-sided single, it was decided that the two new songs would not be included on The Beatles' upcoming album. As a result, the plan to create a unifying concept based on The Beatles' childhood memories would have to be scrapped and/or reworked. In retrospect, they had already covered the subject matter beautifully with both 'Strawberry Fields Forever' and 'Penny Lane'. Rising to the challenge, it was Paul who came up with a fascinating new idea for a project. The Beatles could pretend they were another band and record the entire album from that band's point of view.[27]

Sgt. Pepper's Lonely Hearts Club Band would ultimately feature a number of remarkable songs. However, the one that seemed to connect most directly with the childhood themes of 'Strawberry Fields Forever' and 'Penny Lane' was 'Lucy in the Sky with Diamonds', a song inspired by Lennon's son, Julian. Many listeners believed that the title was a coded message regarding LSD. However, in an interview for *The Dick Cavett Show* on 8 September 1971, John described the song's true origins: 'my son came home with a drawing and showed me this strange-looking woman flying around. I said, "What is it?" He said, "It's Lucy in the sky with diamonds." And I thought, "That's beautiful"'.[28]

The drawing in question suggests a keen interest in the emotional power of colour. Set against a background that contains shades of yellow, orange, and red, one sees various dynamic shapes (diamonds) and a human figure that is assumedly the 'Lucy' of the title. Each of these shapes, which are impressive in their detail, seem to float freely through the colour field as if in water rather than air. The effect suggests the kind of sonic imagery created in the production of 'Strawberry Fields Forever' and 'Penny Lane'. In an interesting flip, each of those tracks seems to have provided the guidelines for translating this drawing into song.

The imagery was Alice in the boat. And also the image of this female who would come and save me – this secret love that was going to come one day. So it turned out to be Yoko, though, and I hadn't met Yoko then. But she was my imaginary girl that we all have.[29]

Like 'Strawberry Fields Forever', the track opens with the sound of an exotic keyboard. The keyboard plays an extended arpeggiation in the key of A major over a repeated descending bassline. Following the completion of the verse, the music shifts up one half-step to B flat major for a transition that links to a full contrasting section in G major. Thus, we now have three tonal centres at work. Also, as compared with the previous section, which floated dreamily along, this new section drives decisively forward.

The recording of 'Lucy in the Sky with Diamonds' was one of the fastest of the *Sgt. Pepper* sessions. It officially began in EMI Studio Two on 1 March 1967, but the band had also spent the previous day evolving the arrangement without actually recording anything. During the session on 1 March, however, they recorded a rhythm track that featured drums, maracas, guitar, piano, and a Hammond organ set to sound like a celeste. The next day, they added vocals with the tape machine running at various speeds so as to make them sound higher on final playback.[30]

'Penny Lane' and 'Strawberry Fields Forever' each presented spaces in which everyday experience became the source of wonder. From the gardens next door to bankers in motorcars; from trees that can be high or low to pretty nurses selling poppies, the mundane had now become decidedly magical. Curiously, 'Lucy in the Sky with Diamonds' seems to reverse this process by making wondrous places seem rather mundane. Strange appositions abound that generate interest, but not much excitement. The pop art quality of the various sights described along the river seems to ultimately suggest the kind of sensory fatigue associated with an extended visit to a museum.

On 30 March 1967, The Beatles were scheduled to attend a recording session for the song 'With a Little Help from My Friends'. That session, however, started rather late. The reason for the late start was that the band had a prior appointment in Chelsea. They had travelled to Chelsea Manor Studios to be photographed by Michael Cooper. During the shoot, a series of photos were taken, from which would be chosen those versions that would adorn the cover of their new album.[31]

Sgt. Pepper's Lonely Hearts Club Band was released on 1 June 1967 to widespread popular acclaim.[32] The album cover was designed by pop artist Peter Blake from sketch ideas created by Paul McCartney. Mike Love of The Beach Boys has described how, unlike his own band, The Beatles themselves were deeply involved in the look and layout of the new album: 'In one conversation, he [McCartney] mentioned that we ought to take more care with our album covers. Paul was the mastermind behind the *Sgt. Pepper* album cover, which was detailed and brilliant'.[33]

The cover photo of the album featured The Beatles standing in front of a hodgepodge of their cultural heroes. In the process, they revealed that their influences covered musicians and performers of both high and low art. There were also politicians, philosophers, film stars, and even holy men in the mix. Also included were a number of interesting figures from the fine arts such as Aubrey Beardsley, Larry Bell, Wallace Berman, Richard Lindner, Simon Rodia, and H.C. Westermann. Finally, on the far left is the image of none other than a Hamburg-era Stuart Sutcliffe, who stands with his former bandmates in their moment of artistic triumph.[34]

Magical Mystery Tour

Following the release of *Sgt. Pepper's Lonely Hearts Club Band*, The Beatles appeared on a global television broadcast that showed them at EMI Studios recording a new song/track called 'All You Need Is Love'.[35] In the process, they extended the canvas of music creation and sound recording around the entire planet. For their next project, they decided to make a film. They had already appeared as performers in two films, but now they sought a new balance and unity with their recorded works by creating and supervising the entire project themselves. The idea for the new film was that the band and their various companions would take a magical journey through the English countryside. Beyond that basic outline, there wasn't much more to go on.

The strategy employed for creating the script was similar to the approach taken for the painting *Images of a Woman*. There, each of The Beatles had been responsible for one quarter of a canvas. For the script, McCartney simply drew a circle with eight sections that represented the proposed narrative: 1. Commercial introduction. Get on the coach. Courier introduces; 2. Coach people meet each other / (Song, Fool on the Hill?); 3. marathon – laboratory sequence; 4. smiling face. LUNCH. mangoes, tropical. (magician); 5. and 6. Dreams; 7. Stripper & band; 8. Song; END. Paul then assigned various sections of the circle to the other Beatles and asked them to each write something to be filmed.[36] And with that, The Beatles embarked enthusiastically on this new project.

The title track of *Magical Mystery Tour* seems to be an attempt to respond to the musical and magical challenges of 'Lucy in the Sky with Diamonds'. The mundanity of the former is countered during the song's introduction, which suggests a rock translation of a circus fanfare. The song then drives forward with a climbing, appropriately modern-sounding chord progression as the singer extolls the benefits of embarking on a mystery tour. Next comes the contrasting section that counters the harmonic asperity of the previous section with a stirring vocal melody that unfolds over a steadily descending bass. Taken together, these two sections echo 'Penny Lane' and 'Lucy in the Sky with Diamonds' in that they appear in two different keys a whole step apart. As the song progresses, one notices that each of the two main sections regularly employs harmonic elements more commonly associated with the other. In the process, the two keys are blended to create new musical colours as the song unfolds.

In addition to the two main sections described above, the song also features two short instrumental passages that further the blending of musical colour: The first is a short two-chord progression that then links back to the opening section. This brief link alternates a B major chord with an F sharp minor chord before moving to a full cadence in E major. In the process, it decisively asserts the tonal centre of the opening section. The second instrumental passage is a remarkable coda that begins in the tonal centre of the contrasting section (D major) before transforming into D minor. The piano freely improvises in this new key as the music dissolves into a fading field of sonic colour.

Sessions for the title track of the new film project began on 25 April 1967, almost immediately following the end of the recording sessions for *Sgt. Pepper*. Work on the basic track by all four Beatles continued for the next week. Bus sound effects were also added during these sessions. An appropriate brass overdub was realized on 3 May. Initially, McCartney tried to hum the sounds he wanted for each of the musicians, but ultimately relented and worked with producer George Martin to write out proper parts.[37] Following the creation of a tentative final mix on 4 May, the song was put aside until 7 November when a final McCartney vocal and additional sound effects were recorded.[38]

As in 'Penny Lane', the coda of 'Magical Mystery Tour' seems to be the song's main point all along. It's almost as if the main sections existed merely to justify the presentation of this remarkable moment in the track. The space here seems colourful and circular and suggests rebirth and renewal. During the fade, as the various elements begin to fragment, this quality seems to intensify. Decades later, artists in a variety of styles would use these kinds of soundscapes as backdrops for entire tracks.

'I Am the Walrus'

Lennon's sole musical composition for the *Magical Mystery Tour* project was a unique song/track entitled 'I Am the Walrus'. Here, the references to Lewis Carroll become even more overt. The lyric and title were inspired by 'The Walrus and the Carpenter', a poem featured in the fourth chapter of *Through the Looking Glass and What Alice Found There*. Lennon retains the ominous undercurrent of the original poem but crafts his own unique imagery, which was well suited to the freeform narrative of *Magical Mystery Tour*. As a result, the sequence created as the backdrop for 'I Am the Walrus' is one of the highpoints of the film.

'I Am the Walrus' begins with a melodic motive that was reportedly inspired by a police siren. Harmonically, the song seems to reference 'Penny Lane' in that its two contrasting sections are respectively in the keys of B major and A major. However, in a clever reversal of that song's harmonic strategy, the primary section here is in A major, while the contrasting section is in B major. Curiously, the harmonic material of the contrasting section initially appears in the guise of an introduction at the beginning of the song. Even curiouser is how the contrasting section is later disguised as an instrumental interlude before it appears under the lyric in its full form.

In addition to the two main sections described above, the song also features an extended coda built on a descending bassline that travels in a seemingly never-ending journey downwards. At the same time, strings in the upper register counter the bass line by ascending ever upward. The two lines complement one another as they proceed. Ultimately, they each do arrive on the tonic pitch, but like Alice and the Red Queen in *Through the Looking Glass*, they have to travel in opposite directions in order to get there. During the coda, the ensemble is also joined by a choir singing a nonsense lyric that reads like a modern variation on the language of Wonderland. Gradually, the entire mass of sound begins to fade slowly into the distance.

In the late 1960s, it was standard practice to create mono and stereo mixes of completed tracks. In the case of 'I Am the Walrus', this practice led to a remarkably expressive outcome. Seemingly inspired by the idea of 'radio-as-music',[39] Lennon had asked for a radio set to be fed directly into the mixing board during the mono mixing session. Scanning across the dial, he came upon a performance of Shakespeare's *King Lear*. Fascinated by the sounds from the live performance, he blended them into the latter sections of 'I Am the Walrus'.[40]

When it was time to do the stereo mix, the radio performance was not available, so the stereo version was completed without those elements. When Lennon heard the stereo mix, he missed the spoken-word excerpts from *King Lear* and asked if they could somehow be added to the stereo mix as well. Unfortunately, those elements were derived from a live broadcast and were not isolated on a track. After some consideration, an edit was proposed that echoed the one used to complete 'Strawberry Fields Forever'. It was decided that the track could open with the stereo mix, but conclude with the mono mix that featured the radio broadcast.[41]

The space created for 'I Am the Walrus' is one that is decidedly close and confining. The various sounds seem to morph and grow as the track progresses. These qualities intensify with the move from stereo into mono. In the coda, an interesting contrast occurs: the contraction of the auditory field is countered by the expansion of the two instrumental lines, one ascending and the other descending, that ultimately meet on the tonic note. The suggestion here might be that as we contract and compress, we are also continually expanding outward into infinity.

Looking-Glass Galleries

The Beatles' recording activities of 1967 had been varied and extensive. As the band took more time in the studio, the quality and depth evident in their material was greatly enhanced. They now seemed to be thinking about their music recordings not just as products but also as artworks in their own right. This, however, created an interesting problem. Considering the sheer quantity of the band's recent output, the earlier notion of an LP as a gallery of recorded sound would likely have to be modified.

In Chapter 2, it was suggested that the US version of *Rubber Soul* by Capitol Records was more consistent with The Beatles' aesthetic direction than its British counterpart. Something similar seems to have occurred with *Magical Mystery Tour*. In late 1967, Parlophone released the six songs from the film soundtrack as a double-EP, but Capitol was concerned about how that format would be received in the American market. As a result, they decided to take an interesting step. They selected a number of the non-album tracks from the previous year, added them to the material from the film soundtrack, and released a full-length LP entitled *Magical Mystery Tour*.

The results of the Capitol repackaging of Beatles tracks were more useful than might have been suspected at the time. Taken together, the *Sgt. Pepper's Lonely Hearts Club Band* LP and the Capitol version of *Magical Mystery Tour* provided listeners with a balanced overview of The Beatles' recent work. Revisiting the Lewis Carroll theme, one might regard *Sgt. Pepper* as a very public matter, an entertainment that takes place in the real world. In contrast, *Magical Mystery Tour* seems to take place on the other side of the looking glass, a world in which the real world is reversed and distorted.

Moving through the material on these two LPs chronologically, or even at random, reveals the remarkable creative distance the band had been travelling in the space of only twelve months. It also suggests that, for The Beatles, a single LP was no longer enough to create a satisfying and effective gallery of sound. They would now have to expand fully into the double-LP format. The following year, they did just that.

The Lennon Play: In His Own Write

Actor Victor Spinetti had given superb performances in the first two Beatles films. His appearance as a neurotic television director in *A Hard Day's Night* (1964) was arguably worthy of a major award ('A likely story').[42] Subsequently, his role as the diabolical but inept Professor Foot in *Help!* (1965) meshed beautifully with the band's own brand of anarchic humour ('MIT was after me, you know. Wanted me to rule the world for them').[43] When The Beatles were casting *Magical Mystery Tour*, Lennon had asked Spinetti to sign on to play the part of the courier, Jolly Jimmy Johnson.[44] Although scheduling conflicts prevented him from taking on that role, he did agree to a smaller part as an army sergeant in which he brilliantly uttered a seemingly endless stream of loud, warlike gibberish.[45]

In the autumn of 1966, while performing in London with Jack Klugman in a West End production of Neil Simon's *The Odd Couple*, Spinetti was approached by renowned American playwright Adrienne Kennedy. She told him that she had adapted and combined John Lennon's first two books, *In His Own Write* (1964) and *A Spaniard in the Works* (1965), into a play and that she would like Spinetti to appear in it. This led to conversations with critic Kenneth Tynan, and then Lawrence Olivier, in which it was proposed that the work could and should be produced at the National Theatre. Spinetti contacted Lennon, who liked the idea, and the two began working earnestly on the new project.[46]

Spinetti was well suited to the task at hand. He'd had an extensive career on the stage and worked closely with director Joan Littlewood at the legendary *Theatre Workshop*. In 1963, he appeared in Littlewood's landmark production of *Oh, What a Lovely War!* and later won a Tony award when the show moved to New York. On

3 December 1967, a one-night-only workshop performance of the piece under the title *Scene Three Act One* took place at the Old Vic, then home of the National Theatre.[47] This was followed by six more months of further development and rehearsal.

Finally, on 18 June 1968, *The Lennon Play: In His Own Write* had its official premiere as part of an evening of three one-act plays at the National Theatre. In an interview for the BBC 2 programme *Release*, Lennon described how the adaptation had affected him personally:

> When I saw the rehearsal of it, I got quite emotional … I mean, I knew, in my heart of hearts, who was who and what the book was saying, but not enough. I was too involved with it when it was written, and any criticism it had – was either just 'Rubbish' or still only writing about what was on the paper. So, it took something like this to happen to make me see what I was about then.[48]

In the six months between the workshop performance of *The Lennon Play* and its full premiere in June 1968, a good deal happened. The Beatles had embarked, with various friends and family in tow, on an extended trip to India. The plan was to study meditation with the Maharishi Mahesh Yogi and take a break from the pressures of writing and recording. Ironically, the trip to India turned out to be a busman's holiday in that when The Beatles returned to the UK, they had a trove of new songs to record. Upon their return, they gathered at George Harrison's home studio to record demos of the new material.[49]

'Revolution 9'

Sessions for what was to become the double LP *The Beatles* (1968) commenced at EMI Studios at the end of May 1968. The first song recorded was Lennon's musical meditation on social and cultural change. This remarkable piece would eventually appear in three different versions. Two were accessible to pop listeners in that they were based on familiar rock and roll forms. The third, however, was an abstract audio collage that suggested the influence of avant-garde composer Karlheinz Stockhausen.[50]

Sgt. Pepper's Lonely Hearts Club Band and *Magical Mystery Tour* had each featured songs/tracks in which the coda had suggested interesting expressive possibilities beyond that of a typical conclusion. 'Penny Lane', 'Strawberry Fields Forever', 'Magical Mystery Tour', and 'I Am the Walrus' had each featured such sections. 'Revolution 9' may well be the highpoint of this development in that sections of it were derived from the extended improvisational section that occurred at the end of the first version of the song, 'Revolution 1'.

The sessions for 'Revolution 9' began on 6 June 1968. The first task at hand was the compiling of various sound effects. According to author Mark Lewisohn, 'Twelve effects were compiled on this day, five marked "Various" and the others titled "Vicars Poems", "Queen's Mess", "Come Dancing Combo", "Organ Last Will

Test" [sic], "Neville Club", "Theatre Outing" and "Applause/TV Jingle"'.[51] Lennon then added a variety of sounds compiled from the EMI Studio sound library, newly recorded passages, and effects that were originally prepared by Lennon and Victor Spinetti for *The Lennon Play: In His Own Write*. The compiling and recording of various sounds continued until 20 June when a full mix was created.

> It was a busy night for all concerned, John Lennon commandeering the use of all three studios at Abbey Road for the spinning in and recording of the myriad tape loops. Just like the 7 April 1966 'Tomorrow Never Knows' session, there were people all over EMI Studios spooling loops onto tape machines with pencils. But instead of Geoff Emerick sitting at the console fading them in and out in a live mix, it was John Lennon, with Yoko [Ono] closely by his side.[52]

Yoko Ono was a well-known member of the Fluxus art movement. Founded by students of composer John Cage,[53] the Fluxus artists 'sought to bridge the gaps between different artistic mediums and between art and life'.[54] Lennon had first met Ono in November 1966 at the Indica Gallery in London. He was particularly taken with the decidedly positive message of her piece *Ceiling Painting (YES Painting)* which consisted of a step ladder, a spyglass, and a canvas on the ceiling. Viewers of the work were directed to climb the ladder and use the spyglass to read a tiny white dot printed on the black canvas that contained the word, 'YES'.[55] In 1980, Lennon described the conversation that followed:

> Then I went up to this thing that said, 'Hammer a nail in'. I said, 'Can I hammer a nail in?' and she said no, because the gallery was actually opening the next day. So the owner, Dunbar, says, 'Let him hammer a nail in'. It was 'He's a millionaire. He might buy it' ... So there was this little conference and she finally said, 'OK, you can hammer a nail in for five shillings'. So smartass here says, 'Well, I'll give you an imaginary five shillings and hammer an imaginary nail in'. And that's when we really met.[56]

The following year, Yoko sent John a copy of her book *Grapefruit* (1964).[55] Steeped in the Fluxus aesthetic, the book contained a series of fascinating 'event scores', conceptual works in which 'everyday actions are framed as minimalistic performances or, occasionally, as imaginary and impossible experiments with everyday situations'.[57] Lennon was impressed and the two continued to stay in touch.[58,59]

In retrospect, Yoko Ono was essential to the realization of 'Revolution 9'. She helped and encouraged Lennon in what must have been a daunting creative task. For this track, he seems to have been intent on abandoning all he knew about musical form and process in order to work with raw sound as the primary work materials of the track. Evidently reaching back to his time at the Liverpool College of Art, he began to shape the loops and sounds with an ear (eye) towards their characteristics as pure sound. He also seemed focused on how the activity of these sounds would help define the virtual landscape of the finished track.

'Revolution 9' creates a dynamic space in which the various sonic elements can move slowly or at breakneck speed. The unpredictable motion of the sounds repeatedly defies attempts at orientation on the part of the listener. In that regard, it suggests an auditory equivalent of the rapid cutting that can be a feature in film or video. As 'Revolution 9' reaches its conclusion, the sonic image begins to morph into a realistic setting in which football fans enthusiastically cheer in support of their team. Gradually, these voices begin to fade away in a loop that swings from side to side in the stereo mix.

The network of sound presented in 'Revolution 9', combined with the song's length (eight minutes and twenty-two seconds), suggests conscious connections with the process of painting. Here, the sounds seem to move dynamically across a large canvas of silence in a manner that calls to mind the work of Jackson Pollock in paintings such as *Lavender Mist* (1950) and *Autumn Rhythm* (1950). In an article on the artist featured in *Gardner's Art Through the Ages: A Global History* (2013), it is asserted that 'Pollock's paintings emphasize the creative process. His mural-size canvases consist of rhythmic drips, splatters, and dribbles of paint that envelop viewers, drawing them into a lacy spider web'.[60] 'Revolution 9' creates a similar kind of web, but one that is made solely of sound.

'Blackbird'

Paul McCartney's contributions to *The Beatles* (1968) include two delicate pieces that continue to develop the notion of music as painting: 'Blackbird' and 'Mother Nature's Son'. 'Blackbird' is composed in G major and consists of two main sections that work in alternation. This gentle track may be the pinnacle of McCartney's ability to craft musical works in geometric terms. Two lines work together to create the kind of musical scaffold associated with the works of J.S. Bach. As it turns out, 'Blackbird' was modelled on a work by Bach, as Paul himself pointed out:

> I've always credited 'Blackbird' to a Bach thing which George and I used to play when we were kids [Bourrée in E minor, learned from Chet Atkins' version]. There's a bass thing that goes with it, and those progressions I always loved. I made 'Blackbird' out of that, in my mind, though other people say it's nothing like it.[61]

One of the most distinctive features of 'Blackbird' is the guitar strum that is featured throughout. Rather than use a standard picking pattern, Paul alternately plucks the outer strings and strums the inner strings to complete the chord. The pattern is distinctive, original, and also allows for what seems to be an Indian influence to coming through via the rhythmic variety of the part. Although one might consider this influence to be the result of The Beatles' recent trip to Rishikesh, there is another precedent that may be surprising. Take 1 of 'Yesterday' features the same strummed pattern before McCartney settles into the familiar part featured on the released version of the song.

'Blackbird' was recorded in EMI Studio Two on 11 June 1968. The track features Paul on acoustic guitar and vocal. There are also sounds of actual blackbirds that were added from an EMI effects tape recorded by Stuart Eltham in 1965, the same year Paul recorded 'Yesterday'.[62] The soft clicking sound in the background of the track seems like a metronome. However, a film of the session suggests that the sound is actually McCartney's feet tapping, and this may well be the actual source of the sound on the track.[63]

The use of bird sounds combined with the subtle treatment of the acoustics of the vocal and guitar parts suggests an exterior space. However, the foot tapping seems to firmly place the sound indoors. The concept at work here appears to suggest an opening up of the spaces of EMI Studio Two in order to create a blend of interior and exterior spaces. One imagines the presence of an open window in the studio so that the sounds of birds chirping outside might appear on the track. Of course, this would undermine the nature of the sound studio, which is designed to mask exterior sounds.

'Mother Nature's Son'

Now we come to one of the most remarkable tracks recorded by Paul during his time with The Beatles. Composed in the key of D major, 'Mother Nature's Son' features the same kind of guitar strum employed in 'Blackbird'. Remarkable colour shifts are achieved by the use of alternating tonic major and minor chords throughout. The instrumentation is also innovative in that it features brass instruments and percussion behind McCartney's acoustic guitar and vocal. The final seventh chord is a remarkable rhetorical flourish that author Tim Riley described as the musical equivalent of a question mark.[64]

Initial recordings for 'Mother Nature's Son' took place in EMI Studio Two on 9 August 1968 and were continued during an overnight session that began on 20 August 1968. Paul provided vocals, acoustic guitar, drums, and tympani. He also worked with George Martin to come up with parts for a brass overdub. They settled on an arrangement for two trumpets and two trombones.[65] Perhaps the most memorable aspect of the recording was its unique mood, a described to Mark Lewisohn by technical engineer Alan Brown who worked on the session:

> It was quite late at night, the whole building was quiet, and there was Paul playing this enchanting song. I love the phrase 'sitting in my field of grass'. It has a completeness about it. It isn't just any old field, it's a field of grass. We were all moved by it.[66]

As on 'Blackbird', the recording of 'Mother Nature's Son' seems to be an attempt to extend the space of EMI Studio Two. The session actually stretched out past the confines of the studio down to the stairwell at the back of the building. It was there that McCartney recorded the distinctive drum part heard on the song.[67] The effect that Paul creates here suggests the sounds of thunder approaching from a distance. It seems that nourishing rain may soon begin to fall on the 'field of grass' mentioned in the lyric.

'Happiness Is a Warm Gun'

The Lennon Play: In His Own Write shows the author and his collaborators (Adrienne Kennedy and Victor Spinetti) blending two books together into a unified theatrical presentation. Now John Lennon would apply the lessons he had learned from that experience to meet a new challenge. The task was to somehow extend the double-A-side-as-diptych idea while also setting it free from the 45-rpm format. If one could create a piece in which the panels were adjacent as on a continuous track, one could also add additional panels provided that one could make it work. The song/track that Lennon ultimately came up with was adapted from a phrase in an American gun magazine.[68]

'Happiness Is a Warm Gun' originally appeared in an unfinished form among the demos recorded at Harrison's home studio following The Beatles' return from their trip to India. On that version, John seems to be trying out ideas for different sections/panels. Ultimately, 'Happiness Is a Warm Gun' would comprise three:

Panel One ('She's Not a Girl Who Misses Much') is built on the kind of finger-picking technique for acoustic guitar that the composer had learned from Donovan during The Beatles' recent trip to India.[69] Applied here to electric guitar, it would become a signature sound for Lennon over the next few years. In the process, he seems to echo Bob Dylan's famous switch to electric guitar a few years earlier. The panel seems to begin in E minor, but quickly changes its direction to reveal that A minor is its actual key area. This is reinforced by an alternation of the subdominant chord and the tonic for the remainder of the section that now includes subtle metric shifts dependent on the lyrical phrase.

Panel Two ('I Need a Fix') arrives suddenly in the key of A major. It consists of two distinct sections. The first features a languorous groove built on two chords a minor third apart (A and C). In addition, the underlying rhythmic groupings have moved from twos to threes, but are couched in an unusual grouping. The second section features a rolling melodic riff over the original progression, which has now been modified to include a G7 chord. The rhythmic games continue here as a kind of back-and-forth struggle between twos and threes, with twos winning out in order to transition us over the G7 chord and into the next panel.

Panel Three ('Happiness Is a Warm Gun') is the most conventional of the three panels in that it is largely based on a classic rock and roll progression

(I–vi–IV–V). This familiar pattern provides a sense of arrival, as if the previous two panels have been moving us backwards in time. Here, the composer seems to be masking the musical sophistication at work with an established and highly accessible form. At one point, the groups of threes heard in the previous panel briefly reassert themselves, but in a manner consistent with early rock and roll styles. Finally, we arrive at a full and conclusive cadence that seems to settle the oppositions at work throughout the piece.

The basic tracks of 'Happiness Is a Warm Gun' were recorded in EMI Studio Two on 23, 24, and 25 September 1968. During the sessions, The Beatles recorded a total of seventy takes in order to master the challenging metric changes featured in the song. The final version was an edit of Takes 53 and 65. The group then overdubbed lead and backing vocals along with additional instrumentation.[70] The musicians on the track were John Lennon on vocals and guitar; Paul McCartney on bass and backing vocals; George Harrison on guitar and backing vocals; and Ringo Starr on drums.[71]

The space created on Panel One ('She's Not a Girl Who Misses Much') seems to be Lennon's take on a rainy afternoon. It connects with McCartney's portrayal of such a scene in 'Things We Said Today'. However, while McCartney's piece emphasized the thunder and the chance of an impending storm, Lennon seems more focused on the rainfall itself. The guitar evokes the sound perfectly and includes interesting shifts that suggest the seemingly random nature of change. Finally, we move into a space that seems more internal than external.

The space created on Panel Two ('I Need a Fix') seems focused on the singer's internal surrender to forces beyond his control. He seems to have given up on something or someone in a way that has led to a state of despair. Rather than attempting to deal with that situation directly, he instead chooses intoxication as a means of escape. After he attains his desired high, he begins to consider the random variations existing in the world around him. The pattern he uncovers leads ultimately to a personal oasis.

On one level, the space of Panel Three ('Happiness Is a Warm Gun') is comforting and familiar. The regular patterns in the musical sounds offer a level of safety and predictability. On another level, we also hear a lyric that is decidedly disturbing in its content. The character of the previous section seems to have found a means by which to resolve the various internal conflicts that led to his dilemma. Unfortunately, the resolution he has arrived at seems to involve the use of violent action.

'Happiness Is a Warm Gun' was a remarkable achievement for The Beatles. Here, they managed to expand the two-panel diptych idea of the double-A-side single into three panels. In the process, they effectively created the musical equivalent of a triptych; that is, a 'three-paneled painting, ivory plaque, or *altarpiece*'.[72] They were also able to place the panels adjacent to one another so that the track could be played as one continuous work. The next step was to enlarge this idea towards the dimensions of 'Revolution 9'.

Galleries

The pairing of *Magical Mystery Tour* with *Sgt. Pepper's Lonely Hearts Club Band* had been serendipitous. Now, with additional spaces to fill and design, the overall contour of their new double LP was larger than anything the band had attempted before. Rising to the challenge, they chose to feature a series of relatively short pieces that held specific meaning(s) within the context of musical history up to that point. As a result, the album can suggest a collection of discarded, or soon to be discarded, cultural fragments of human experience. In that respect, one song/track stands out in particular – a gentle ballad by Paul McCartney entitled 'Junk'.

'Junk' had been recorded in demo form at George Harrison's home studio prior to the beginning of sessions at EMI. Unfortunately, The Beatles never actually recorded a full studio version of the song/track.[73] In retrospect, this seems rather strange since the song's lyric, which explores the emotional power of discarded artefacts, connects well with the conceptual strategy adopted for the final album. For whatever reason, 'Junk' was not included. However, within two years, it would itself be retrieved to become the centrepiece of Paul McCartney's first solo LP.

The double-LP design was ideal for the exhibition of an extended and ambitious work like 'Revolution 9'. Side four seems to have been specifically set aside for that purpose. The room opens with 'Revolution 1', the original source of the sound collage. We then move on to a design layout that features one song/track each from McCartney ('Honey Pie'), Harrison ('Savoy Truffle'), and Lennon ('Cry Baby Cry'). These seem to prepare the listener/viewer for the main event, the sprawling canvas of 'Revolution 9'. At the end of the side/room, listeners/viewers are soothed during their departure from the exhibit with the soft, cloudy strains of Lennon's 'Good Night'.

Following the release of the LP *The Beatles*, the band members took a well-deserved break for the holidays. However, they regrouped in early January 1969 to revisit the idea of how one might blend film with music. The plan was to film The Beatles developing songs for a new album and then conclude with a full live concert in an exotic setting. When it became clear that both the film and the album would take longer to complete and make suitable for general release, The Beatles decided to make yet another new album. Released later that year, it was ultimately named after the location of London's EMI Studios.

Songs for the album that would become *Abbey Road* were recorded over the spring and summer of 1969. These were reminiscent of the material that had appeared on *The Beatles* but infused with a renewed sense of the band's corporate identity. Side one made this point clear by featuring tracks from individual members that nevertheless feel like statements from the entire band; for example, 'Come Together' (Lennon), 'Something' (Harrison), 'Oh, Darling' (McCartney), and 'Octopus's Garden' (Starr). Despite the impressive quality of the material on side one, it was the second side that was the real treat. Following another gem from George Harrison entitled 'Here Comes the Sun', the band offered something entirely new.

As noted, the double-LP design of *The Beatles* was ideal for an ambitious work like 'Revolution 9'. Side four of that album might be considered in terms of a large room especially designed for the exhibition of such a work. For *Abbey Road*, they would revisit this idea and use the second side to present an ambitious piece that would take its structural cues from 'Happiness Is a Warm Gun'. This extended work, which is sometimes described as a 'medley', might also be regarded as a musical triptych in large form.[74] Here, through the masterful blending of the LP as gallery-of-sound with the extended multi-panelled work, The Beatles offered up what may well be the finest achievement of their career.

Notes

1 John Lennon, *In His Own Write* (London: Jonathan Cape, 1964), 68.
2 Mark Lewisohn, *The Complete Beatles Chronicle* (New York: Harmony Books, 1992), 210–214.
3 Philip Norman, *Shout! The Beatles in Their Generation* (New York: Simon & Schuster, 2005), 310.
4 Philip Norman, *Shout! The Beatles in Their Generation* (New York: Simon & Schuster, 2005), 306.
5 Mark Lewisohn, *The Complete Beatles Chronicle* (New York: Harmony Books, 1992), 210–231.
6 David Sheff, *All We Are Saying: The Last Major Interview with John Lennon and Yoko Ono* (New York: St. Martin's Griffin, 2000), 155.
7 Barry Miles and Paul McCartney, *Many Years from Now* (New York: H. Holt, 1997), 307.
8 Mark Lewisohn, *The Beatles Recording Sessions* (New York: Harmony Books, 1988), 89.
9 Mark Lewisohn, *The Beatles Recording Sessions* (New York: Harmony Books, 1988), 87.
10 Mark Lewisohn, *The Complete Beatles Chronicle* (New York: Harmony Books, 1992), 232–233.
11 'John Lennon – Not Only ... but Also [HD] [Best Quality]'. YouTube. Techrick, 14 January 2018. https://youtu.be/0qAo0wx--C0 (dialogue transcribed by author).
12 Mark Lewisohn, *The Beatles Recording Sessions* (New York: Harmony Books, 1988), 89.
13 Mark Lewisohn, *The Beatles Recording Sessions* (New York: Harmony Books, 1988), 89–90.
14 Kevin Ryan and Brian Kehew, *Recording The Beatles: The Studio Equipment and Techniques Used to Create Their Classic Albums* (Houston, TX: Curvebender Publishers, 2006), 439.
15 Barry Miles and Paul McCartney, *Many Years from Now* (New York: H. Holt, 1997), 307–308.
16 Mark Lewisohn, *The Beatles Recording Sessions* (New York: Harmony Books, 1988), 91.
17 Kevin Ryan and Brian Kehew, *Recording The Beatles: The Studio Equipment and Techniques Used to Create Their Classic Albums* (Houston, TX: Curvebender Publishers, 2006), 442.
18 Mark Lewisohn, *The Beatles Recording Sessions* (New York: Harmony Books, 1988), 93.
19 Richard Brian Davis, *Alice in Wonderland and Philosophy: Curiouser and Curiouser* (Hoboken, NJ: John Wiley & Sons, 2010), 210.
20 Mark Lewisohn, *The Complete Beatles Chronicle* (New York: Harmony Books, 1992), 242.
21 Mark Lewisohn, *The Beatles Recording Sessions* (New York: Harmony Books, 1988), 84.
22 Fred S. Kleiner, *Gardner's Art Through the Ages: A Global History* (Boston, MA: Thompson Wadsworth, 2013), 1090.
23 Arthur, C. Danto, *Andy Warhol* (Yale University Press, 2010), 41.

24 Michael Kennedy, *The Concise Oxford Dictionary of Music* (Oxford: Oxford University Press, 2004), 594–595.

25 Michael Kennedy, *The Concise Oxford Dictionary of Music* (Oxford: Oxford University Press, 2004), 653–654.

26 'Andy Warhol Documentary Film Part 1 of 2'. YouTube. The Art Channel, 9 November 2013. https://youtu.be/UQXpqQO4vaE?t=4570.

27 Paul Du Noyer, *Conversations with McCartney* (New York: The Overlook Press, 2016), 67.

28 'John Lennon on "Lucy in the Sky with Diamonds" and LSD: The Dick Cavett Show'. YouTube. The Dick Cavett Show, 5 October 2018. https://youtu.be/umF60jXiYBI.

29 David Sheff, *All We Are Saying: The Last Major Interview with John Lennon and Yoko Ono* (New York: St. Martin's Griffin, 2000), 182.

30 Mark Lewisohn, *The Beatles Recording Sessions* (New York: Harmony Books, 1988), 100.

31 Mark Lewisohn, *The Beatles Recording Sessions* (New York: Harmony Books, 1988), 106.

32 Mark Lewisohn, *The Beatles Recording Sessions* (New York: Harmony Books, 1988), 114.

33 Charles L. Granata, *Wouldn't It Be Nice: Brian Wilson and the Making of The Beach Boys' Pet Sounds* (Chicago, IL: Chicago Review Press, 2003), 166.

34 'Sgt Pepper and Friends'. Oxford Dictionary of National Biography. Oxford University Press, 2022. www.oxforddnb.com/page/sgt-pepper-and-friends.

35 Ian MacDonald, *Revolution in the Head: The Beatles' Records and the Sixties* (London: Vintage, 2008), 261.

36 Barry Miles and Paul McCartney, *Many Years from Now* (New York: H. Holt, 1997), 358.

37 Mark Lewisohn, *The Beatles Recording Sessions* (New York: Harmony Books, 1988), 110–111.

38 Mark Lewisohn, *The Beatles Recording Sessions* (New York: Harmony Books, 1988), 130.

39 Ian Peel, *The Unknown Paul McCartney: McCartney and the Avant-Garde* (London and Richmond, Surrey: Reynolds & Hearn, 2002), 96.

40 Mark Lewisohn, *The Beatles Recording Sessions* (New York: Harmony Books, 1988), 128.

41 Mark Lewisohn, *The Beatles Recording Sessions* (New York: Harmony Books, 1988), 130.

42 *A Hard Day's Night*, directed by Richard Lester (1964; Burbank, CA: The Criterion Collection, 2014), DVD.

43 *Help!*, directed by Richard Lester (1965; Hollywood, CA: Capitol Records/Apple, 2007), DVD.

44 Philip Norman, *John Lennon: The Life* (Toronto: Anchor Canada, 2009), 523.

45 *Magical Mystery Tour*, directed by The Beatles (1967; Hollywood, CA: EMI Records Limited: Apple Films Limited, 2012), DVD.

46 'Theatre Archive Project – Sounds.bl.uk'. British Library Online Services. British Library, 1 September 2008. https://sounds.bl.uk/related-content/TRANSCRIPTS/024T-C1142X000292-0100A0.pdf.

47 Lennon, John. 'Scene Three Act One'. Theatricalia. A Matthew Somerville production. Accessed 19 March 2022. https://theatricalia.com/play/a7a/scene-three-act-one/production/mrq.

48 'John Lennon – Poignant Interview (BBC 2 Release Program 1968) HD'. YouTube. Poetic Sunsets, 4 April 2021. https://youtu.be/LwbVeGNa_lA (transcribed by author).

49 Mark Lewisohn, *The Beatles Recording Sessions* (New York: Harmony Books, 1988), 135.

50 Ian MacDonald, *Revolution in the Head: The Beatles' Records and the Sixties* (London: Vintage, 2008), 291.

51 Mark Lewisohn, *The Beatles Recording Sessions* (New York: Harmony Books, 1988), 137.

52 Mark Lewisohn, *The Beatles Recording Sessions* (New York: Harmony Books, 1988), 138.

53 Fred S. Kleiner, *Gardner's Art Through the Ages: A Global History* (Boston, MA: Thompson Wadsworth, 2013), 903.

54 'Introduction'. MoMA.org. Charting Fluxus: George Maciunas's Ambitious Art History. MoMA. Accessed 19 March 2022. www.moma.org/interactives/exhibitions/2013/char ting_fluxus.

55 Alan Clayson, *Woman: The Incredible Life of Yoko Ono* (New Malden: Chrome Dreams, 2004), 55.

56 David Sheff, *All We Are Saying: The Last Major Interview with John Lennon and Yoko Ono* (New York: St. Martin's Griffin, 2000), 104.

57 John Lennon and Yoko Ono, *Imagine John Yoko* (London: Thames & Hudson, Ltd., 2018), 28.

58 Hannah Higgins, *Fluxus Experience* (Berkeley, CA: University of California Press, 2002), 2.

59 Alan Clayson, *Woman: The Incredible Life of Yoko Ono* (New Malden: Chrome Dreams, 2004), 57.

60 Fred S. Kleiner, *Gardner's Art Through the Ages: A Global History* (Boston, MA: Thompson Wadsworth, 2013), 903.

61 Paul Du Noyer, *Conversations with McCartney* (New York: The Overlook Press, 2016), 209.

62 Mark Lewisohn, *The Beatles Recording Sessions* (New York: Harmony Books, 1988), 137.

63 Anykey679. 'Apple Promo Film #2 – Blackbird (Studio)'. YouTube. The Beatles Day, 4 March 2015. www.youtube.com/watch?v=7HI0fgeHTgE&t=142s.

64 Tim Riley, *Tell Me Why: A Beatles Commentary* (New York: Alfred A. Knopf, 1988), 279.

65 Ian MacDonald, *Revolution in the Head: The Beatles' Records and the Sixties* (London: Vintage, 2008), 305.

66 Mark Lewisohn, *The Beatles Recording Sessions* (New York: Harmony Books, 1988), 150.

67 Ken Scott, *From Abbey Road to Ziggy Stardust* (Los Angeles, CA: Alfred Music Publishing, 2012), 10.

68 Ian MacDonald, *Revolution in the Head: The Beatles' Records and the Sixties* (London: Vintage, 2008), 318.

69 Ian MacDonald, *Revolution in the Head: The Beatles' Records and the Sixties* (London: Vintage, 2008), 300.

70 Mark Lewisohn, *The Beatles Recording Sessions* (New York: Harmony Books, 1988), 157.

71 Ian MacDonald, *Revolution in the Head: The Beatles' Records and the Sixties* (London: Vintage, 2008), 120.

72 Fred S. Kleiner, *Gardner's Art Through the Ages: A Global History* (Boston, MA: Thompson Wadsworth, 2013), 1101.

73 Mark Lewisohn, *The Complete Beatles Chronicle* (New York: Harmony Books, 1992), 283–284.

74 Additional examples of musical triptychs include *New England Triptych* (1956) by William Schuman (*The Concise Oxford Dictionary of Music*, 2004, 654); *American Triptych* (1965) by Gunther Schuller (*The Harvard Concise Dictionary of Music and Musicians*, 1999, 596); and *Triptych* (1978) by Christopher Brown (*The Concise Oxford Dictionary of Music*, 2004, 104).

PART II
Extending the Space

4

A SEPARATE CANVAS

Following the release of *Abbey Road* (1969), The Beatles attended to the remaining business at hand; that is, the completion of the film/LP project they had begun earlier that year. Originally called *Get Back* after the single of the same name, they now settled on *Let It Be*, the title of one of the strongest songs/tracks on hand. The artistic ambition of the project is still impressive in its scope. Once again, as on their previous hands-on film project *Magical Mystery Tour*, they were attempting to create a bridge between art forms. The difference is that on *Magical Mystery Tour* The Beatles had attempted to invent the content; with *Let It Be*, they themselves became the content.

The Beatles would be filmed in documentary fashion rehearsing songs for a new album. Given the band's stellar history at EMI, it would seem a logical choice for them to complete the project there. Instead, they assembled at Twickenham Film Studios determined to play their new songs in unadorned fashion without the sophisticated recording techniques that had characterized their finest work to date.[1,2] The film, directed by Michael Lindsey-Hogg, would maintain the concept in that it would largely feature live, unadorned performances from the band. The accompanying album release was another matter entirely. Producer Glyn Johns had initially tried to organize the material into a workable sequence that would be suitable for general release. However, The Beatles ultimately relented and resorted to various tried and true studio techniques to finish the album.

On 30 January 1969 The Beatles had given a midday concert on the roof of their Apple business offices in London.[3] This rooftop set was heard by a number of people in nearby office buildings as well as passers-by on the streets below. Several of these onlookers were interviewed by a camera crew during the performance. One man, in particular, managed to succinctly express all the goodwill the band had generated over the course of their career:

DOI: 10.4324/9781003300212-7

I think The Beatles are crackin'. You can't beat 'em, I say. They're all out on their own, a style of their own. And they, in my opinion, I think they're a lovely crowd. They've got good qualities; they sing well. And well, what else can I say but that they're all good people.[4]

'Across the Universe'

During a day of filming at Twickenham, The Beatles had begun to play a John Lennon song called 'Across the Universe'. They had already recorded a version of this song in early 1968, and had intended to release it as a single. However, that plan was soon abandoned and instead 'Across the Universe' was donated to comedian Spike Milligan to be part of a charity album he was organizing for the World Wildlife Fund.[5] That album, entitled *No One's Gonna Change Our World*, would ultimately be released in December 1969. In the meantime, 'Across the Universe' had resurfaced as a possible contender for the new film/album project.

Here, Lennon managed to create something rather unique in The Beatles catalogue. Throughout the piece, he maintains a remarkably deep connection between music and text. His lyrics seem directly connected to the poetic variations that are an essential part of the musical process. As a result, when considering the song/ track, one is often not sure where the music ends and the lyric begins.

As the *Let It Be* project dragged on, Beatles manager Allen Klein contracted legendary producer Phil Spector to complete the tracks for the album.[6] Spector went back to the original version of 'Across the Universe' that had been donated to the World Wildlife Fund project and remixed it in preparation for further overdubs. That recording had featured an intimate, acoustic setting reminiscent of tracks from *Rubber Soul* (1965). Spector, however, believed that the song would benefit from a grander setting, so he decided to add strings, brass, choir, and drums to the arrangement. These were recorded in a marathon session that took place at EMI Studios on 1 April 1970.[7]

The space created on the version of 'Across the Universe' that was included on *Let It Be* is rich and expansive, with colours that suggest a unified sensorium of sight and sound. A curious aspect of the recording concerns its unusual choice of key area. The original version of the song was in D major, but by the time it was released on the World Wildlife Fund charity album, it had been sped up to sound one half-step higher in E flat major. Curiously, by the time it was released on *Let It Be*, 'Across the Universe' had been slowed down from the original version to sound one half-step lower in D flat major.[8] Perhaps Lennon was looking for a suitable space between key areas that would best ground the musical/lyrical metaphors mentioned above.

'Junk'

Conspicuous in his absence from the final recording sessions for *Let It Be* was Paul McCartney. In September 1969, Lennon had announced to his fellow Beatles and their new manager, Allen Klein, that he was leaving the group, but had been persuaded to say nothing publicly while a new contract was being negotiated.[9] McCartney had disagreed with the choice of Allen Klein as manager the previous year, and as he was unable to convince the other Beatles, he opted to withdraw from the situation and consider his options. In December 1969, he received delivery of a Studer four-track recorded at his home in St John's Wood, London. He then began experimenting with overdubbing all the parts himself using only one microphone plugged directly into the back of the machine. This process continued over the next few months with additional work done at Morgan Studios and EMI Studios, at the end of which he had his first solo album.[10]

During the 1970s, both Lennon and McCartney would revisit *The Beatles* (1968) in order to extend and develop the various threads that had been suggested by that collection. Here, with his first solo album, Paul revisits a theme embedded in that remarkable album. It concerned the discarded fragments of human experience. This is best exemplified by the album's centrepiece: 'Junk', a seeming reference to William Butler Yeats' 'rag-and-bone shop of the heart'.[11] Discarded by the band for both *The Beatles* (1968) and *Abbey Road* (1969), the song would now be retrieved.

'Junk' is a gentle waltz that consists of two main sections. The primary section is built on a lilting chord progression in F sharp minor. The contrasting section then opens with an unusual suspension over a D minor chord before moving decisively to the relative major (A major). The overall arrangement is soft and delicate, consisting of acoustic guitars, an exceptionally melodic electric bass, and colourful lead and backing vocals. The song then concludes with a coda over a descending chromatic line and leads finally to an interesting improvisational dance between the acoustic guitars.

As mentioned, the lyric seems to reference 'The Circus Animals' Desertion' by William Butler Yeats.[12] The shop mentioned in the song suggests the 'rag-and-bone shop' of Yeats' poem.[13] Here, the various items on display seem to be crying out in an effort to emphasize the value of the human feeling that has been infused within them.

As he'd do later on 'Backwards Traveller' from *London Town* (1978), McCartney seems to be clueing us in on the nature of his creative process. Over the course of his career, he would return again and again to the discarded elements of human experience that wait patiently to be retrieved. By the same token, the music for 'Junk' blends beautifully with the song's lyric in a manner reminiscent of Lennon's work on 'Across the Universe'. The lament he sings for the various items described in the text is itself a cliché and thus in danger of being discarded. As a result, the song's thematic focus, as manifest in both the music and the lyric, continually circles back on itself in search of renewal.

'Junk' was among those tracks from the *McCartney* LP that were begun at home in December 1969 and finished at Morgan Studios in February 1970. At his home, he recorded bass, acoustic guitars, and a lead vocal. At Morgan Studios in Willesden, London he transferred the contents of the four-track tape to eight-track format to make room for additional overdubs.[14] He then added a harmony vocal and percussion.[15] According to notes by the composer provided in a press release for the album, the track arrangement for the song resembled that shown in Example 1.[16]

EXAMPLE 1 MULTI-TRACK OUTLINE FOR 'JUNK'

Track 1	Acoustic guitar (St John's Wood)
Track 2	Acoustic guitar (St John's Wood)
Track 3	Bass (St John's Wood)
Track 4	Vocal (St John's Wood)
Track 5	Percussion (bass drum) (Morgan Studios)
Track 6	Percussion (snare with brushes) (Morgan Studios)
Track 7	Percussion (small xylophone) (Morgan Studios)
Track 8	Harmony vocal (Morgan Studios)

When McCartney received the four-track recorder, he reportedly placed it in his 'back room', the room that had become his home studio space.[17] The sound space of this room seems audible on several of the tracks from the album, 'Junk' included. In connection with this idea, it's interesting to consider how the creative process can be enhanced when it occurs in the house in which we live.[18] As compared with Paul's prior work in professional recording studios, there is a relaxation evident in these performances, suggesting that the artist is learning to abide more comfortably within himself, as he described to Paul Du Noyer:

> Home was being natural, being myself. I either made it at home – I got a machine from EMI, a four-track – or went down to a little studio, Morgan in Willesden, just working with one engineer. Me and Lin and the baby in the control room. It was joyous.[19]

In addition to the retrieved (or continuing) theme of discarded fragments/artefacts of human experience, the *McCartney* LP had another interesting concept at work. Several of the tracks on display such as 'Every Night', 'Man We Was Lonely', and 'Maybe I'm Amazed' sound fully realized. Others, however, seem noticeably incomplete. For example, the brief opening track entitled 'The Lovely Linda' suggests a rough preliminary sketch for a much larger work to be completed at a later date. The implication is that within the virtual space of the LP format, listeners have been invited into an artist's creative space to explore and consider his process.

Through its clever variation on the LP-as-gallery theme, the *McCartney* LP was able to make use of works that were fragments in search of a larger context. One of the most interesting examples of this idea was a track called 'Hot as Sun/Glasses'. Even though only two elements are referenced by the title, this track is essentially in three parts. The first, 'Hot as Sun', was an instrumental that dated back to the early Beatles; the second, 'Glasses', was a sound experiment involving glasses filled with water and played randomly; the third, 'Suicide', was a brief excerpt of a comic song that McCartney hoped Frank Sinatra might agree to record. He didn't.[20]

'Hot as Sun' was recorded at Morgan Studios in February 1970.[21] During the session, McCartney added a much-needed middle section for the piece, and, in an impressive display of skill, played all the instruments on the track himself.[22] 'Glasses' was recorded in EMI Studio Three and engineered by Phil McDonald.[23] The track was succinctly described by its composer as 'Wineglasses played at random and overdubbed on top of each other'.[24] The final section, 'Suicide', was evidently a quick snippet of McCartney on piano and vocal playing a song that he recorded at his home in St John's Wood.[25]

'Hot as Sun/Glasses' creates an interesting contrast between musical spaces. The opening section is a modern recording of a track that was written years earlier in an early rock style. As previously noted, the middle section was added during the session in a seeming attempt to reach back to that earlier style. During the song's repeating coda, which may also have been created during the session, there is a sudden cut to a sea of sounds in which random pitch shifts resonate in a timeless space. Suddenly, out of this sound mass there appears a voice and a piano in mid-song, and in a style that suggests we are hearing a broadcast from an earlier era of popular music (the 1930s).

The tracks from *McCartney* discussed thus far trace an interesting creative journey. It began in St John's Wood, London where McCartney had established a proper home studio and completed a series of recordings that would form the basis for the new album. This was followed by trips to Morgan Studios in Willesden, London, where the four-track master tapes created in St John's Wood were transferred to eight-track for mixing, editing, and further recording. The last stop was EMI Studios for the final mastering of the completed tracks, and where Paul also took the opportunity to record two new tracks, one of which was called 'Every Night'.[26] This new song was a gentle folk ballad built on a unique chord pattern played on acoustic guitar. Echoing its assumed model of 'Everyday' by Buddy Holly, the song continues with a series of interesting harmonic shifts before finally arriving at a basic progression built on primary chords, over which McCartney improvises a melodic vocal line reminiscent of the coda from 'Junk'. The format then repeats in its entirety and the song begins to gently fade away.

'Every Night' was recorded at EMI Studios on 22 February 1970. As previously noted, McCartney travelled there to begin the final mastering process for the album. This session was booked to create stereo mixes of two tracks, 'That Would Be Something' and 'Valentine Day'.[27] However, during the session, he was inspired to continue the recording process, this time in the familiar ambience of EMI. According to notes by the composer provided in a press release for the *McCartney* album, the arrangement and track layout was as in Example 2.[28]

EXAMPLE 2 MULTI-TRACK OUTLINE FOR 'EVERY NIGHT'

Track 1	Vocal and …
Track 2	Acoustic guitar
Track 3	Drums
Track 4	Bass
Track 5	Lead guitar (acoustic)
Track 6	Harmony to the lead guitar
Track 7	Double-tracked vocal in parts
Track 8	Electric guitar (not used)

Although it is not clearly indicated, the suggestion is that the first two tracks of 'Vocal and acoustic guitar' were recorded together while the rest of the overdubs may have been created sequentially from Tracks 3 to 7. Thus, the next parts would likely have been drums on Track 4 followed by electric bass on Track 5. Next could have come a lead part on acoustic guitar recorded onto Track 5 and a harmony to that same part on Track 6. Finally, McCartney would have double-tracked his vocal in parts on Track 7, and then tried out a part on electric guitar that was ultimately not used. The track notes for 'Every Night' also suggest the presence of a ninth track on the master tape. Since it is not clear exactly what this is meant to indicate, it has been omitted from the track layout in Example 2.

The space defined by the sounds of 'Every Night' suggests an aquatic environment in which the parts flow back and forth. The gentle ease of this performance is quite remarkable when one considers that it was recorded entirely at EMI Studios rather than in St John's Wood. The mood is similar to that of 'Hot as Sun' but even more spacious and relaxed. The suggestion is that McCartney has managed to extend the ease that was audible on the initial tracks recorded at home through Morgan Studios and then on to EMI. Thus, the album's ultimate aesthetic innovation may well lie in the way it merges the relaxation of the home demo with the polish of the professional recording studio.

'Kreen-Akrore'

Paul ended his first album with an extraordinary track called 'Kreen-Akrore'. The piece was reportedly inspired by *The Tribe That Hides from Man* (1970), a documentary that focused on attempts to establish contact with an elusive South American tribe.[29] The opening section features a drum part that moves steadily but carefully along. It is followed by a contrasting passage in which a band plays a brief progression before disappearing back into the darkness. These sections alternate throughout the piece with subtle textural variations employed during each appearance.

'Kreen-Akrore' was recorded at Morgan Studios on 12 February 1970. McCartney provided drums, piano, bass, electric guitar, organ, and percussion. He and Linda McCartney sang backing vocals and added various effects.[30] According to Paul, the two drum tracks were recorded first. These were augmented with add-itional instrumental parts and effects that served to extend the texture and the concept. He also describes how they lit a fire in the studio but opted instead for the sound of breaking twigs to create the same effect.[31] According to notes by the composer provided in a press release for the *McCartney* album, the arrangement and track layout was as shown in Example 3.[32]

EXAMPLE 3 MULTI-TRACK OUTLINE FOR 'KREEN-AKRORE'

Track 1   Drums 1 (Paul)
Track 2   Drums 2 (Paul)
Track 3   Piano (Paul)
Track 4   Guitar (Paul)
Track 5   Organ (Paul)
Track 6   Vocals (Paul and Linda)
Track 7   Vocals (Paul and Linda)
Track 8   Effects (Paul and Linda)

The soundscape of 'Kreen-Akrore' is varied and compelling. Session notes provided by Paul assert that the track was driven by the concept of a hunt.[33] As the track unfolds, the drum parts approximate the increasingly rapid heartbeat of both predator and prey. The ambience of a forest at night is created by various effects that include the sounds of birds. Ultimately, 'Kreen-Akrore' works as a veritable painting in sound.

The release of *McCartney* created yet another logistical problem for The Beatles. Paul was understandably enthusiastic about his new solo album and wanted it released as soon as possible. The other band members preferred that the release be postponed until after *Let It Be* in order to maximize the public's focus on The Beatles' final project. McCartney, however, was determined that his LP be made available at an earlier date. After the others relented, Paul made it known to the press that The Beatles were no more.[34]

The breakup of The Beatles was a sobering experience. It seemed to close the book on the optimism that had been fuelling the previous decade. Still, it also allowed for an assessment on all that had been achieved culturally up to that point. In that regard, The Beatles' accomplishments became much clearer. In the book *The Ambient Century: From Mahler to Moby* (2003), author Mark Prendergast described the significance of The Beatles' studio work:

> Their contribution was a quantum leap in terms of sound and quality on almost everything that had come before them. By the late 1960s each of their albums had become an event, a benchmark example of what could be done inside a studio with the best technology and a group of musicians at the very apex of their creativity.[35]

'Remember'

Like McCartney, Lennon had also been revisiting and further developing ideas that were first explored on *The Beatles* (1968). Over the previous year, he had released the singles 'Give Peace a Chance', 'Cold Turkey', and 'Instant Karma', each of which had explored the power of raw sound as a kind of broad musical brushstroke. Now he would extend this idea into an entire album called *John Lennon/Plastic Ono Band* (1970). Produced by Phil Spector, Yoko Ono, and Lennon, the album featured a remarkable collection of tracks that grapple with issues of personal identity. In this connection, Lennon described his new band as '[a] conceptual group which exists only in the mind. You're in it. Everybody's in the Plastic Ono Band. We're all members of the Plastic Ono Band. We're all members of the conceptual Utopia'.[36]

'Remember' begins side two of *John Lennon/Plastic Ono Band* with an insistent riff played on acoustic piano. This riff is remarkable in that it veers repeatedly into the instrument's lower register, and thus risks blurring the song's harmonic colour. The pattern deliberately distorts the rhythmic flow before settling on a descending chromatic line in the bass as the foundation for the song's primary section. This section is abruptly interrupted by a dead stop, followed by an anthemic section in which the rising motion of the melody seems to counter the compelling yet perilous descent of the opening section. The coda builds on the descending bass line of the primary section before culminating in the sounds of a massive explosion.

The master version of 'Remember' (Take 13) was recorded in EMI Studio Three on 9 October 1970, John Lennon's thirtieth birthday. The musicians were Ringo Starr on drums (Tracks 3 and 4), Klaus Voormann on electric bass (Track 2), and Lennon himself on piano (Track 5), lead vocals (Track 7), harmony vocals (Track 1), and jaw harp (Tracks 1 and 8). Track 1 had originally featured an organ, presumably played by Lennon himself and recorded on 10 October. However, this part was eventually erased to make room for an additional overdub of jaw harp and an intermittent harmony vocal (Example 4).[37]

EXAMPLE 4 MULTI-TRACK OUTLINE FOR 'REMEMBER'[38]

Track 1	John Lennon (jaw harp and harmony vocal – Take 3) (originally organ)
Track 2	Klaus Voormann (bass)
Track 3	Starr (drums – left)
Track 4	Starr (drums – right)
Track 5	Lennon (piano)
Track 6	Lennon (vocal – Take 3)
Track 7	Lennon (vocal – Take 3 – best)
Track 8	Lennon (jaw harp – Take 3)

The sound of the jaw harp is difficult to discern on the final mix, but its presence is made clearer on an alternate mix provided on *John Lennon/Plastic Ono Band – The Ultimate Collection* released in 2021. Comparing that mix with the released version demonstrates how the sound of the instrument was evidently blended with the acoustic piano. Its presence seems to have reduced some of the ambiguity created by playing the low-register piano.

Like many of the songs on *John Lennon/Plastic Ono Band*, the electric bass and the bass drums are featured in what seems to be an extreme close-up, suggesting that 'Remember' was produced with an awareness of the power of proximity. The resulting effect evokes the darker aspects of memory and/or the cavernous spaces of a nightmare. As the pressure seems to build to the point of a complete overload, a new space suddenly opens, and the nightmare ends. The motion through this new space is smoothly reassuring and suggests that wisdom and confidence have been attained through earlier struggles. Soon, however, the cycle resumes and leads ultimately to what seems to be a violent completion of the journey.

'Love'

In keeping with the sharp contrasts that characterize *John Lennon/Plastic Ono Band*, the song that follows 'Remember' is a gentle ballad entitled 'Love'. The song essentially consists of guitar and voice but also features accompaniment on parlour piano. An unusual feature during the introduction is the way in which the piano fades in from far away. The process then repeats itself in the coda, during which, after the song comes to a full stop, the piano fades in once again before disappearing slowly into the distance. This remarkable production effect suggests a dream in which the more elusive elements are always just out of reach.

'Love' was one of the most uncomplicated recordings on the entire album. It featured only John Lennon on acoustic guitar and vocals and Phil Spector on piano.[39] However, that version created some interesting complications later on in the process. The problem was that the version of 'Love' included on the original LP release was a mono mix that contained a noticeable amount of excess noise. Subsequent stereo versions simulated the introduction and coda in order to reduce this noise and, in the process, make a case for the original version being the authentic one.[40]

The space created for 'Love' seems to evoke the hypnogogic state of mind just prior to sleep. The gentle strum of the guitar and the rocking motion of the piano part recall a lullaby, while Lennon's tender vocal performance adds to the effect. As the track unfolds, the listener is gradually lulled into a pleasant slumber. Once there, the deeper meanings explored in the text can begin to reveal themselves. Love can be understood in its essence, beyond the superficial concerns of waking life.

'Why'

One of the most interesting unused sequences filmed for *Let It Be* takes place on 25 January 1969, after The Beatles had moved from Twickenham Film Studios to a newly created recording studio at the band's business offices in Savile Row, London.[41] The footage shows Yoko Ono in the background while The Beatles are sketching out an arrangement for 'Two of Us'. As they continue to play, Ono sets up some blank paper on the wall of the studio and begins to paint a series of ideograms.[42] Here, she seems to be making a statement about the connections between recording studio and art studio. The implications are interesting to consider when one listens to her album, *Yoko Ono/Plastic Ono Band*.

Recorded primarily at Abbey Road, this fascinating collection seems to sit somewhere in the crossroads between rock, jazz, and avant-garde experimentation. Bassist and graphic artist Klaus Voormann described the development of this eclectic approach:

> We knew Yoko was gonna do her album. We didn't know how it was actually going to work or what she was going to do. We heard a few tracks she did and I found that very interesting. There was some great horn player, I think it was Ornette Coleman. She had some great musicians and three jazz players, really really good. So we tried to do the same thing and John was open to it.[43]

Throughout the album, Ono uses her voice to paint freely on the canvas created by the studio space. In retrospect, her approach suggests the influence of Jackson Pollock, so much so that many of the tracks might best be described as 'action paintings' in sound.

In a gesture of solidarity between the two *Plastic Ono Band* projects, the first single release was a pairing of the opening tracks from each LP. The A-side was 'Mother', a harrowing yet undeniably powerful track in which Lennon began to purge the trauma associated with his fractured family history. The B-side was 'Why', a passionate eruption of sound that began with Lennon's lead guitar morphing into Ono's anguished high-pitched vocals. Lennon described this moment in terms of the collaborative space created on the session:

> There's a point on the first song where the guitar comes in and even Yoko thought it was her voice. It became like a dialogue rather than a monologue and I like that, stimulating each other. And that happened in the drumming and bass too, they get like that too. And it's very interesting that you don't know who is really inspiring who, it just goes on like that.[44]

Two Galleries

Part of the brilliance of Paul McCartney's work on his first solo album was the way in which he reinvented the idea of LP as gallery. Essentially, he blends it with the notion of studio space as workshop and then invites listeners in to consider the various tracks on display as works in progress. Additionally, the journey from his home in St John's Wood, to Morgan Studios, and then back to EMI seems to have allowed him an opportunity to reconsider his own recording process. As a result, he began to deepen his already considerable understanding of music, space, and imagery and then made it a feature of his solo debut. More than fifty years later, the results of this innovative project are still impressive.

In contrast with McCartney, Lennon began his album at EMI Studios, seemingly trying to turn it into his own workshop or gallery. Like McCartney, his work displays a newfound ease in the space. This may well have been because the production team assembled for the project resembles the group he and Sutcliffe had envisioned back in the days when they were one half of the Dissenters. In addition to Lennon himself and ex-Beatle Ringo drumming, the core team consisted of graphic artist Klaus Voormann on bass and conceptual artist Yoko Ono, who was co-producing with Lennon and Phil Spector. Anyone looking in during the sessions might have wondered if a group of artists had taken over the space!

Although Yoko Ono didn't perform on the Lennon sessions, her influence can be felt throughout. Also, since *John Lennon/Plastic Ono Band* and *Yoko Ono/Plastic Ono Band* were recorded in near-concurrent fashion and later paired on release, it may be reasonable to consider the two as a double LP. In that regard, there is an interesting flow between them. Lennon's disc can be seen as the result of a singer/songwriter, known for an expressive yet highly structured approach, moving back towards the source – that is, raw – sound. In contrast, Ono's process seemed to involve starting from raw sound and moving gradually towards structural forms. Thus, the two albums can be seen as moving in contrary motion to one another before meeting somewhere in the middle.

Ram

In 1971, Paul McCartney would deliver on the promise of his solo debut with *Ram*. Created in collaboration with his wife Linda, the album blends sonic experimentation with musical whimsy. The sessions began at CBS Studios in New York City in October 1970. In response to critics who complained that his first solo album had lacked the professional lustre of The Beatles, McCartney hired top New York session players for the new project. Guitarists David Spinozza and Hugh McCracken, along with drummer Denny Seiwell, joined him to become the core band for *Ram*. The first single released from the sessions was a charming piece entitled 'Another Day'.

'Another Day' is a mid-tempo folk-rock song built on two sections of considerable length that each lend gravitas to the melancholy message of the text. McCartney's flair for melody is widely known, but his rhythmic subtleties are sometimes overlooked. Here, his vocal opens the track and is quickly joined by an intriguing rhythmic pattern that cleverly alternates groups of three against groups of two. The rhythmic play continues in the extended contrasting section in which groups of twos and threes are repeatedly layered over one another. The song concludes with a decisive coda that features an arrival point seemingly predetermined by all that has come before.

Sessions for 'Another Day' began on 12 October 1970 at CBS Studios, Studio B.[45] As previously noted, the journey for McCartney over the previous year had been one marked by changing recording formats. It started on four-track at his home in St John's Wood, followed by moves to eight-track at both Morgan Studios and EMI. The new project would extend that journey in that it would be recorded on a sixteen-track machine. An additional factor would be the size of the room, which rivalled the large recording spaces McCartney had grown accustomed to at EMI. Engineer Tim Geelan described the recording format, the layout of Studio B, and his memories of McCartney in the studio:

> We had a 3M MM-1000 16-track recorder and a homemade console at CBS. Studio B was a big room, about 40 or 50 feet long and 50 feet wide with a 40-foot-high ceiling. We didn't worry about bleeding at all. The setup was real tight and everyone had headsets. Paul was absolutely the best. I was impressed with his musicianship and command of the studio.[46]

The recording schedule was regular in that there would be meetings in the morning in which Paul would introduce the material to the core musicians. This would be followed by the working out of appropriate arrangements. After breaking for lunch, they would return to begin recording the basic tracks. Example 5 collates the available information on the recording sessions of 'Another Day', which began at CBS Studios on 12 October 1970 and continued at A&R Studios in January 1971.[47]

EXAMPLE 5 MULTI-TRACK OUTLINE FOR 'ANOTHER DAY'[48]

Track 1   Bass drum (Denny Seiwell)
Track 2   Hi-hat, snare, small tom (Denny Seiwell)
Track 3   Floor tom (Denny Seiwell)
Track 4   Snare and bass drum fill (Denny Seiwell) (TAPS)
Track 5   Bass (Paul McCartney)
Track 6   Acoustic guitar (David Spinozza)
Track 7   Acoustic guitar (Paul McCartney)
Track 8   Sax sounds and guitar fills (Paul McCartney)
Track 9   Amp guitar #1 (David Spinozza and Paul McCartney)
Track 10   Amp guitar #2 (David Spinozza and Paul McCartney)
Track 11   Harmony at end + crowd (Paul and Linda McCartney) (1/21/71)
Track 12   Harmony at end + crowd doubled (Paul and Linda McCartney) (1/21/71)
Track 13   Lead vocal (Paul McCartney) (1/21/71)
Track 14   Lead vocal doubled (Paul McCartney) (1/21/71)
Track 15   Background + high voice (Paul and Linda McCartney) (1/21/71)
Track 16   Background + high voice doubled (Paul and Linda McCartney) (1/21/71)

The finished track seems to evoke a rainy afternoon in which intermittent showers alternate with a mist or fog that hangs gently over the landscape. As the track unfolds, the various instrumental sounds seem to explore and define the space. Of particular interest is the bass line played by McCartney himself. Using the bass guitar as a kind of musical paintbrush, he creates a line that is strong and assured, yet also light and playful in its inventive rhythmic gestures. Throughout the track, he seems to use the bass to infuse the space/scene with rich and vibrant colour.

'Another Day' was chosen as the first single release from the *Ram* sessions largely on the recommendation of Dixon Van Winkle. The engineer had prepared the track for radio airplay but was subsequently concerned that some of his choices during mixing may have been too extreme:

> I mixed the track and David Crawford cut about 100 copies of it in a back room at A&R for the radio stations. The next day when I heard it on the air, I realized it was a disaster! We got carried away with the bass part, and when it hit the radio station's compressor, it pumped like crazy! I learned that lesson real quick! But we never remixed the song, and Paul never said anything about it.[49]

Based on the impressions provided through the discussion of 'Another Day' provided above, as well as the song's lingering appeal, Van Winkle needn't have worried. His choices in preparing the mix were spot on.

'Uncle Albert/Admiral Halsey'

Several tracks on *McCartney* had extended the idea of musical diptych ('Momma Miss America') or even triptych ('Hot as Sun/Glasses'). These certainly connect with the thrust of The Beatles' work, and also emphasize Paul's facility with this form. Nevertheless, their sketch-like quality might cause them to be overlooked by some as mere trifles. With 'Uncle Albert/Admiral Halsey', however, Paul and Linda unveiled a fully developed diptych that was worthy of similar works by The Beatles. In fact, the song/track's release as a single in the USA in the summer of 1971 led some youthful listeners to believe that the band had, in fact, reformed.

> **Panel One** is a mellow yet atmospheric character sketch entitled 'Uncle Albert'. This section has an interesting structure in that even though it feels very much like a detailed portrait of the title character, we never actually get to meet the man. Instead, we hear one side of a phone conversation in which the singer apologizes for a lack of information and also for not keeping in touch. This section makes effective use of harmonic and melodic structures that often seem to suggest the influence of Burt Bacharach. If all this wasn't enough, it also employs the sounds of a rainstorm complete with thunder as a transition into the next panel.

Panel Two is a bouncy music hall–styled number called 'Admiral Halsey'. Musically, it extends the Bacharach references from the first panel through the use of a melodic hook played on flugelhorn. This part seems to be an homage to Bacharach's distinctive touch in writing for that instrument as demonstrated on many of his recordings released throughout the 1960s. As in the first panel, the composition concerns a character that we never actually get to meet. We do, however, get an account of a conversation that the Admiral had with the singer, in which he describes what he needs ('a bath') in order to carry out his schedule.

The basic tracks for 'Uncle Albert/Admiral Halsey' were recorded on 6 November 1970 at Columbia Studios in New York City. Orchestral overdubs took place on 3 and 11 January 1971, this time at A&R Studios in New York City. Further overdubs were completed at Sunset Sound Recorders Studio in Los Angeles in March and April 1971. In addition to Paul McCartney on acoustic and electric guitars, bass, piano, and vocals, the song also featured Linda McCartney on backing vocals, Denny Seiwell on drums, Hugh McCracken on acoustic and electric guitars, and Paul Beaver on synthesizer. George Martin provided the orchestration for the track, but the score was conducted by McCartney himself.[50]

Paul was reportedly confident and well prepared in the studio. He was also open and flexible regarding musical arrangements for his songs. Guitarist Hugh McCracken described how the distinctive guitar lines featured on 'Uncle Albert/Admiral Halsey' came about:

> He sees and hears everything he wants, and would give specific instructions to me and the drummer. But he didn't know what he wanted the guitar part to be like on this song. I asked him to trust me and he did. After I came up with the parts, he was very pleased. For the rest of the record, Paul let me try things out before making any suggestions.[51]

The narrative space of 'Uncle Albert/Admiral Halsey' seems built on a shared cultural history between Britain and the United States. Paul did have an Uncle Albert, who was married to his Aunt Milly.[52] However, it is also interesting to take note of how P.L. Travers featured a character by that name in *Mary Poppins*. There, Travers paints Uncle Albert as an eccentric Edwardian given to fits of laughter that cause him to float upwards towards the ceiling of his room.[53] The 'Admiral Halsey' featured in Panel Two seems to be a reference to William 'Bull' Halsey. A famous war hero, Halsey commanded the Third Fleet in the Pacific Ocean during the Second World War.[54] Thus, McCartney may have been creating an associative link between a fictional character floating on air during the heights of the British Empire and an American naval hero who helped to defend that empire when it was in danger.

'Monkberry Moon Delight'

Side two of the *Ram* album contains a remarkable extended track entitled 'Monkberry Moon Delight'. Here, McCartney employs his Little Richard-inspired vocal style to deliver what might best be described as frenzied folk music. The song is performed in C minor, but the elemental chord progression suggests that the material may have been transposed up from A minor. The main section presents an extended narrative in what seems to be nonsense verse that echoes the works of Lewis Carroll. The contrasting section reveals the central image: a delicious drink called 'Monkberry Moon Delight' that, when consumed, generates the kind of physical and emotional exhilaration that is exhibited by the singer of the song.

The basic tracks for 'Monkberry Moon Delight' were recorded in the autumn of 1970 during the initial sessions for the *Ram* album at CBS Studios, New York City. Additional parts would then have been added in Los Angeles in early 1971. The musicians on the final track are Paul McCartney on piano, guitar, bass, and vocals; Linda McCartney on vocals; Denny Seiwell on drums and percussion; and Hugh McCracken on guitar. There is also an indication that someone is playing a mandolin, possibly McCracken. Following the overdub sessions, the song was then mixed for inclusion on *Ram*.[55]

Although no obvious effects are used, the space created by the various sounds present on the track suggests a scene taking place in a primordial forest. Here, the secrets of nature reveal themselves through a delicious drink made from the juice of wild berries. Of particular interest is the coda in which the lead singer begins to abandon words completely in order to express a sense of wonder by means of pure, improvised vocal melody. In a manner similar to the action of the bass guitar in 'Another Day', the lead vocal seems to be painting on the canvas of the natural world. The continuous stream of motivic material in the vocal suggests that the source of the singer's inspiration is eternal.

'Eat at Home'

'Eat at Home' is one of the most straightforward works on the *Ram* album, and also one of the most effective. Reaching back to the early guitar-based styles that had inspired him, Paul offers an unpretentious yet stylish slice of bluesy rock and roll. The unpretentiousness lies in the alternation between the two main sections built on primary chords. The stylishness rests in the chromatic filigree that he adds as transitional material between the two sections. Although 'Eat at Home' initially may seem like padding for the second side, the song has come to be regarded as one of the best tracks on *Ram* (Example 6).

EXAMPLE 6 MULTI-TRACK OUTLINE FOR 'EAT AT HOME'[56]

Track 1	Bass drum (Denny Seiwell)
Track 2	Hi-hat, snare, small tom (Denny Seiwell)
Track 3	Floor tom (Denny Seiwell)
Track 4	Bass #1 (Paul McCartney)
Track 5	Bass #2 (Paul McCartney)
Track 6	Amp guitar (David Spinozza)
Track 7	Acoustic guitar (Paul McCartney)
Track 8	Rough lead vocal (Paul McCartney) (evidently unused)
Track 9	(blank)
Track 10	Lead vocal (Paul McCartney) (3/30/71)
Track 11	Lead vocal (main?) (Paul McCartney) (3/30/71)
Track 12	Lead vocal (Linda McCartney) (3/30/71)
Track 13	Lead vocal (doubled) (Linda McCartney) (3/30/71)
Track 14	Cowbell (McCartney) (erased) (3/30/71)
Track 15	Guitar (McCartney?) (erased) (3/30/71)
Track 16	Lead guitar (Paul McCartney) (erased) (3/30/71)

Available documentation indicates that the basic tracks for 'Eat at Home' began shortly after the initial sessions for 'Another Day'. The sixteen-track recording sheet on which both songs are listed indicates an identical setup for Denny Seiwell's drum kit. McCartney had recorded two bass parts, both of which may have been used in various sections of the song. According to the sheet, the song was set aside until 30 March 1971 when lead and backing vocals were added along with unused tracks of percussion and electric guitar. These were evidently recorded at Sunset Sound Studios in Los Angeles, after which the song would have been mixed for inclusion on the *Ram* album.[57]

One of the most striking aspects of 'Eat at Home' is the varied tuning evident on some of the instruments on the track. On one level, this suggests the casual space of a local club in which a spirited new band is in live performance. As such, it lends a certain degree of authenticity to the sounds. On another level, the varied tuning of 'Eat at Home' suggests a blurred or smeared painted image. The effect recalls The Beatles' 'Strawberry Fields Forever' in which vari-speed effects revealed the bright colours that exist between the spaces of standard tuning.

Extending the Studio/Gallery

As previously noted, the brilliance of *McCartney* (1970) arguably lies in how it reinvents the LP as gallery by blending it with the notion of studio space as workshop. Listeners were then invited in to consider the various tracks on display as works in progress. With *Ram* (1971), Paul expands on this idea by taking it on the road to major American studios. Although the process in these studios was state-of-the-art for the time, McCartney seemed to work largely the way that he had in his home studio at St John's Wood. As a result, he arguably helped transform the way in which popular music was approached and recorded in mainstream studios.

Later that year, Lennon would respond with *Imagine* (1971), a remarkable collection that built on the work he and Yoko had done on the *Plastic Ono Band* projects, but this time tailored for a mainstream pop audience. Also, evidently inspired by his ex-partner's first solo album, he began the process of creating a home studio of his own at Tittenhurst Park. Engineer Eddie Veale described how the creation of what was to become Ascot Sound Studios was guided by how John and Yoko inhabited the space:

> John wanted his own studio. If I'd looked back at the period, it was probably that John wanted to get out of town, he wanted the release, somewhere that he could work peacefully and relax. After some discussion, John decided that the annex would be the best place for the studio because it was close to the kitchen, for all the usual teas and snacks and stuff, and sufficiently away from the house that it didn't impact on the domestic scene.[58]

When the studio was complete, the sessions for the album began in earnest. The basic tracks recorded at Ascot Sound Studios were produced by Lennon, Yoko Ono, and Phil Spector. Additional sessions took place at the Record Plant in New York.[59] The album's track sequence is a masterpiece of programming in terms of the idea of LP as gallery. Here we seem to have three overlapping rooms in which the various works on display can generally be grouped in terms of their dominant musical characteristics: piano ballads with strings; blues/rock songs with full band; and acoustic folk songs with small ensemble. However, the various songs/tracks cross-reference one another in that an individual element commonly associated with one group can also be featured in another. As previously noted, *Imagine* was produced with the idea of reaching a mainstream audience; the album's opening track did just that.

'Imagine'

'Imagine' is another gentle piano ballad in the style for which Lennon would become increasingly known during his solo career. He had gotten the idea for the song from a poem included in Yoko Ono's book *Grapefruit* (1964) entitled 'Cloud Piece'.[60] Written in the spring of 1963, 'Cloud Piece' consisted of two lines: 'Imagine the clouds dripping. Dig a hole in your garden to put them in.'[61] Lennon's lyric extends this idea to a reconsideration of the entirety of human affairs. In his version, the implication is that the structural elements of our society, good and bad, are derived from the imaginings of the human mind. And if they are just imaginings, perhaps they can be reimagined. And, what then?

Throughout their collaboration, John and Yoko had tapped into what was arguably the central issue of their time: the quest for peace. The significance of this achievement was not lost on the arts community. In an essay entitled 'Constant's

New Babylon – Pushing the Zeitgeist to Its Limit', author Laura Stamps stressed the importance of this particular song in terms of the calamitous history of the twentieth century:

> The brilliant thing about the song is that it does not address hippies or anarchists but people outside these subcultures. These are the people Lennon calls upon to imagine a new, better world. 'You may say I'm a dreamer, but I'm not the only one'. His timing was perfect. After the horrors of the Second World War, Europe had an urgent desire to build a new and better world on the ruins of the old one. This need was expressed with growing urgency in the political, social, and cultural domains of the 1950s and 1960s. Lennon's messianic call came just as the way had been paved for his message.[62]

The concise imagery of Ono's poem also seems to have inspired Lennon's approach to the pacing of his musical setting. One of the most remarkable and recognizable elements of the song is the piano riff that underpins the main section. Moving gracefully through the upper part of the scale, the melodic line of this riff reaches up to a ninth before looping back to repeat the pattern. During the song's contrasting section, Lennon playfully evokes a sense of nostalgia by employing chords that suggest the harmonic innovations of the early Beatles. Here, however, they are woven into a mature style that seems more focused on the expressive effects of the image being created rather than on the jubilant act of creation itself.

The tracking sessions for 'Imagine' began in Ascot Sound Studios in Tittenhurst Park on 27 May 1971. The musicians were Alan White on drums, Klaus Voormann on bass, and Lennon himself on piano and vocals.[63] John and Yoko travelled to New York City that summer to record various overdubs at the Record Plant.[64] They added orchestrations for several of the LP's tracks, including 'Imagine'. A stereo mix of the existing eight-track master had been prepared at Ascot Sound Studios and later transferred to sixteen-track for the string players to hear as they recorded their parts. These orchestrations were prepared by Torrie Zito and performed by various members of the New York Philharmonic, credited on the album as The Flux Fiddlers (Example 7).[65]

EXAMPLE 7 MULTI-TRACK OUTLINE FOR 'IMAGINE'[66]

Track 1	Bass (Klaus Voormann)
Track 2	Drums (Alan White)
Track 3	(unused)
Track 4	Piano overdub onto Take 10 (Lennon)
Track 5	Piano (Lennon, Takes 2–10)
Track 6	Vocal overdub onto Take 10 (Lennon)
Track 7	Vocals (Lennon)
Track 8	(unused)

The space created for 'Imagine' recalls 'Strawberry Fields Forever' in that it feels like a personal refuge. Thus, connections between sanctuary and creative thought are considered. The emergence of the space seems to be sourced in the reverb of the gently rocking piano part that plays throughout. Within that part, the above-mentioned melodic riff line that reaches up to the ninth seems to trigger the clouds mentioned in Ono's poem and also depicted on the LP cover. These are then embodied in the gentle orchestration that forms a soft mist, gradually embracing the listener. Finally, the images of the poem, the re-imaginings suggested in Lennon's lyric, and the soundspace revealed by the various musical elements all blend gracefully into one.

'Mrs. Lennon'

During the sessions for *Imagine*, John Lennon and Yoko Ono recorded a follow-up to *Yoko Ono/Plastic Ono Band* entitled *Fly*. Emerging two weeks after the release of the *Imagine* album, this impressive double LP extended the approach of Ono's previous work in various directions. In the title track, she takes experimental sound painting a step further by using her solo voice in combination with various tape-driven effects. At the same time, she also embraced standard rock and ballad forms in a way that helped expand the potential appeal of her work. One of these was a gentle acoustic ballad called 'Mrs. Lennon'.

'Mrs. Lennon' seems to exist in the same soundspace as 'Imagine'. It begins with a gentle pattern on acoustic guitar that provides the foundation for the piano that enters shortly thereafter. Reinforced by organ, the piano reverb once again creates the impression of a misty landscape. The music is built on a circular minor key chord progression that cycles repeatedly as the song unfolds. Within this circular pattern, the bass seems liberated in that it takes several improvisational turns that perfectly complement the reserved piano and organ parts. As the piece progresses, the text moves from personal concerns to issues that are decidedly global in nature. This quality is then emphasized by the sound of bells, which makes it clear that this particular song/track is a meditative space in which the global and the local intersect.

Commenting on the song, Yoko said that '"Mrs. Lennon" was meant to be an ironic joke on me, by me, and an anti-war song. The lyrics were made in 1969, the music was finished in New York during the recording sessions'. With regard to irony, it seems remarkable that, in spite of her status in the art world and her collaborative role in John Lennon's projects both with The Beatles and on his own, Yoko had to continually deal with being treated like a second-class citizen. Lennon himself pointed this out with regard to their work in the recording studio:

> She would say to an engineer, 'I'd like a little more bass', and they'd look at me and say, 'What did you say, John?' Those days I didn't even notice it myself. Now I know what she's talking about. In Japan, when I ask for a cup of tea in Japanese, they look at Yoko and ask, 'He wants a cup of tea?' in Japanese.[67]

'Oh My Love'

A fully credited collaboration between John and Yoko, 'Oh My Love' is one of the most enchanting songs in the solo Beatles catalogue. A standard form involving two alternating sections throughout, the piece is unusual in that one of its organizational elements is the interval of a fifth. Seemingly written on guitar in the established late-Beatle and post-Beatle style of John Lennon, it also translates well to piano in its barest form. There is also a second piano line that breaks free to dance in variation with the main line. Lennon's gentle vocal grounds the delicate surrounding elements as the song unfolds (Example 8).

EXAMPLE 8 MULTI-TRACK OUTLINE FOR 'OH MY LOVE'[68]

Track 1	Klaus Voormann (bass)
Track 2	Alan White (Tibetan cymbals – Takes 1–5)
Track 3	George Harrison (electric guitar)
Track 4	Nicky Hopkins (electric piano)
Track 5	John Lennon (piano)
Track 6	John Lennon (vocal overdub onto Take 20)
Track 7	John Lennon (vocal); John Lennon (vocal overdub onto Take 20)
Track 8	Alan White (Tibetan cymbals overdub onto Take 20)

The basic tracks for 'Oh My Love' were recorded at Ascot Sound Studios on 28 May 1971. The musicians were John Lennon on piano and vocals; George Harrison on electric guitar; Klaus Voormann on bass; Nicky Hopkins on electric piano; and Alan White on Tibetan cymbals. White's Tibetan cymbal part was originally recorded live on Track 2 during Takes 1–5. However, after some discussion, it was decided to add them as an overdub instead. The final version of the song/track was mixed from Take 20.[69]

The world created for 'Oh My Love' is an extraordinary blend of interior and exterior spaces. The piano seems to occupy the interior of a chapel or a church, each of which can feature a glowing resonance. The guitar, however, occupies an exterior space in which its delicate tones move softly as if through a forest or glade. The combination of these two soundscapes creates a remarkable blend of colour throughout the track. One gets the impression that through the work of the artist the two have become inseparable.

'How Do You Sleep?'

Among the songs recorded for *Imagine* (1971) was a pointed jab at Paul McCartney entitled 'How Do You Sleep?'. Some of the lyrics in 'Too Many People', the opening track from *Ram*, had been read by Lennon as coded messages that were critical of both he and Yoko. As a result, he felt it was necessary to respond in kind. In what is arguably one of his finest pieces of post-Beatles music, Lennon produced a scathing lyric that was rather insulting to his former partner's credibility. However, in an interview with *Playboy* magazine in 1980, he suggested that it was all just a part of the process:

> You know, I wasn't really feeling that vicious at the time. But I was using my resentment toward Paul to create a song, let's put it that way. He saw that it pointedly refers to him, and people kept hounding him about it. But, you know, there were a few digs on his album before mine. He's so obscure other people didn't notice them, but I heard them. I thought, Well, I'm not obscure, I just get right down to the nitty-gritty. So he'd done it his way and I did it mine.[70]

Written appropriately in a minor key, 'How Do You Sleep?' opens with a precipitous slow-motion descent to the dominant chord before leaping back up to the tonic to start the whole process once again. The contrasting section is built on a compelling and durable riff that is soon revealed as the basic motif upon which the entire song is built. This riff becomes even more compelling when the orchestra joins in to emphasize the point and drive it home. The climax of the piece is the instrumental solo on slide guitar, which takes the track to a new level. There, the various microtonal gestures by George Harrison portray the powerful emotional content of the song/track as something beyond the scope of standard tuning.

EXAMPLE 9 MULTI-TRACK OUTLINE FOR 'HOW DO YOU SLEEP?'[71]

Track 1	Klaus Voormann (bass)
Track 2	Alan White (drums)
Track 3	George Harrison (electric guitar)
Track 4	John Lennon (electric guitar)
Track 5	John Lennon (vocal overdub onto Take 11)
Track 6	Nicky Hopkins (electric piano)
Track 7	John Lennon (vocal overdub onto Take 11)
Track 8	John Lennon (vocal FX overdub onto Take 11)

The tracking sessions for 'How Do You Sleep?' took place in Ascot Sound Studios in Tittenhurst Park on 26 May 1971. The musicians on the final mix were Alan White on drums, Klaus Voormann on bass, George Harrison on electric guitar, and Lennon himself on electric guitar and vocals. Orchestrations for 'How Do You Sleep?' were added at the Record Plant in New York City during the summer of

1971. Once again, a prepared stereo mix of the eight-track master was transferred to sixteen-track format. This was what The Flux Fiddlers heard as they recorded Torrie Zito's marvellous orchestration for the song.[72]

The space created for 'How Do You Sleep?' seems to be a photo negative of the one created for 'Imagine'. There, the space seemed like a personal refuge from the troubles of the world. Here, it seems as if a storm is brewing and its awesome power will not be denied. The gestural effects in the string orchestration suggest the rough blending of colours on a palette. When considered in combination with the microtonal gestures of Harrison's slide guitar, they seem to indicate that the storm is about to break.

Notes

1 Nick Johnstone, *Yoko Ono 'Talking'* (London: Omnibus Press, 2005), 20.
2 Once the filming at Twickenham had concluded, The Beatles regrouped at the Apple Offices in Savile Row where recording equipment had been installed. Once there, they continued rehearsing and taping songs for the film. Mark Lewisohn, *The Beatles Recording Sessions* (New York: Harmony Books, 1988), 164.
3 Mark Lewisohn, *The Beatles Recording Sessions* (New York: Harmony Books, 1988), 169.
4 *Let It Be*, directed by Michael Lindsay-Hogg (1970; Burbank, CA: Warner Home Video, 1984), VHS.
5 Mark Lewisohn, *The Beatles Recording Sessions* (New York: Harmony Books, 1988), 134.
6 Paul Du Noyer, *Conversations with McCartney* (New York: The Overlook Press, 2016), 74.
7 Mark Lewisohn, *The Beatles Recording Sessions* (New York: Harmony Books, 1988), 198–199.
8 Ian MacDonald, *Revolution in the Head: The Beatles' Records and the Sixties* (London: Vintage, 2008), 277.
9 Mark Lewisohn, *The Complete Beatles Chronicle* (New York: Harmony Books, 1992), 340.
10 Paul Du Noyer, *Conversations with McCartney* (New York: The Overlook Press, 2016), 85.
11 Richard J. Finneran (ed.), *The Collected Poems of W. B. Yeats* (New York: Scribner Paperback Poetry, 1996), 346–348.
12 Richard J. Finneran (ed.), *The Collected Poems of W. B. Yeats* (New York: Scribner Paperback Poetry, 1996), 346–348.
13 Paul McCartney, *The Lyrics: 1956 to the Present* (New York: Liveright, 2021), 389.
14 This version of 'Junk' featuring vocals was reportedly Take 2 of the song. However, Take 1 would itself be retrieved to create the instrumental 'Singalong Junk'. Chip Madinger and Mark Easter, *Eight Arms to Hold You: The Solo Beatles Compendium* (Chesterfield, MO: 44.1 Productions, 2000), 156.
15 Chip Madinger and Mark Easter, *Eight Arms to Hold You: The Solo Beatles Compendium* (Chesterfield, MO: 44.1 Productions, 2000), 154.
16 Example 1 was created using McCartney's comments regarding the recording of the track. His description of the sequence in which the various parts were recorded guided the estimated placement of the instruments here ('McCartney (Album)'. McCartney Times, 3 May 2017. www.mccartney.com/?p=8656).
17 Chip Madinger and Mark Easter, *Eight Arms to Hold You: The Solo Beatles Compendium* (Chesterfield, MO: 44.1 Productions, 2000), 154.
18 Gaston Bachelard, *The Poetics of Space* (Boston, MA: Beacon Press, 1994), xxxvii.
19 Paul Du Noyer, *Conversations with McCartney* (New York: The Overlook Press, 2016), 85.

20 Paul Du Noyer, *Conversations with McCartney* (New York: The Overlook Press, 2016), 194–195.

21 Mark Lewisohn, *The Complete Beatles Chronicle* (New York: Harmony Books, 1992), 345.

22 'McCartney (Album)'. McCartney Times, 3 May 2017. www.mccartney.com/?p=8656.

23 Luca Perasi, *Paul McCartney: Recording Sessions (1969–2013)* (Milan: L.I.L.Y. Publishing, 2014), 21.

24 'McCartney (Album)'. McCartney Times, 3 May 2017. www.mccartney.com/?p=8656.

25 Luca Perasi, *Paul McCartney: Recording Sessions (1969–2013)* (Milan: L.I.L.Y. Publishing, 2014), 21.

26 Mark Lewisohn, *The Complete Beatles Chronicle* (New York: Harmony Books, 1992), 346.

27 Mark Lewisohn, *The Complete Beatles Chronicle* (New York: Harmony Books, 1992), 346.

28 'McCartney (Album)'. McCartney Times, 3 May 2017. www.mccartney.com/?p=8656.

29 Chip Madinger and Mark Easter, *Eight Arms to Hold You: The Solo Beatles Compendium* (Chesterfield, MO: 44.1 Productions, 2000), 156.

30 Luca Perasi, *Paul McCartney: Recording Sessions (1969–2013)* (Milan: L.I.L.Y. Publishing, 2014), 19–20.

31 'McCartney (Album)'. McCartney Times, 3 May 2017. www.mccartney.com/?p=8656.

32 'McCartney (Album)'. McCartney Times, 3 May 2017. www.mccartney.com/?p=8656.

33 'McCartney (Album)'. McCartney Times, 3 May 2017. www.mccartney.com/?p=8656.

34 Howard Sounes, *Fab: An Intimate Life of Paul McCartney* (Cambridge, MA: Da Capo Press, 2010), 250.

35 Mark Prendergast, *The Ambient Century: From Mahler to Moby* (London: Bloomsbury, 2003), 179–180.

36 Simon Hilton (ed.), *John Lennon/Plastic Ono Band* (London: Universal Music Ltd., 2021), 12.

37 Simon Hilton (ed.), *John Lennon/Plastic Ono Band* (London: Universal Music Ltd., 2021), 66–67.

38 Simon Hilton (ed.), *John Lennon/Plastic Ono Band* (London: Universal Music Ltd., 2021), 66–67.

39 Bruce Spizer, *The Beatles Solo on Apple Records* (New Orleans, LA: 498 Productions, 2005), 35.

40 Chip Madinger and Mark Easter, *Eight Arms to Hold You: The Solo Beatles Compendium* (Chesterfield, MO: 44.1 Productions, 2000), 38.

41 Doug Sulpy and Ray Schweighardt, *Get Back: The Unauthorized Chronicle of The Beatles' 'Let It Be' Disaster* (New York: St. Martin's Press, 1997), 259.

42 Doug Sulpy and Ray Schweighardt, *Get Back: The Unauthorized Chronicle of The Beatles' 'Let It Be' Disaster* (New York: St. Martin's Press, 1997), 261.

43 Simon Hilton (ed.), *John Lennon/Plastic Ono Band* (London: Universal Music Ltd., 2021), 118.

44 Simon Hilton (ed.), *John Lennon/Plastic Ono Band* (London: Universal Music Ltd., 2021), 118.

45 Eric Iozzi, 'Another Day (Paul McCartney Song)'. Wikipedia. Wikimedia Foundation, 28 January 2022. https://en.wikipedia.org/wiki/Another_Day_(Paul_McCartney_song)#/media/File:Record_Sheet_01.jpg. (The printing on this track sheet appears to be in McCartney's own hand.)

46 Gary Eskow, 'Classic Tracks: Paul McCartney's "Uncle Albert/Admiral Halsey"'. Mixonline, 1 August 2004. https://web.archive.org/web/20180924131254/https://www.mixonline.com/recording/classic-tracks-paul-mccartneys-uncle-albertadmiral-halsey-375127.

47 Chip Madinger and Mark Easter, *Eight Arms to Hold You: The Solo Beatles Compendium* (Chesterfield, MO: 44.1 Productions, 2000), 157.

48 Eric Iozzi, 'Another Day (Paul McCartney Song)'. Wikipedia. Wikimedia Foundation, 28 January 2022. https://en.wikipedia.org/wiki/Another_Day_(Paul_McCartney_song)#/media/File:Record_Sheet_01.jpg. Eric Iozzi, File: Record Sheet 01.jpg. Wikimedia Commons, 3 June 2019.

49 Gary Eskow, 'Classic Tracks: Paul McCartney's "Uncle Albert/Admiral Halsey"'. Mixonline, 1 August 2004. https://web.archive.org/web/20180924131254/https://www.mixonline.com/recording/classic-tracks-paul-mccartneys-uncle-albertadmiral-halsey-375127.

50 Luca Perasi, *Paul McCartney: Recording Sessions (1969–2013)* (Milan: L.I.L.Y. Publishing, 2014), 45–50.

51 Gary Eskow, 'Classic Tracks: Paul McCartney's "Uncle Albert/Admiral Halsey"'. Mixonline, 1 August 2004. https://web.archive.org/web/20180924131254/https://www.mixonline.com/recording/classic-tracks-paul-mccartneys-uncle-albertadmiral-halsey-375127.

52 Paul Du Noyer, *Conversations with McCartney* (New York: The Overlook Press, 2016), 331.

53 P.L. Travers, *Mary Poppins: 80th Anniversary Collection* (New York: Houghton Mifflin Harcourt, 2014), 45–46.

54 John Wukovits, *Admiral "Bull" Halsey: The Life and Wars of the Navy's Most Controversial Commander* (New York: Palgrave Macmillan, 2010), xii.

55 Chip Madinger and Mark Easter, *Eight Arms to Hold You: The Solo Beatles Compendium* (Chesterfield, MO: 44.1 Productions, 2000), 157.

56 Eric Iozzi, 'Another Day (Paul McCartney Song)'. Wikipedia. Wikimedia Foundation, 28 January 2022. https://en.wikipedia.org/wiki/Another_Day_(Paul_McCartney_song)#/media/File:Record_Sheet_01.jpg.

57 Chip Madinger and Mark Easter, *Eight Arms to Hold You: The Solo Beatles Compendium* (Chesterfield, MO: 44.1 Productions, 2000), 157.

58 *John and Yoko: Above Us Only Sky*, directed by Michael Epstein (2019; Wandsworth, London: Eagle Vision, 2019), DVD.

59 Chip Madinger and Mark Easter, *Eight Arms to Hold You: The Solo Beatles Compendium* (Chesterfield, MO: 44.1 Productions, 2000), 45.

60 Chip Madinger and Mark Easter, *Eight Arms to Hold You: The Solo Beatles Compendium* (Chesterfield, MO: 44.1 Productions, 2000), 48.

61 Simon Hilton (ed.), *Imagine: John Lennon* (London: Universal Music Ltd., 2018), 32.

62 Manuel Borja-Villel, *Constant: New Babylon* (Amsterdam: MNCARS, 2015), 13.

63 John Blaney, *John Lennon: Listen to This Book* (Guildford: Paper Jukebox, 2005), 82.

64 John Lennon and Yoko Ono, *Imagine John Yoko* (London: Thames & Hudson, Ltd., 2018), 156.

65 Simon Hilton (ed.), *Imagine: John Lennon* (London: Universal Music Ltd., 2018), 36.

66 Simon Hilton (ed.), *Imagine: John Lennon* (London: Universal Music Ltd., 2018), 36–37.

67 John Lennon and Yoko Ono, *Imagine John Yoko* (London: Thames & Hudson, Ltd., 2018), 239.

68 Simon Hilton (ed.), *Imagine: John Lennon* (London: Universal Music Ltd., 2018), 60–61.

69 Simon Hilton (ed.), *Imagine: John Lennon* (London: Universal Music Ltd., 2018), 60–61.

70 '1980 Playboy Interview With John Lennon And Yoko Ono'. Namedat.com, 31 January 2020. www.namedat.com/1980-playboy-interview-with-john-lennon-and-yoko-ono.

71 Simon Hilton (ed.), *Imagine: John Lennon* (London: Universal Music Ltd., 2018), 64–65.

72 Simon Hilton (ed.), *Imagine: John Lennon* (London: Universal Music Ltd., 2018), 36.

5
HANDS ACROSS THE WATER

During the *Ram* sessions, Paul and Linda McCartney had evolved a unique sound that they evidently wished to develop further. However, in order to get to the next level, they would need a band. This would enable them to develop their sound and enhance it with additional influences brought in by other musicians. The group that emerged was called Wings. In addition to Paul and Linda, it featured Denny Laine from the Moody Blues on guitar and vocals and drummer Denny Seiwell from the *Ram* sessions. Wings would form the basis for McCartney's musical activities for the rest of the decade.[1]

Wings released their first album, *Wild Life*, in 1971. Building on the sound of *Ram*, the album featured an eclectic mix of folk, rock, and mellow pop. Evidently not wanting to get mired in the recording process, McCartney was determined to record his new band's debut as quickly as possible.[2] The process was so rapid, in fact, that the majority of songs featured were done in first or second takes.[3] The album's opening track neatly documents this sense of urgency in that it includes Paul's cue to engineer Tony Clark to begin recording the performance, which was by then fully in progress.[4]

'Mumbo'

'Mumbo' finds Wings in full forward motion. As a passionate rock song, it displays a rhythmic urgency that seems relentless. Seemingly echoing the vocal approach of 'Monkberry Moon Delight', the song takes the idea a step further by dispensing with lyrics entirely. Built on two chords in the key of F major, 'Mumbo' relies on a curious stream of vocal gibberish and bluesy guitar riffs to make its point. And what exactly is that point?

Listening closely to the track, certain words do become audible. For instance, the opening line begins with 'Well ...', before melting back into nonsense syllables. The

DOI: 10.4324/9781003300212-8

line then concludes with what sounds like the phrase 'break it'. This pattern continues throughout the song/track with certain words and phrases emerging briefly before subsiding once again into a mass of pure sound. The effect is fascinating in that one definitely gets the sense that an urgent message being sent, albeit one that defies specificity. Paul's own take on the piece is interesting to consider:

> 'Mumbo' is just a big scream of no words. A wacky idea, cos it was just 'Whuurrrgghh A-hurrgghhh!' and we mixed it back so it was like 'Louie Louie'. Everyone's going, What are the words of that? Just hope they don't ask for the sheet music. Which no one ever did, luckily.[5]

The track was recorded at Abbey Road during the summer and early autumn of 1971. As mentioned, Tony Clark was the engineer. The musicians were Paul on bass, vocals, and electric guitar (and possibly tambourine); Linda on piano and organ; Denny Laine on electric guitar; and Denny Seiwell on drums (and possibly tambourine).[6] As he had done on the extended coda of 'Monkberry Moon Delight', McCartney seems to be working again like an action painter in that he fills the space with colourful vocal sound. The familiar surroundings must have been comforting to revisit since they seem to have allowed him to begin the process of resolving his musical past. This is most evident in 'Mumbo', which seems to work both as a form of closure and a new beginning.

'Bip Bop'

The next track on *Wild Life* seems to take its cue from the gibberish of 'Mumbo'. Built on the nonsense phrase 'bip bop', the lyric develops this idea as a recurring hook throughout the song. Interspersed, we also hear a fragmented narrative concerning a young couple enjoying a night on the town. The musical setting is centred around a persistent electric guitar part that creates the basis for the nonsensical phrases of the text, while also underpinning the narrative described above. Periodically, the guitar initiates a rising Beatles-esque chord progression that loops back into the main idea.

'Bip Bop' was recorded quickly at Abbey Road during sessions that took place during the summer and early autumn of 1971. The musicians on the track were Paul on electric guitar, bass, and lead vocals; Linda on backing vocals and possibly a tambourine; Denny Laine on electric guitar; and Denny Seiwell on drums and possibly a tambourine.[7] Overall, the playing is loose and relaxed, but the initial riff seems somewhat uncertain. It's as if the guitarist is trying to find his feet within the clever rhythmic pattern. Things quickly settle down, however, as the players soon discover that the ingenious riff continually renews its energies as the track unfolds.

The earthy ambience of 'Bip Bop' is pervasive and very effective. The groove consists of familiar musical gestures drawn out of country and western and rock and roll. The resulting blend creates a trance-like quality throughout. This is emphasized by the timbre of the lead vocal in which Paul blends masculine and feminine elements within the same performance. Ultimately, 'Bip Bop' creates a space that might best be described as meditative.

During the recording session for 'Bip Bop', Paul also put down a twelve-string acoustic guitar instrumental that seemed to be reaching back to 'Blackbird'. Entitled 'Bip Bop Link', the track follows 'I Am Your Singer' but curiously was not listed in the liner notes of the original LP. This omission was later corrected when the album was released on compact disc.[8] Here, as on 'Blackbird', Paul plucks away on the outer strings of his guitar while alternately strumming the inner strings to complete the chord. This pattern, along with the momentum generated by the descending harmonic progression, made 'Bip Bop Link' one of the artist's most compelling solo performances to date.

'Tomorrow'

If 'Mumbo' represented a new beginning, then the penultimate track from *Wild Life* is another journey back into the past. Just as 'Bip Bop Link' had referenced 'Blackbird' from *The Beatles* (1968), 'Tomorrow' seems to recall McCartney's own most famous song, 'Yesterday'. This notion is supported by the opening chord progression, which features a similarly distinctive cadence into the relative minor. The song's contrasting section is certainly effective, but it is the extended coda that is most remarkable. There, the band shifts into a triplet rhythm characteristic of early rock and roll as Paul sings a spirited melody in the upper reaches of his vocal register.

'Tomorrow' was recorded between 25 and 27 July 1971 at EMI Studios in London. The basic tracks along with additional overdubs seem to have been recorded on those dates. The musicians were Paul on vocals and piano, with Linda possibly playing some keyboards as well. Denny Laine played the bass and Denny Seiwell manned the drum kit. Paul and Denny then worked out parts for electric guitars as an overdub. Paul, Linda, and Denny then developed the backing vocals, which were recorded around the same microphone. At this point in the band's career, they seemed to be evolving their distinctive harmony vocal style as they went along.[9]

The space of 'Tomorrow' combines clarity with subtle shades of reverberance. The opening section that highlights piano and vocal is exceedingly dry and rather plain. There, the band seems to be playing in a small room with limited resonance. This dry quality is countered in the song's contrasting section where generous amounts of reverb are applied, particularly to the vocal harmonies. The extended coda blends the two qualities with noticeably dry vocals and rather heavily reverbed electric guitar.

'Tomorrow' remains a relatively obscure gem from the Wings back catalogue. This is rather curious since it becomes clear on repeated listenings that the song is an example of composition at a rather high level. In an interview for *Rolling Stone* magazine published on 31 January 1974, Paul discussed the song's obscurity, and connected it with his ongoing interest in the works of Pablo Picasso:

Yeah, 'Tomorrow' is one of them. It's like, when I'm talking to people about Picasso or something and they say, well, his blue period was his only one that was any good. But for me, if the guy does some great things then even his downer moments are interesting. His lesser moments, rather, because they make up the final picture. Some moments seem less, he was going through kind of a pressure period. You know, you can't live your life without pressure periods. No one I know has.[10]

'Dear Friend'

After eighteen months of simmering hostility between Lennon and McCartney, Paul felt that the time had come to bury the hatchet. 'Dear Friend', the final track from the new album, was a touching lament for their current situation. In it, he reached out in a way intended to bypass the bitterness and connect with his former partner on a personal level. In conversation with author Paul Du Noyer, McCartney described the song as 'A bit of longing about John … You know, "Let's have a glass of wine and forget it"'.[11]

Featuring only Paul on bass, piano, and vocals, Denny Seiwell on drums and percussion, and Richard Hewson's orchestration, 'Dear Friend' seems to sit in a separate space from the rest of the songs on the album. The song is built on a steady descending bass line in the mournful key of C minor. Over the repeating line, Paul adds some interesting clusters on piano that suggest the influence of jazz harmony. The orchestration extends this influence as it subtly paints the track with mysterious patches of instrumental colour. These patches emerge mysteriously out of the sound mass before disappearing wearily into the darkness.

The space created on the track for 'Dear Friend' is one that is well suited to the song's intention. Here, the singer's regret over the estrangement and the palpable sense of longing for resolution is almost too much to bear. The basic unadorned piano part suggests that the intention is an honest one. Better still is the ambience created by the orchestral arrangement. Throughout, it gives an appropriately nebulous form to the raw emotion driving the piece.

Conceptual Galleries

Wild Life was not well received on its original release. Repeated listenings, however, reveal not only the easy charm of the songwriting but also the spirited performances from a new band still finding its way. Consequently, it has managed, over time, to win over fans and critics alike. During an appearance on *The Mike Douglas Show* on 18 February 1972, John Lennon was complimentary about the album:

I quite enjoyed some of it, yeah. You know, I think it's very hard, you know, to listen to your friend … Some of it's alright. I thought it was getting better. Some of it wasn't as good and some was better. I think he's going in the right direction.[12]

In terms of the LP-as-gallery idea, McCartney seems to have been bringing back fresh ideas from his time in America. These, combined with the familiarity of working at what had been his home studio with The Beatles, gives the music an ease of expression that lends credence to the apparent concept of getting back to a more natural approach.

In the meantime, John and Yoko seemed to be moving in the opposite direction. As previously noted, during the final phase of the sessions for *Imagine*, they had gone to New York to record overdubs. While there, the idea of relocating to the United States was becoming more and more appealing to them both. In *John and Yoko: Above Us Only Sky* (2018), author and journalist Ray Connolly described why he thought America was a logical move for them:

> I think John loved the energy of New York City, there's no question about that. And I think he loved that it was an opportunity for him to become an American. He saw New York as being kind of a bit like Liverpool, or the Liverpool 8 area, where the art college was. And Yoko was, in a way, American. I know she's Japanese, but she's mainly American.[13]

During their trip to New York in the summer of 1971, John and Yoko had met Jim Harithas, director of the Everson Museum in Syracuse, New York. Together, they hatched the idea of a new art exhibit. Entitled *This Is Not Here*, the show opened at the Everson Museum on 9 October 1971 and was built around Yoko's idea that the participation of the viewer completes the artwork. Among the various rooms set up for the exhibit, there was one that allowed viewers to paint on canvases in various colours. Another, called 'Dialogue Room', featured works by John and Yoko that were set up so as to stress how a creative conversation was taking place between them.[14]

Another of their most interesting conceptual projects was an 'exhibit' at the Museum of Modern Art (MoMA) that never actually took place. Yoko described the event this way: 'It's a conceptual art show … It's just in my mind, it's a concept'. Nevertheless, many people showed up in response to an advert that had been placed in the newspapers by John and Yoko.[15] In an interview included on the MoMA website, Ono discussed how she documented the response to the show: 'So I had a cameraman standing there and asking questions: "How did you like the Yoko show?" And some people said, "Yeah, it was okay." Some people said, "I looked for it, but we couldn't find Yoko's show."'[16]

In connection, it is interesting to consider how John and Yoko's recording work over the previous few years had influenced this particular presentation. They had recently been working almost exclusively on recording music in the spirit of the visual arts. Now, they had reversed the process by taking the notion of virtual gallery back into the artworld from where it originated. An idea one can take away from this reversal of process is that anywhere on the entire planet can be considered a gallery and/or a workspace. That is, the globe itself can be considered not simply as a static backdrop but as an organic space for presentation as well as creation.

Around this time, John and Yoko had also taken the opportunity to immerse themselves in American politics. The ideas they explored soon found expression on *Some Time in New York City* (1972), an LP with cover art that mimicked the style of a daily newspaper. Reaching for the immediacy of painting, they had created music that sought to directly address the pressing social issues of the day. The problem they faced was that by the time *Some Time in New York City* was released, many of the issues it attempted to address had either been resolved or forgotten. Thus, topics that once seemed so immediate had effectively become yesterday's news.

In terms of the LP as gallery, *Some Time in New York City* continued exploring the aesthetic potential of the double-album. Building on *John Lennon/Plastic Ono Band* and *Yoko Ono/Plastic Ono Band*, the new album seemed to contrast a formal song-driven approach with one that was more expressive and experimental in nature. The difference was that on *Some Time in New York City* the expressive/ experimental aspect was represented by live performances from 1969 (side three) and 1971 (side four). The 1969 performance was from the Lyceum Ballroom in London and featured George Harrison. The performance from 1971 was from the Fillmore East in New York City and featured Frank Zappa and the Mothers of Invention.[17]

'Live and Let Die'

Over the previous year, Paul McCartney and Wings began the process of finding their way as a performing band and also to prepare for a new album. First, they expanded the Wings line-up by adding guitarist Henry McCullough. Next, they embarked on a casual tour of the UK during which they would show up at various colleges unannounced and ask if the students might be interested in hearing Paul McCartney's new band in live performance.[18] This was followed by a brief tour at various venues around Europe.[19] Along the way, the band had recorded and released a few singles and had also begun the arduous task of creating a suitable follow-up to *Wild Life*.

Paul McCartney and Wings' second album would ultimately be released under the title of *Red Rose Speedway*. Originally conceived as a double LP, the album seemed to be an attempt to combine the whimsy of *Ram* with the bold experimentation of late-period Beatles. During the sessions, however, Paul had received a rather daunting request. He was asked through Ron Kass, formerly of Apple Records, and now with Cubby Broccoli, to write the theme for the upcoming James Bond film, *Live and Let Die*.[20] Rising to the challenge, he proved his mettle as a composer by creating one of the most memorable Bond themes yet written.

'Live and Let Die' opens in typical McCartney fashion with the composer singing and playing his piano. As this harmonious section reaches its climax, he is suddenly joined by the band with full orchestra playing a sequence of power chords. This sequence leads directly into a contrasting instrumental section built on an orchestral riff with full band in tow that somehow manages to match the iconic guitar line forever associated with James Bond. As this new riff reaches its peak, it suddenly spills over into a rolling reggae groove that releases the accumulated energy generated by the previous section. The orchestral riff section then returns, only to lower us into a transition derived from the opening material that is then followed by the return of Paul at his piano. One last orchestral riff follows before the song ends on an inconclusive harmony that drifts away slowly into the darkness.

'Live and Let Die' was recorded at AIR Studios in late 1972. Overdubs were added the following day. In addition to the various members of Paul McCartney and Wings (Paul and Linda McCartney, Denny Seiwell, Denny Laine, and Henry McCullough), the track also featured Ray Cooper on percussion. George Martin conducted the orchestra from his own original score. The track was engineered by Bill Price and Geoff Emerick.[21]

The Beatles had been creating music for film since 1964. The difference here is that with 'Live and Let Die', McCartney seems to have effectively blended pop songwriting and classic film-scoring techniques. While there is no specific scene that he, as the composer, is scoring, the orchestral riff sections certainly have that quality. In the process, he seems to build a viable bridge between the two forms. Years before the widespread use of the pop film score, he creates a song/track that seems to simultaneously occupy filmic space and the virtual spaces of popular music.

The burst of creativity that had characterized the *Ram* sessions would continue to feed Paul's process for the next few years. For instance, the recording of 'Little Woman Love', the B-side to 'Mary Had a Little Lamb', had begun during the sessions for *Ram*; 'Big Barn Bed', the opening track of *Red Rose Speedway*, was first heard as a short vocal improvisation at the end of the reprise of the song 'Ram On'; and 'Little Lamb Dragonfly', the closing track to side one of *Red Rose Speedway*, was first attempted during sessions for the *Ram* album.[22] Finally, we come to a track that traces its origins back to the first week of sessions at CBS Studios in New York City.

'Get on the Right Thing'

Presented in the key of E major, 'Get on the Right Thing' actually suggests an F major piano piece that may have been transposed during the compositional process to accommodate both guitar and bass, which are notoriously more comfortable in that key. The song's opening section features a rising chord progression over a rocking piano octave on E. This progression is nuanced with chromatic motion as it unfolds before leading to a full cadence in D major. After a repetition of this section, a new contrasting section appears that alternates E major and A major chords under the title line. The two sections then repeat, and the song fades out, instruments first, and then vocals (Example 10).

EXAMPLE 10 MULTI-TRACK OUTLINE FOR 'GET ON THE RIGHT THING'[23]

Track 1	Bass drum (Denny Seiwell)
Track 2	Hi-hat, snare, small tom (Denny Seiwell)
Track 3	Floor tom (Denny Seiwell)
Track 4	Bass #2 (Paul McCartney)
Track 5	Bass #1 (Paul McCartney) (unused)
Track 6	Amp guitar #1 (basic hold) (David Spinozza)
Track 7	Piano (Paul McCartney)
Track 8	Rough lead vocal (Paul McCartney) (2/11/71)
Track 9	Amp guitar feedback #1 (Paul McCartney)
Track 10	Amp guitar backwards #1 (David Spinozza)
Track 11	Amp guitar backwards #2 (David Spinozza)
Track 12	Amp guitar feedback #2 (Paul McCartney)
Track 13	Solo break guitar #2 ending (David Spinozza?)
Track 14	Group vocal bounce (Paul and Linda McCartney) (2/11/71)
Track 15	Lead vocal (Paul McCartney) (2/10/71)
Track 16	Piano and guitar bounce (solo at/before end) (Pal McCartney on both?)

According to available documentation, the basic tracks for 'Get on the Right Thing' were recorded at CBS Studios in New York on 12 October 1970. The previously mentioned sixteen-track recording sheet for the song, which also contains track notes for 'Another Day' and 'Eat at Home', indicates an identical setup for Seiwell's drum kit. Additional vocal parts were recorded at A&R Studios in New York City in February 1971. Between *Ram* and *Red Rose Speedway*, reverb seems to have been added to the entire track since the initial version sounded much drier. Early mixes suggest that the idea of fading the instruments down so that the vocals dominate during the final moments of the coda may have been present from the outset.

The space of 'Get on the Right Thing' seems somewhat indeterminate. It doesn't appear to fit with the experimental tone of the rest of *Ram*. At the same time, there is a looseness about the approach that seems somewhat at odds with the mainstream polish that is a feature of *Red Rose Speedway*. Thus, the song/track appears to lack a proper context, sitting somewhere between two distinctly different LP concepts. One wonders if 'Get on the Right Thing' would have fit better in the original plan for the *Red Rose Speedway* LP.

In Chapter 4 it was suggested that Paul McCartney's first solo album seemed to be developing ideas originally introduced on *The Beatles* (1968). John Lennon and Yoko Ono had gone in a similar direction with both editions of *Plastic Ono Band* (1970). Yoko's next solo album, *Fly* (1971), went further still by seemingly approaching the entire space of a double LP as a large canvas. Initially, the plan for Wings' second album was in line with this trend. It seems that *Red Rose Speedway* was originally intended as a double LP. Drummer Denny Seiwell had retained acetates of one of the planned sequences. These were dated 13 December 1972, and for many years this was the only reliable information about the alternate version.[24] However, in 2018, researchers working with Paul McCartney on his Archive Collections project discovered information about a subsequent double-LP sequence that was likely the last version considered before the plan was abandoned in favour of a single LP.[25]

Both the single-LP and double-LP versions of *Red Rose Speedway* included four songs that might be regarded as the musical equivalent of a tetraptych; that is, a painting in four parts. On the final single LP, this medley is placed on side two in a manner similar to the medley on *Abbey Road*. However, the original track layout for the double-LP version of *Red Rose Speedway* has it placed at the end of side three, just past the midpoint of the entire album. This alternate placement seems to better serve the four-panelled form and arguably provides a nicer shape to the album as a whole.

'My Love'

The song that saved *Red Rose Speedway* also seemed to sink the concept of the album as a kind of whimsical sequel to *The Beatles* (1968). 'My Love' was a heartfelt tribute from Paul to Linda that actually seems to have been written several years earlier.[26] Composed in F major in a standard musical form, the song floats along with a buoyancy that suggests relaxed acceptance all around. The sense of urgency that is a feature of rock and roll has seemingly been dissipated by marital bliss. The implication is that the two lovers have found a safe harbour from the world and all its cares.

'My Love' was recorded at Abbey Road Studios on 25 January 1973.[27] The musicians on the track were Paul on vocals and electric piano; Linda on backing vocals; Denny Laine on bass and backing vocals; Henry McCullough on electric guitar; and Denny Seiwell on drums.[28] The orchestration, which was recorded live with the full band, was created by Richard Hewson.[29] The session highlighted tensions emerging within the band, as McCartney himself pointed out:

> In this studio, we did 'My Love', a ballad that we were doing. And we'd worked it out, we'd rehearsed it, and we had a full orchestra. It was live. That was recorded live and played and sang live. And, uh, we had the whole orchestra all waiting, you know, for the downbeat. And Henry McCullough, the guitar player, the Irish guitar player there, he comes over to me. Now, we're ready to go. 'Just a minute. What's that?' And he says, 'Do you mind if I change the solo?' 'Not at all, you go ahead.' And actually it's one of the best solos he ever played, that. He just made it up on the session.[30]

As mentioned above, 'My Love' was recorded as a live take with full orchestra. As a result, the space created for/by the song seems to be derived by the unique ambience generated by the full ensemble. From the outset, there seems to be an unusual softness at work here. This soft quality is enhanced by the electric piano, which provides the song's primary harmonic drive. The one exception to the prevailing softness is the electric lead guitar, which provides a cutting yet lyrical quality that completes the soundscape with the appropriate colour.

'Mind Games'

At the end of 1972, John Lennon and Yoko Ono premiered *Imagine*, a film for television. Shot in New York City and at Tittenhurst Park, the film featured videos for all the songs from the *Imagine* album along with several tracks from *Fly*. There were also cameo appearances by Fred Astaire, Dick Cavett, Jonas Mekas, Jack Palance, and George Harrison.[31] Arguably, the film's most memorable sequence is the one created for *Imagine*. There, John performs the song at a white piano at Tittenhurst Park, while Yoko opens the shutters to let in the light.

John would return later that year with *Mind Games*, a seeming attempt to extend the LP-as-gallery approach of *Imagine* (1971) into new and interesting areas. In the book *The Beatles Solo on Apple Records* (2005), author Bruce Spizer cited May Pang's assertion that the eighteen-month gap in his recording activities was due to a series of challenges that had emerged in his professional and personal life:

> [T]he negative reaction to *Some Time In New York City* shook John's confidence and kept him out of the recording studio for over a year. This, combined with developing tensions in his relationship with Yoko, kept John from being significantly involved in Yoko's 1973 album *Feeling the Space*. Yoko had drummer Jim Keltner line up some of New York's finest session musicians to back her on the project. When John finally attended one of the sessions, he was impressed with the players and got the bug to record again.[32]

The LP's title track was begun several years earlier as 'Make Love, Not War'.[33] In the late 1960s this was a provocative idea, but by the early 1970s it seemed to have lost some of its intellectual lustre. In the meantime, Lennon had become fascinated by a book written by Robert Masters and Jean Houston, whose earlier works had included *The Varieties of Psychedelic Experience* (1966) and *Psychedelic Art* (1968). Their new book was called *Mind Games* (1972), and it consisted of a series of exercises designed to strengthen and expand the abilities of human consciousness. The subject matter seemed better connected to the mood of the time, and thus Lennon had a proper title for his song and a concept for his new album.[34]

'Mind Games' begins with a descending harmonic progression built around a repeated pattern on slide guitar. This pattern suggests a brushstroke that seems to be driving the rhythmic juggernaut below, while at the same time deriving energy from it. The robustness of this figure warrants a lot of repetition, and Lennon provides it. Eventually, however, he yields to the need for variety by creating a contrasting section that seems decidedly minimal. However, it does set up the return of the opening progression and guitar pattern, which begins to appear eternally renewable as the song/track unfolds.

'Mind Games' was recorded at the Record Plant East in New York City during July and August 1973. In addition to John Lennon on vocals and guitar, the track featured Ken Ascher on keyboards, Gordon Edwards on bass, Jim Keltner on drums, and *Ram* veteran David Spinozza on guitar.[35] As previously mentioned, this was a new group of musicians that Lennon had heard during his visit to Yoko's sessions for her album *Feeling the Space*.[36] The players here pick up on the compelling, anthemic quality of the song and respond accordingly. Their nimble playing provides a drive that had been notably missing from Lennon's recent recordings.

'Mind Games' seems to constitute a journey through the inner spaces suggested in 'Imagine'. The repeated slide guitar pattern suggests an imagined flight at high altitudes. This flight is certainly thrilling but also rather precarious since the height at which we are travelling is considerable. Moreover, since we seem to be moving through the realm of thought, there might come a sudden realization that we lack any real physical support for the journey. We could then begin to tumble downward in a seemingly endless fall.

'I Know (I Know)'

What is particularly interesting about the new material Lennon was producing at this time was how it allowed him to showcase his skills as a composer/producer. At the same time, it also revealed an artist developing new ideas with regard to what might soon be possible in popular music. He was certainly revisiting themes he had initially explored with The Beatles, but he was also soaking up new sounds from the American scene. This combination would ultimately come to define his mature mid-1970s sound. In that regard, one of the most powerful tracks on the album is an energetic message to Yoko called 'I Know (I Know)'.

The initial material of 'I Know (I Know)' is a harmonic riff that recalls The Beatles' 'I've Got a Feeling' from *Let It Be*. Lennon modifies the pattern to give it more variety as the opening section of the song unfolds. The riff then transitions into a contrasting section seemingly inspired by American gospel music. The real treat comes just past the midpoint of the track when Lennon concludes his contrasting section with an unusual metrical pattern that, in combination with a cadence into the relative minor key and a subsequent pause, can only be described as thrilling. This same pattern later becomes part of the song's extended coda, thereby reinforcing the idea that the best composers always seem to go wherever they want to go.

Like the album's title track, 'I Know (I Know)' was recorded at the Record Plant East in New York City during July and August 1973. In addition to Lennon on vocals and guitar, the track featured Ken Ascher on keyboards, Gordon Edwards on bass, Jim Keltner on drums, and David Spinozza on guitar.[37] The musicians navigate the unusual time changes and frequent pauses with ease. They also create a powerful and compelling groove that seems to be inspiring Lennon to reach for more. Here, his lead vocals achieve a level of intensity that calls to mind his spirited performances with the early Beatles.

John's compositional and performance choices on 'I Know (I Know)' create a unique space that seems somehow dangerous. In that regard, his process seems to connect with Gabriel Garcia Lorca's writings on *duende*, which is defined as 'a momentary burst of inspiration, the blush of all that is truly alive, all that the performer is creating at a certain moment'.[38] Lorca also describes how '[e]ach art has a duende different in form and style, but their roots meet in the … essential, uncontrollable, quivering, common base of wood, sound, canvas, and word'.[39] In connection with these ideas, one might view Lennon's sudden and wilful movements through the final moments of 'I Know (I Know)' as inspirations that dispense with formal logic in order to court a kind of creative frenzy.

'Out the Blue'

Seemingly a sister song/track to 'I Know (I Know)', 'Out the Blue' is a true standout in Lennon's solo catalogue. The song opens with an intricate acoustic guitar passage that outlines a melodic figure reminiscent of those composed by his ex-partner Paul. The guitar is then joined by a vocal that is treated with a reverb effect typical of recordings by Elvis Presley. The resulting contrast is quite remarkable since it combines the intimate tones of an acoustic guitar with the kind of vocal effects associated with classic rock and roll. Soon, the full ensemble joins in with a lively groove appropriate to the spirit of the track.

'Out the Blue' was recorded at the Record Plant East in New York City during July and August 1973. In addition to Lennon on vocals and guitar, the track featured Ken Ascher on keyboards, Gordon Edwards on bass, Jim Keltner on drums, David Spinozza on guitar, Sneaky Pete Kleinow on pedal steel, and the vocal group Something Different on backing vocals.[40] As was the case on 'I Know (I Know)', the players here encounter a song structure that is positioned somewhat dangerously. This quality of risk can be sourced in the aforementioned guitar intro and its shift from subdivisions of twos into subdivisions of threes. The way in which the players respond to this shift helps open up a unique virtual space on the track.

'Out the Blue' offers listeners a compelling paradox. It describes the arrival of a loved one as something that is a complete surprise, yet also somehow inevitable. This paradox inspires genuine wonder, along with a series of questions regarding the spiritual nature of love itself. The musical elements featured in the arrangement all seem to be reaching outwards towards this idea. Ultimately, one gets the sense that the virtual space of 'Out the Blue' is functioning as a zone of philosophical inquiry.

'Nutopian International Anthem'

At a press conference in New York City on 1 April 1973, John and Yoko announced that they were forming a new conceptual country called Nutopia.[41] The inner sleeve and lyric sheet began with what was called the Declaration of Nutopia. It was signed by John Ono Lennon and Yoko Ono Lennon and included a mailing address for the Nutopian Embassy in New York City. The final track on side one of the LP was the anthem for this conceptual country.[42] It was quite simply a brief blast of silence.

'Nutopian International Anthem' blends the ideas of John Cage as exemplified in his 4'33", a piece made of listening, with the spirit of Robert Rauschenberg's 'White Paintings', a series of blank canvases. As a master of the medium of sound recording, Lennon offered his own take on the subject. He encouraged listeners to consider silence as the blank canvas of a recorded work. If one was to take away a single message from 'Nutopian International Anthem', it might be 'Listen to this canvas'.

'Nutopian International Anthem' extends the LP-as-gallery theme in interesting ways. As mentioned above, it appears at the end of side one of the original release, which makes it easy to miss when listening to *Mind Games* in its entirety. The resulting effect suggests that the work has been secreted away in a room somewhere off the main gallery.

'Band on the Run'

As a follow-up to *Red Rose Speedway*, Paul McCartney and Wings were planning a series of sessions that would be a bit more exotic in terms of locale. Having heard that EMI maintained studios all around the world, Paul asked their management for a list of what was available: 'I thought Rio or Lagos, because of the rhythmic element ... Being in a climate, you know: if you are in Brazil there's no escaping it, same with Africa. I thought, Africa, yeah, it'll be a great vibe'.[43] Sessions were booked for EMI Studios in Lagos for September 1973.[44]

It was at this point that the various strands of dissatisfaction within Wings resurfaced. Guitarist Henry McCullough had been clashing with McCartney over the direction of the band's music. Paul seemed to prefer a structured approach, while McCullough, who had come out of a blues tradition, liked to work in a manner that was more improvisational. In July 1973, they had a confrontation that resulted in McCullough walking out of rehearsals and not returning. Then, drummer Denny Seiwell, who was generally unhappy with Wings' financial arrangements, called Paul just before the planned departure for Lagos to inform him that he wasn't going:[45]

> A couple of the guys said, 'We just don't wanna go'. Well, thanks. I hated that. I like an easy life, like most people ... I then thought, right, OK, we'll show you. And that was it, very much a motivating drive. We will now make the best album ... Our only alternative was to cancel the whole trip, not make an album, go into a depression.[46]

And so Paul and Linda, along with Denny Laine, decided to go ahead with the plan and make the trip anyway. In addition to his regular duties, Paul would fill in on drums, and he and Denny would play guitar. Linda would provide keyboards and vocals, and all three would pitch in whenever necessary.[47] Fortunately, Paul was also able to enlist the services of Geoff Emerick, the man who had engineered many of The Beatles' best recordings, to come along and help out. Thus began an adventure that would result in the creation of what was arguably Paul McCartney and Wings' best album, *Band on the Run*.

The title track for *Band on the Run* is a remarkable piece that seemed to build on 'Uncle Albert/Admiral Halsey' from *Ram*. There are also references to 'Happiness Is a Warm Gun' and the second side of *Abbey Road*. The song/track consists of three sections/panels that outline a journey to freedom. Each of these sections could arguably work independently of the others. Here, however, they are woven together by the composer to create another musical triptych:

> **Panel One** ('Stuck Inside These Four Walls'): The music begins with a gently descending guitar riff that seems to reference a similar riff from the Beatles' 'Helter Skelter'. Unlike that raucous song, however, the music in this first panel soothes the listener by establishing a mellow, meditative tone. The singer is a prisoner reflecting on his life sentence and on everything he has lost. Particularly painful is the fact that he cannot be with his dearest loved ones ever again. He stresses how no one he will ever meet within the confines of his prison will ever be as kind to him as his own mother.

> **Panel Two** ('If I Ever Get Out of Here'): The reverie of Panel One is suddenly broken by a hard riff played on electric guitar and backed by full band. A two-chord pattern is established that creates a compelling rhythmic groove. This groove provides the basis for the early stages of a plan to escape. The singer then tells us what his next moves would be if he can manage to leave his current situation behind. He would give away all his worldly goods, but also says that he would make sure something was left over to cover the cost of a daily pint.

> **Panel Three** ('Band on the Run'): An extended riff with full band and orchestra introduces the next panel. Here, a bright rhythm on acoustic guitar provides the foundation for a long-awaited journey to freedom. The full band soon joins in as the singer begins to describe how he and his confederates managed their escape. The change in tone of both music and lyric suggests that freedom has also released creativity. The band is not sure of their future, but they are ready to meet whatever comes their way.

In the book *Here, There and Everywhere: My Life Recording the Music of The Beatles* (2006), engineer Geoff Emerick described the procedure for the recording of *Band on the Run*: 'All of the tapes we had recorded in Lagos were eight-track, so our first task was to copy those tracks that would be receiving overdubs to sixteen-track format; doing so would give us eight additional tracks to record on'.[48] Transferring the original eight-track recordings to sixteen-track format allows one to have the best of both worlds. The intimacy and simplicity of the original eight-track master becomes the basis for a larger, more complex soundscape. Here, McCartney and Wings employed a method that recalled John Lennon and Yoko Ono's work on the *Imagine* album, and also how Paul himself had worked creating various tracks for his debut solo album in which he transferred four-track masters recorded at home to an eight-track format at Morgan Studios and EMI.

The space created for 'Band on the Run' suggests a journey from interiors to exteriors. The intimate quality of Panel One features the soft, intimate tones of a close personal space. This is then followed by Panel Two, a larger space that allows for collective sounds to be heard more clearly. Finally, in Panel Three, we burst out into the open air. This new exterior space allows for expanded instrumentation and also for enhanced communication over greater distances. In that regard, the return of the hook line from this panel at the very end of the album stresses the importance of these larger spaces with regard to the theme of *Band on the Run*. In addition to the narrative presented in the lyric of the song, the journey described here could be connected with the development of a musical group. The Beatles, for instance, had started out in small clubs, moved on into the larger spaces of theatres and concert halls, and finally embraced the open-air stadiums of their American concert tours.

'Jet'

'Jet' is a powerful rock song/track that would become one of the most popular entries in the Wings musical catalogue. Although the title seems to have been partly inspired by a black Labrador owned by the McCartney family, the song may well have been a reference to David Bowie's 'Suffragette City' released the year before.[49] 'Jet' opens with a powerful instrumental riff that seems to blend guitar power chords with the kind of brass lines associated with big band jazz. In keeping with the style of its era, the song also makes use of a Moog synthesizer for its distinctive solo section. Throughout, McCartney's vocals seem to be reaching for the kind of jet-engine effect he created for his high-harmony vocals on Beatles tracks such as 'No Reply'.

The musicians on 'Jet' were Paul on drums, guitar, bass, and perhaps keyboards and piano; Linda on keyboards and backing vocals; and Denny Laine on guitar, backing vocals, and perhaps piano; Howie Casey played the saxophone and the Beaux Arts Orchestra provided the strings from an arrangement by Tony Visconti. There are also horns on the track, but it is not known exactly who the musicians were for the session.[50] As previously mentioned, the tracks recorded in Lagos were eight-track and thus had to be transferred later to sixteen-track in order to make room for additional overdubs. When it came to 'Jet', this process nearly ended in disaster.

As Paul and Denny were recording overdubs onto the newly available tracks, Geoff Emerick realized that the tape they were using was shedding oxide particles. As a result, the high end on the track, particularly the cymbal parts, was starting to disappear:

The only thing you could do was to quickly make a second-generation copy of the audio on a good reel of tape and hope that the sound hadn't deteriorated too badly by that point. It was just our luck to have this one bad reel of tape just as we were recording such a great song ... I had to think quickly: do I tell Paul, or don't I? I mulled it over and finally came to the conclusion that there was no point in telling him.[51]

In connection with Emerick's account, it's interesting to consider the unique sound quality of 'Jet' as compared with the rest of the *Band on the Run* LP. As a result of the loss of some of the 'top end', the space seems to have been coloured a bit more by the eight-track source. The resulting effect suggests the pages of vintage books in which the paper has naturally aged to a sepia tone. This quality enhances the vintage imagery featured in the lyrics; for example, 'Sergeant Major' and 'Lady Suffragette'. On another level, one might also liken the effect to a canvas that has been prepared with a particular colour onto which other colours can then be added to create unique effects.

'Picasso's Last Words (Drink to Me)'

The pièce de resistance of *Band on the Run* is a mellow number called 'Picasso's Last Words (Drink to Me)'. Its origins are almost as interesting as the song itself. It was written in response to a challenge from actor Dustin Hoffman, who had read an article on the death of Picasso in which the artist's last spoken words were reportedly, 'Drink to me, drink to my health, you know I can't drink anymore'. Hoffman liked the quote and wondered if Paul could come up with something suitable with those words. A few minutes later, the song began to take shape.[52]

Unlike the majority of tracks on *Band on the Run*, the recording of 'Picasso's Last Words (Drink to Me)' did not begin at EMI Studios in Lagos. Instead, the initial recording session took place at Ginger Baker's ARC Studio, as Geoff Emerick relates:

We ended up doing most of the song 'Picasso's Last Words' – which was intentionally recorded to resemble a Picasso painting, with lots of seemingly unrelated song fragments stuck together – at ARC, although we added a lot of overdubs later when we returned to London, editing them together, along with snatches of other tunes on the album, to try to make one cohesive piece out of it.[53]

In addition to Paul on guitars, bass, drums, keyboards, percussion, and vocals; Linda on backing vocals and percussion; and Denny Laine on guitars, vocals, and percussion, Ginger Baker himself was enlisted to add additional percussion to the track. The narration heard during the French interlude section was spoken by Denis Le Sève and was originally recorded for the BBC programme 'Le Flash Touristique'. The orchestration was prepared and conducted by Tony Visconti and performed by the Beaux Arts Orchestra.[54] Visconti recounted McCartney's direction for the orchestration: 'Just do your thing, but in the style of Motown strings'.[55]

As previously mentioned, the strategy for the recording of 'Picasso's Last Words (Drink to Me)' was to access the kind of Cubist painting techniques associated with Picasso himself.[56] Applying his talent for the geometrics of musical form to 'Picasso's Last Words (Drink to Me)', McCartney keeps his listeners on their toes by repeatedly playing with their expectations for a decisive point of view.[57] Revisiting something he'd last attempted on *Red Rose Speedway*, he presents a work that contains multiple panels. Expanding on that work, in which the melodic hooks of the first three panels were heard in a reprise over the final track, the various sections here seem to be rearranging and reforming themselves as the piece unfolds. Moreover, two of the panels contain elements from tracks heard earlier in the LP sequence: 'Jet' and 'Mrs. Vandebilt'. Thus, 'Picasso's Last Words (Drink to Me)' becomes a kind of miniature gallery derived from the larger sonic gallery that is *Band on the Run*. Reconsidering this idea, one wonders how many of the other tracks on the LP might be intermingled in this way.

Galleries in Motion

Since the dissolution of The Beatles, the creative dialogue between John Lennon and Paul McCartney had entered a new phase. The sense of friendly competition upon which the band was built had now become a long-distance conversation. Remarkably, this new relationship seemed to be driven by the same kind of friendly one-upmanship that had resulted in some of their best songs/tracks with The Beatles. Each new solo project that came along seemed to indicate that these ex-partners were carefully taking note of each other's work. That awareness resulted in solo material from each that seemed to effectively say, 'Okay, that's good. But how about this?'

In Chapter 4 it was noted how the *Imagine* LP seems to advance the notion of LP as gallery of recorded sound. In that space, one encounters what seem to be three overlapping rooms in which the works on display are effectively grouped in terms of their dominant musical characteristics: piano ballads; blues/rock songs; and acoustic folk songs. Entries in each group also seem to reference one another as the album progresses, thereby suggesting that the various elements might be rearranged by the listener in unique and interesting ways. Here, Lennon seems to have been laying down a firm challenge regarding what was possible in the field. Paul McCartney's third album with Wings clearly rose to that challenge.

Band on the Run (1973) is much more than an adequate response to *Imagine* (1971). It embodies all of McCartney's strengths as composer, producer, and performer. The transposable nature of various songs/tracks as demonstrated by 'Picasso's Last Words (Drink to Me)' reveals an organic depth to the entire collection. This is further enhanced by the return of a section of the title track that occurs right at the end of the album. Accessing the theme of LP as narrative form, *Band on the Run* also seems to relate the story of Wings and the difficulties Paul and the group were having in trying to break free from restrictive definitions of what a rock band could or should be. The narrative could also be seen to reach back to The Beatles and their attempts to break free from their earlier image as pop stars in order to become full-time creative artists in the studio.

Notes

1 Howard Sounes, *Fab: An Intimate Life of Paul McCartney* (Cambridge, MA: Da Capo Press, 2010), 269–270.

2 Howard Sounes, *Fab: An Intimate Life of Paul McCartney* (Cambridge, MA: Da Capo Press, 2010), 278–279.

3 Bruce Spizer, *The Beatles Solo on Apple Records* (New Orleans, LA: 498 Productions, 2005), 142.

4 Luca Perasi, *Paul McCartney: Recording Sessions (1969–2013)* (Milan: L.I.L.Y. Publishing, 2014), 67–68.

5 Paul Du Noyer, *Conversations with McCartney* (New York: The Overlook Press, 2016), 103.

6 Luca Perasi, *Paul McCartney: Recording Sessions (1969–2013)* (Milan: L.I.L.Y. Publishing, 2014), 67–68.

7 Luca Perasi, *Paul McCartney: Recording Sessions (1969–2013)* (Milan: L.I.L.Y. Publishing, 2014), 68–69.

8 Paul Du Noyer, *Conversations with McCartney* (New York: The Overlook Press, 2016), 302–303.

9 Luca Perasi, *Paul McCartney: Recording Sessions (1969–2013)* (Milan: L.I.L.Y. Publishing, 2014), 72–73.

10 Paul Gambaccini, 'Paul McCartney: The Rolling Stone Interview'. *Rolling Stone*, 25 June 2018. www.rollingstone.com/music/music-features/paul-mccartney-the-rolling-stone-interview-3-241349.

11 Paul Du Noyer, *Conversations with McCartney* (New York: The Overlook Press, 2016), 103.

12 'John Lennon Yoko Ono on the Mike Douglas Show Day 5 Feb 18, 1972 YouTube'. YouTube. manibep, 24 December 2016. https://youtu.be/dB8ei4GcvQY?t=1006 (transcribed by author).

13 *John and Yoko: Above Us Only Sky*, directed by Michael Epstein (2019; Wandsworth, London: Eagle Vision, 2019), DVD.

14 John Lennon and Yoko Ono, *Imagine John Yoko* (London: Thames & Hudson, Ltd., 2018), 286.

15 *John and Yoko: Above Us Only Sky*, directed by Michael Epstein (2019; Wandsworth, London: Eagle Vision, 2019), DVD.

16 'Yoko Ono. Museum of Modern (f)Art. 1971: Moma'. The Museum of Modern Art. MoMA. Accessed 20 March 2022. www.moma.org/audio/playlist/15/384.

17 Bruce Spizer, *The Beatles Solo on Apple Records* (New Orleans, LA: 498 Productions, 2005), 69–70.

18 Howard Sounes, *Fab: An Intimate Life of Paul McCartney* (Cambridge, MA: Da Capo Press, 2010), 276–277.

19 Howard Sounes, *Fab: An Intimate Life of Paul McCartney* (Cambridge, MA: Da Capo Press, 2010), 279–280.

20 Bruce Spizer, *The Beatles Solo on Apple Records* (New Orleans, LA: 498 Productions, 2005), 163.

21 Luca Perasi, *Paul McCartney: Recording Sessions (1969–2013)* (Milan: L.I.L.Y. Publishing, 2014), 90–91.

22 Bruce Spizer, *The Beatles Solo on Apple Records* (New Orleans, LA: 498 Productions, 2005), 156–157.

23 Eric Iozzi, 'Another Day (Paul McCartney Song)'. Wikipedia. Wikimedia Foundation, 28 January 2022. https://en.wikipedia.org/wiki/Another_Day_(Paul_McCartney_s ong)#/media/File:Record_Sheet_01.jpg. (The printing on this track sheet appears to be in McCartney's own hand.)

24 Luca Perasi, *Paul McCartney: Recording Sessions (1969–2013)* (Milan: L.I.L.Y. Publishing, 2014), 96.

25 'Red Rose Speedway "the Double Album"'. PaulMcCartney.com, 27 April 2020. www. paulmccartney.com/news-blogs/news/red-rose-speedway-the-double-album.

26 Luca Perasi, *Paul McCartney: Recording Sessions (1969–2013)* (Milan: L.I.L.Y. Publishing, 2014), 86–88.

27 'My Love (Song)'. The Paul McCartney project, 26 March 2020. www.the-paulmccart ney-project.com/song/my-love.

28 Luca Perasi, *Paul McCartney: Recording Sessions (1969–2013)* (Milan: L.I.L.Y. Publishing, 2014), 88.

29 Chip Madinger and Mark Easter, *Eight Arms to Hold You: The Solo Beatles Compendium* (Chesterfield, MO: 44.1 Productions, 2000), 176.

30 'The Paul McCartney Special'. YouTube. sirpaulru, 21 November 2020. www.youtube. com/watch?v=krwYODnCOHQ (transcribed by author).

31 John Lennon and Yoko Ono, *Imagine John Yoko* (London: Thames & Hudson, Ltd., 2018), 256.

32 Bruce Spizer, *The Beatles Solo on Apple Records* (New Orleans, LA: 498 Productions, 2005), 74.

33 Chip Madinger and Mark Easter, *Eight Arms to Hold You: The Solo Beatles Compendium* (Chesterfield, MO: 44.1 Productions, 2000), 87.

34 John Blaney, *John Lennon: Listen to This Book* (Guildford: Paper Jukebox, 2005), 126.

35 John Blaney, *John Lennon: Listen to This Book* (Guildford: Paper Jukebox, 2005), 130.

36 Bruce Spizer, *The Beatles Solo on Apple Records* (New Orleans, LA: 498 Productions, 2005), 74.

37 John Blaney, *John Lennon: Listen to This Book* (Guildford: Paper Jukebox, 2005), 134.

38 Gabriel Garcia Lorca, *In Search of Duende* (New York: New Direction Books, 1998), viii.

39 Gabriel Garcia Lorca, *In Search of Duende* (New York: New Direction Books, 1998), 61.

40 John Blaney, *John Lennon: Listen to This Book* (Guildford: Paper Jukebox, 2005), 132.

41 Philip Norman, *John Lennon: The Life* (Toronto: Anchor Canada, 2009), 708.

42 *Mind Games*, Apple, 1973.

43 Paul Du Noyer, *Conversations with McCartney* (New York: The Overlook Press, 2016), 108.

44 Howard Sounes, *Fab: An Intimate Life of Paul McCartney* (Cambridge, MA: Da Capo Press, 2010), 289.

45 Howard Sounes, *Fab: An Intimate Life of Paul McCartney* (Cambridge, MA: Da Capo Press, 2010), 290–291.

46 Paul Du Noyer, *Conversations with McCartney* (New York: The Overlook Press, 2016), 109.

47 Geoff Emerick and Howard Massey, *Here, There, and Everywhere: My Life Recording the Music of The Beatles* (New York: Gotham Books, 2006), 346.

48 Geoff Emerick and Howard Massey, *Here, There, and Everywhere: My Life Recording the Music of The Beatles* (New York: Gotham Books, 2006), 350.

49 Luca Perasi, *Paul McCartney: Recording Sessions (1969–2013)* (Milan: L.I.L.Y. Publishing, 2014), 112–113.

50 Luca Perasi, *Paul McCartney: Recording Sessions (1969–2013)* (Milan: L.I.L.Y. Publishing, 2014), 112–114.

51 Geoff Emerick and Howard Massey, *Here, There, and Everywhere: My Life Recording the Music of The Beatles* (New York: Gotham Books, 2006), 351.

52 Howard Sounes, *Fab: An Intimate Life of Paul McCartney* (Cambridge, MA: Da Capo Press, 2010), 293.

53 Geoff Emerick and Howard Massey, *Here, There, and Everywhere: My Life Recording the Music of The Beatles* (New York: Gotham Books, 2006), 345–346.

54 Luca Perasi, *Paul McCartney: Recording Sessions (1969–2013)* (Milan: L.I.L.Y. Publishing, 2014), 112.

55 Tony Visconti, *Bowie, Bolan, and the Brooklyn Boy* (New York: HarperCollins, 2007), 204.

56 Paul Gambaccini (ed.), *Paul McCartney: In His Own Words* (London: Omnibus Press, 1976), 79.

57 Hans L.C. Jaffe, *Picasso* (New York: Harry N. Abrams, Inc., 1983), 28.

6

RIDING THE WAVE

Following the success of *Band on the Run*, no one would have blamed Wings for taking some well-deserved time off. The band did take a break, but it turned out to be another busman's holiday. They spent some time with family by writing and recording a new album with Paul's brother Mike, who was known profession-ally as Mike McGear.[1] That album, entitled *McGear* (1974), provided a window onto Wings' creative process at a crucial time in the band's career; that is, halfway between *Band on the Run* (1973) and *Venus and Mars* (1975). In fact, the final track from *McGear* sounds like a missing link in the Wings catalogue.

'The Man Who Found God on the Moon' links together three different story ideas. The first concerned balloons flying above the motorway seen by Mike McGear while he was driving home from London to Liverpool.[2] McGear described how the second idea ('Make Me Happy') was inspired by a young girl who was selling books and flowers for Krishna, and a doorman who was rather rude to the girl:

> He was going to kick her out, but I said, 'It's all right'. I might have bought a flower off her. As she was leaving, she turned around, looked at both of us, and very quietly, very innocently, said, 'Hare Krishna', and walked out the bloody door. That's the way to get out aggression in this life: disarm with complete honesty.[3]

The song's third story idea concerned the Apollo 11 moon landing. The lyrics in this final section referenced how a number of astronauts experienced a 'spiritual awakening' following their return from space. This section effectively combines the themes from the first two stories with an assertion that a journey out into the unknown can effectively lead to a deeper sense of connection and inner peace.

As with the majority of tracks on the *McGear* album, the recording of 'The Man Who Found God on the Moon' took place at Strawberry Studios in the winter of

DOI: 10.4324/9781003300212-9

1974. In addition to McGear and Wings, 10cc's Graham Gouldman and Lol Creme may also have contributed to the recording, but were not credited.[4] McCartney also took the opportunity to begin replenishing the ranks of his own band. He brought in a young Scottish guitarist named Jimmy McCulloch who would soon become a full-time member of Wings.[5]

In addition to the musical elements handled by the various personnel listed above, 'The Man Who Found God on the Moon' is especially noteworthy for its expressive use of audio effects. Over the years, the source for these effects had been rather obscure. Finally, in August 2021, all of the material was identified and played on The Consequences Podcast.[6] It had also become available on the website of Sean Macreavy Media.[7] The source was a reel-to-reel tape labelled SRS (Strawberry Recording Studios) containing various sounds prepared by Paul, three of which were included on 'The Man Who Found God on the Moon': 'Dougal bits', 'Moon talk', and 'Mike's Kids: Harry K'.

'Mike's Kids: Harry K' features the sounds of the Hare Krishna chant being sung by Mike McGear's daughters. This can be heard during the song's second section. 'Moon Talk' occurs during the song's third section and features the sounds of the Apollo 11 transmissions shortly after astronauts Neil Armstrong and Buzz Aldrin had set foot on the moon. Finally, 'Dougal bits' is the source for the voice heard during the extended fade-out which says, 'So, there you are, then: quite a difference. Yes, the answer is LP'. The line came from a 1971 BBC informational film narrated by Robert Dougal that concerned changes to the British currency. Within the context of the song, 'LP' seemed to refer to the long-playing record as a medium, suggesting a link between the subject matter of the track and the technology that was used to create it. However, as pointed out by Sean Macreavy, the original reference in the Robert Dougal narration was to 'Pounds (new) Pence'.[8] So, there you are, then.

The skilful blending of sounds creates a unique colour field for 'The Man Who Found God on the Moon'. This painterly process seems to have been the means of bringing the three distinct story elements together into one flowing narrative line. In what is arguably the most remarkable moment in the entire piece, Mike McGear reaches up for a brief vocal improvisation just before the return of the opening section. Paul McCartney then overlaps with his brother and continues the ascent of the line into his upper register. This compelling brushstroke in sound at once suggests balloons in flight, astronauts walking on the moon, and the cooperation derived from human connection and feeling that made both achievements possible.

'Whatever Gets You Through the Night'

In 1974, John Lennon was at something of a loss as to how he should carry on. Yoko Ono had released two albums the previous year and Paul McCartney and Wings were riding high in the wake of *Band on the Run*. Meanwhile, his last album, *Mind Games*, had received a lukewarm response from fans and critics alike. To make matters worse, his marriage to Yoko had foundered in the middle of his struggle to avoid being deported from America. Just when all hope seemed lost, he received support from someone who, though not a blood relative, was thought of as 'family'.[9]

By the time he came to collaborate with John Lennon on the album *Walls and Bridges* (1974), Elton John had been tearing up the pop music playing fields for more than a decade. He was born Reginald Kenneth Dwight on 25 March 1947.[10] A naturally gifted musician, he studied piano from an early age and went on to attend the Royal Academy of Music.[11] During the early 1960s, he played in a group called Bluesology that released an original song by Elton in 1965 called 'Come Back Baby'.[12] As a part of Bluesology, he also gained a tremendous amount of musical and professional experience when the band was hired to back a variety of American R&B acts as they toured through the UK.[13] In a 2009 interview, Elton described the benefits of that early training to Elvis Costello:

> And then after we finished the Major Lance tour, we were offered Patti LaBelle ... I was a huge fan of her music and we rehearsed with her. This was when Cindy Birdsong was in the group, before she joined the Supremes. You learn – I learned so much for my latter-day experience with stagecraft, and how to perform a song, how to talk to an audience, how to work hard.[14]

Dissatisfied with the subsequent direction of Bluesology, Elton answered an advert from Liberty Records in 1967 which announced that they were looking for new talent.[15] He didn't pass the audition but he was paired with Bernie Taupin, a young, aspiring lyricist who had replied to the same advert. Together, they began writing songs, and in order to support this process, Elton took gigs as a session musician while also working at Dick James Music. As Lennon pointed out, this is where Elton, Bernie, and The Beatles had first crossed paths: 'Elton had been working in Dick James's office when we used to send our demos in and there's a long sort of relationship musically with Elton that people don't really know about'.[16]

Between 1969 and late 1971, Elton's recordings of John/Taupin originals resulted in four remarkable LPs that each achieved popular and critical acclaim. Produced by Gus Dudgeon and orchestrated by Paul Buckmaster, these albums created a fascinating blend of rock, classical, folk, country, gospel, and rhythm and blues. In addition, he released a live recording of a New York radio concert and also contributed songs to the soundtrack of a film.[17] By the time he came to collaborate with John on *Walls and Bridges*, he had entered a new phase in his career. Now, he and his collaborators were experimenting with studio techniques that made his newer works sound decidedly bright as compared with the more earthy tones of his earlier records.

Elton had dropped in on the sessions for *Walls and Bridges* while John was recording the planned single, 'Whatever Gets You Through the Night'. Building on the New York sounds that had been a feature of *Mind Games*, the song/track seems to reflect the approach Lennon would soon take on *Rock and Roll* (1975). Essentially a series of R&B-inspired vocal riffs built on an infectious groove, 'Whatever Gets

You Through the Night' never lets up. Here, the participation and stamina of Elton John would turn out to be essential.

The sessions for 'Whatever Gets You Through the Night' took place at the Record Plant East in New York City during the summer of 1974. The track featured Lennon on guitar and vocals; Jesse Ed Davis and Eddie Mottau on guitars; Jim Keltner on drums; Klaus Voormann on bass; Ken Ascher on clavinet; Arthur Jenkins on percussion; and Bobby Keys on saxophone. In addition to playing piano and organ, Elton would also add vocal harmonies to the track. This process, however, was trickier than he had anticipated:[18]

> He put the vocal down first and I had to sing backing vocals, double-tracked, to someone else's phrasing. Now, I'm very quick but that took a long time because Lennon's phrasing was SO weird. It was fantastic but you start to understand why he was a one-off. We did two vocal harmonies in the studio based around his one lead vocal and it was quite nerve-racking.[19]

The space created for the track was reminiscent of the approach taken on *Mind Games* the previous year. However, while tracks from that album tended to leave spaces in the mix, 'Whatever Gets You Through the Night' was filled to the brim with richly hued musical sound. Elton's piano and organ provide a substantial amount of harmonic colour and thus provides a solid foundation for the lead and harmony vocals. It also grounds the wildly melodic saxophone of Bobby Keys, which at times seems in danger of dancing off the edge of the track.

Elton also provided vocal harmony on another song/track for *Walls and Bridges* entitled 'Surprise, Surprise (Sweet Bird of Paradox)'. Grateful for Elton's help, and wishing to return the favour, Lennon agreed to visit Elton for an upcoming session in Colorado. The plan was for Elton and his band to record a cover version of a well-known song by The Beatles.

'Lucy in the Sky with Diamonds' (1974)

On his own double LP *Goodbye Yellow Brick Road* (1973), Elton John successfully conjured up the Summer of Love for a whole new generation of listeners. The album's opening track approached the level of The Beatles with a multi-panelled work, arguably a musical diptych, that was placed prominently on the first side of the album.[20] On *Caribou* (1974), Carl Wilson of The Beach Boys recorded a memorable backing vocal track for 'Don't Let the Sun Go Down on Me'.[21] The implication seems clear: Elton was blending Beatles-inspired pop songcraft with the kinds of musical effects The Beach Boys had been creating for albums like *Pet Sounds* (1966) and *Smiley Smile* (1967). It was this potent mixture that he and his collaborators brought with them into the sessions for 'Lucy in the Sky with Diamonds'.

Elton John's version of 'Lucy in the Sky with Diamonds' was recorded at Caribou Ranch Studio in July 1974.[22] The players on the session were the regular members of the Elton John Band, plus one very special guest. This was Dr. Winston O'Boogie, who added sparkling guitars and backing vocals to the track. He can be heard very clearly during the song's reggae break. Dr. Winston O'Boogie, of course, was a pseudonym for John Lennon, who was giving his blessing to Elton and his new version of the song by actually participating in the session.[23]

As recorded by The Beatles, 'Lucy in the Sky with Diamonds' seems to take place in a relatively small, self-contained space. Elton's version seems cavernous by comparison. The one exception is a section just past the midpoint of the track in which Lennon's vocals and 'reggae' guitars appear in a kind of audio close-up. The larger sound space also seems to have led to a slower groove throughout that makes the track seem almost laid back when compared with the original. These changes had an impact on the perception of the setting. In Elton's capable hands, the pastoral imagery of the English countryside that had been a feature of the first version of the track was now transformed into a landscape of global colour.

'#9 Dream'

Side two of the *Walls and Bridges* LP begins with a song/track that suggests a musical painting cast in the mode of a pop song. Earlier that year, Lennon had produced an LP for Harry Nilsson entitled *Pussy Cats*. That album presented an intriguing mix of Nilsson originals along with inspired cover versions of works by some of his and Lennon's musical heroes. One of these was a version of 'Many Rivers to Cross' by Jimmy Cliff. Nilsson's recording featured a beautiful string arrangement created by Ken Ascher, and it was this arrangement that would become the basis for one of Lennon's most memorable solo compositions, '#9 Dream'.

Introduced by an opening slide guitar gesture that recalls the beginning of *Mind Games*, '#9 Dream' seems to be taking off into the sky. There are three distinct musical sections on offer, and Lennon's mastery is more than aptly demonstrated in the transition he creates from the third section back into section one. There, the players begin to slow down and descend gradually into a brief but full stop that signals the return of section one. This idea recurs just before the end of the piece. There, however, the transition leads us back to section three, which is now repurposed as an extended coda.

'#9 Dream' was recorded at the Record Plant East in New York City during the summer of 1974. In addition to Lennon himself who provided vocals and acoustic guitar, the track also featured Klaus Voormann on bass; Jim Keltner on drums; Arthur Jenkins on percussion; Nicky Hopkins on electric piano; Jesse Ed Davis and Eddie Mottau on guitars; Ken Ascher on clavinet; Bobby Keys on saxophone; and a group called The 44th Street Fairies on backing vocals. The distinctive orchestration was created and conducted by Ken Ascher.[24] The sessions for *Walls and Bridges* created an interesting blend in that they featured players who appeared on *Imagine* working with musicians from the New York scene that had previously played on *Mind Games*. As a result, the moods and colours that had characterized each project were blended together to tremendous effect.

The space created in '#9 Dream' suggests connections with both 'Imagine' and 'Mind Games'. The take-off enacted at the beginning of the track leads us into an open sky in which the dripping clouds of *Imagine* and 'Cloud Piece' are present. Soon, we are flying in a manner that suggests the mental journey of 'Mind Games'. However, while that trip often seemed precarious, the flying here is soft and easy. We are able to touch down and take off again at will, navigating through open space with grace and style.

After the session for 'Whatever Gets You Through the Night', Elton John was convinced that the record would reach number one on the charts. He told this to John who promised that if it did happen, he would appear live onstage with Elton. Since Lennon had never had a number one record on his own, it must have seemed a safe promise. However, when the prediction came true, he had to make good. On Thanksgiving night (28 November 1974), he performed live with Elton and his band at Madison Square Garden in New York City.[25]

By all accounts, the night was very emotional. Lennon found out, through the crowd's enthusiasm, just how much he was loved. Elton fulfilled a lifelong ambition by performing with one of his biggest musical heroes. The fans in the audience were witness to history as a member of the band that had been lost to them four years earlier had now returned to take an active role in the musical scene he'd helped create. And finally, Yoko Ono, who had arranged to be present in the audience that fateful evening, began to take steps towards ending her separation from John.[26]

It was clearly a time for giving thanks and also for tying up loose ends. The previous year, Lennon had agreed to complete an album as a means of settling a potential lawsuit. That project had been initiated in response to a claim by the owners of the copyright for 'You Can't Catch Me' by Chuck Berry. Their claim was that 'Come Together' by The Beatles had borrowed too much of its melodic line and a bit of lyric from Berry's classic song. Rather than challenge the claim, Lennon agreed to record three songs from Berry's catalogue, including 'You Can't Catch Me'.[27]

In February 1975, Lennon released *Rock 'n' Roll*, a self-curated collection of his early influences. Co-produced with Phil Spector, sessions began at Record Plant West in late 1973 and were completed at Record Plant East the following year.[28] The version of 'You Can't Catch Me' that was included was a masterful rendering of the song. It employed tasty Latin percussion to activate the verses and a full ensemble blasting away on the chorus in a manner that recalled the intensity of early Little Richard. Another standout from the album was 'Stand by Me' by Ben E. King, in which Lennon's interpretation suggested a link between late-period Beatles and classic rhythm and blues.

'Love in Song'

1974 was a deceptively quiet year for Paul McCartney and Wings. Even though they didn't play live or release a new album, the band had spent the summer in

Nashville recording new material and also recruiting new members. In addition to Jimmy McCulloch who played guitar on the sessions for the *McGear* album, they also added drummer Geoff Britton to the fold. Later that year, they released the 45-rpm single 'Junior's Farm'.[29] That track cleverly showcased the newly refurbished Wings line-up, and also provided clues as to where the band would be going musically in the coming year.

In a seeming attempt to duplicate the serendipitous process that had made *Band on the Run* so compelling, Wings' next LP would be recorded in another exotic locale known for high-quality music. This time, the location would be New Orleans and the album would be called *Venus and Mars*. Although tuneful and impressive, what seemed to be missing from *Venus and Mars* was a sense of danger. During the *Band on the* Run sessions, Wings were up against it, and had to prove themselves by digging deep to find their magic. This time around, they were on a roll, but seemed to be finding it difficult to get their songs to take hold. Nevertheless, several tracks stood out and served to showcase Paul's painterly skills as a composer. The first was a haunting ballad that seemed to somehow connect with the band's prior struggles.

Apparently a typical McCartney folk ballad, 'Love in Song' is nevertheless quite unique in both its concept and its realization. The creeping introduction that becomes the foundation for the main section suggests a deep spirituality. As a result, the main section that follows sounds more like a prayer than a pop song. This quality is soon offset by the contrasting section, which is far more conventional in its melodic and harmonic structure and suggests the influence of an adult commercial style. As alternations of the secular and the sacred, these sections provide mutual relief in a way that suggests renewal and continuing growth. Inevitably, however, the energy begins to dissipate, and 'Love in Song' dissolves back into the personal space from which it came.

The recording of 'Love in Song' began during sessions that took place at EMI Studios in November and December 1974.[30] The players were Paul on vocals, bass, piano, and hand bells, with possible input on the orchestration; Linda on backing vocals, hand bells, and Moog; Denny Laine on piano, electric guitar, and backing vocals; Jimmy McCulloch on twelve-string guitar; and Geoff Britton on drums and milk bottles. At this point, Britton was still Wings' drummer, but would soon be replaced by an American named Joe English. The strings heard on the track were recorded at Wally Heider Studios in Los Angeles on 10 March 1975.[31] The orchestration was created by Tony Dorsey and played by the Sid Sharp Strings. Gayle Levant played the harp.[32] Additional overdubs may also have been recorded earlier that year at Sea Saint Studios in New Orleans.[33]

The space created for 'Love in Song' is arguably more memorable than the musical materials themselves. This is not a criticism of the composer or the band. It's simply that the space created is so unique in the McCartney and Wings catalogue that it seems to stay in the memory longer than the various musical elements that are used to reveal it. Here, the sounds cast shadows that move steadily across the space as the track unfolds. Ultimately, after the brief respite of a sunny day, they recede slowly into the darkness from which they initially emerged.

'You Gave Me the Answer'

The next standout track from *Venus and Mars* was another in a series of period pieces by Paul. Earlier examples of this approach include 'When I'm Sixty-Four' and 'Honey Pie', but there are subtle references to 'Blackbird' here as well. Built around a meticulous piano part in D major, the song recreates the sound of a dance hall number of the 1930s. The lead vocal is heard through an appropriately pinched megaphone effect in the style of Fred Astaire or Rudy Vallee. Although it returns to familiar McCartney territory, the song is musically more adventurous than any of its antecedents and remains a little-known gem in the Wings recorded catalogue.

The basic tracks of 'You Gave Me the Answer' were recorded between mid-January and late February 1975 at Sea Saint Studios in New Orleans. Overdubs were completed in March 1975 at Wally Heider Studios in Los Angeles.[34] The musicians on the track were Paul on piano, bass, and lead vocals, with possible input on the orchestration; Linda McCartney on backing vocals; Jimmy McCulloch on electric guitar; and Joe English on drums and backing vocals. The orchestration for the track was created by Tony Dorsey and featured Michael J. Pierce and Vito Platomone on clarinet; Carlos Klejman and Russell Joseph Bobrowski on violin; Ronald B. Benko on trumpet; John K. Branch on viola; Harold Joseph Ballam on bassoon; and Bernard S. Richterman on the cello.[35]

'You Gave Me the Answer' recreates the soundspace of an earlier era in popular music. This quality is enhanced by the production, which tries to accent the qualities of early recording technology. This was the era of elegant dance bands, of Rudy Vallee and Ray Noble. However, it was also marked by the deliberate ignorance of an encroaching danger. The dreams of then and now, it seems, would ultimately be undone by the harsh realities of the modern world.

'Listen to What the Man Said'

Here was an infectiously appealing track with a rather unusual provenance. The song seems to blend elements of piano and guitar in a way that suggests that McCartney may have been writing across two instruments. The main riff is played on electric guitar, but seems more natural to the piano. In similar manner, the piano is the rhythm instrument, but the progression and key area seem more native to the guitar. As in so many of the tracks discussed thus far, the real treat is the coda in which strings enhance an already colourful scene with bright patches of instrumental colour.

The basic tracks of 'Listen to What the Man Said' were recorded at Sea Saint Studios in New Orleans between 16 January and 24 February 1975. Overdubs were completed in March 1975 at Wally Heider Studios in Los Angeles. The musicians on the track were Paul on vocals, electric piano, bass, and possibly synthesizer and percussion; Linda McCartney on backing vocals and possibly keyboards; Denny Laine on backing vocals and electric guitar; Jimmy McCulloch on electric guitar; Joe English on drums and possibly percussion; and Tom Scott on soprano saxophone.[36] The orchestration was prepared by Tony Dorsey and played by the Sid Sharp Strings. Gayle Levant played the harp.[37]

'Listen to What the Man Said' effectively creates the mood and space of a street fair. In that regard, the mix seems deliberately cluttered with sounds that overlap one another throughout the scene/song/track. This blend of sounds creates a harmonic mist that becomes the atmosphere of the scene. Finally, we arrive at a final passage (coda) that serves to release the energies that have been building over the course of the track. The effect is that of a field of colourful flowers that have just begun to bloom in the sun.

Shaved Fish

Later that year, Lennon curated a collection of his solo works entitled *Shaved Fish*. The LP included hard-to-find early singles by the Plastic Ono Band. Perhaps because they had initially been released prior to The Beatles' breakup, powerful records such as 'Give Peace a Chance', 'Cold Turkey', and 'Instant Karma' all seemed to have vanished from the public mind. *Shaved Fish* would seek to remedy that situation. The collection would create a chronology for mid-1970s music listeners that would help them better understand the trajectory of John and Yoko's work since the late 1960s.

Shaved Fish was released in autumn 1975 in the weeks following the birth of John and Yoko's son, Sean. Earlier that month, Lennon had won his lengthy battle to remain in the United States. In February 1976, his contract with Capitol Records expired, and he chose not to renew it. Instead, he used the opportunity to segue into a temporary retirement from the music business.[38] For the first time since 1962, when he and The Beatles had signed on as recording artists, he was free.

Following Lennon's graceful departure from the musical stage, McCartney was faced with an interesting challenge. Up to this point, whether together or at a distance, he had always been able to bounce off his partner's artistic sensibilities. This worked well because Paul seemed inherently adept at a multi-panel approach, while John had a natural flair for the LP-as-gallery idea. Thus, whether together or apart, each partner could access the speciality of the other while also maintaining a personal creative flow. Now, with Lennon going into retirement, McCartney would have to do it all.

In March 1976, Wings would release the democratically conceived LP *Wings at the Speed of Sound*. It featured vocal performances by every member of the band and was made in preparation for a tour of Europe and America that Wings would undertake that year.[39] As with *McGear* (1974), this new album became a window on the band's creative process. Musically, it veered deftly from arena rock ('Beware My Love') to contemporary pop ('Silly Love Songs') to melodic ballads in the classic McCartney style ('Warm and Beautiful'). One of the most unique songs/tracks on offer was a relatively obscure character sketch near the end of side two called 'San Ferry Anne'.

'San Ferry Anne'

As he had done with 'Love in Song', Paul builds his piece on a steadily descending musical line. This time, however, he is back in the familiar tonal landscape of A minor. The contrasting section seems to begin within the same key, but a remarkable transformational effect in what was the tonic harmony signals our arrival in a new tonal space. He settles briefly in E minor before moving decisively back to the original tonic and a repeat of the form. The coda, which features colourful brass and woodwind gestures, uses elements from the opening section now moved into the tonal landscape of D minor.

Sessions for *Wings at the Speed of Sound* took place at Abbey Road Studios in two phases. The first was between August and October 1975, after which the band left for a series of concerts in Australia.[40] The second phase, during which the song 'San Ferry Anne' was recorded, took place in January and February of the following year. The musicians on the track were Paul on acoustic guitar, bass, and vocals; Denny Laine on acoustic guitar; Jimmy McCulloch on electric guitar; and Joe English on drums. Brass and woodwinds were provided by Howie Casey, Tony Dorsey, Steve Howard, and Thaddeus Richard.[41]

The musical brushstrokes used to outline the space of 'San Ferry Anne' suggest that the song might have fit well in the LP gallery of *Venus and Mars*. Together, these brushstrokes create an ambience that evokes a dream space of an earlier time. This space seems to exist solely in the mind of the main character, a woman who moves through the present, but lives decidedly in the past. Her all-day dances might be to the strains of a ballroom orchestra from the 1930s. Perhaps, within this dance, she'll be able to refashion her world into the beautiful dream of a happy life – but it doesn't matter.

'Let 'Em In'

Wings at the Speed of Sound opened with one of the biggest hits of the band's career. Reaching back to the hook line of 'Single Pigeon', McCartney fashions a song that is arguably impossible to dislike. Written in the piano-friendly key of B flat major, the song achieves a unity between its primary and secondary sections through an infectious piano riff played by Paul. The main vocal line yields periodically to a secondary riff from the horn section with little or no loss of focus. The lyrics alternate between exhortations of hospitality and a litany of those who are expected to attend what promises to be a very lively party.

'Let 'Em In' was another product of the second phase of sessions for *Wings at the Speed of Sound*. The song was recorded at Abbey Road Studios in February 1976. The players on the track were Paul McCartney on vocals and piano; Linda McCartney on backing vocals; Denny Laine on backing vocals; Jimmy McCulloch on bass; and Joe English on drums. Flutes and horns were performed by Howie Casey, Thaddeus Richard, Steve Howard, and Tony Dorsey.[42] The track was released with the full album in March 1976, and also as a single later that year.[43]

The space created for 'Let 'Em In' is remarkably soft and supple. Seemingly emanating out of the door-chimes that introduce the song/track, the space appears to be almost completely lacking rough edges. Even the horns sound somehow softened. The one exception is the military drum that gains in volume and intensity as the track proceeds.[44] Finally, it seems to take over and become the most prominent sound in the ensemble.

'Refuge of the Roads'

Paul McCartney's return to America was headline news.[45] In the twelve years since The Beatles had first appeared on *The Ed Sullivan Show*, the times had been confusing and stressful. Predictably, the early 1970s were characterized by a nostalgic yearning for a simpler life. Thus, a return to the States by one of the Fab Four was hotly anticipated. Paul obliged this general desire to revisit the past by peppering the Wings setlist with renditions of Beatles classics, such as 'Yesterday', 'Lady Madonna', 'Blackbird', and 'The Long and Winding Road'.[46]

When creating the logistics for the shows, Paul and Linda were determined to avoid leaving their children at home for an extended period of time. Thus, special arrangements were made to accommodate the family throughout the tour. Homes were secured in various locations where the children would stay while Paul and Linda would fly off to perform at a concert. After the show, they would fly back to be with the kids. When a series of shows were completed, the entourage would then move on to another rented home and continue the same process from there.[47] In addition to the various band members and their friends and families, the Wings tour also featured an artist-in-residence named Humphrey Ocean. His role was to create sketches of the band and the audiences as the shows unfolded.[48]

As Wings were busy preparing the recordings of various shows for a planned live triple LP, an interesting development was occurring across the Atlantic. A singer-songwriter from Canada named Joni Mitchell was using painters' principles to break new ground in pop music. She had been trying to update her musical language and this process was becoming awkward for the session musicians who complained about the eccentric nature of her ideas. It was clear that Joni needed to seek out new collaborators.[49] She had heard of the remarkable work that was being done by jazz musician Jaco Pastorius, so she invited him to overdub bass on four pieces from her recently completed album, *Hejira* (1976).[50]

One of the compositions to which Jaco added his distinctive bass sound was a piece called 'Refuge of the Roads'. As the final track on the original LP, it creates a remarkable, wave-like gesture as it unfolds. Here, Joni seems to suggest that rhythmic momentum itself is a musical element to be shaped and moulded by the composer. Also, as McCartney had done with 'Picasso's Last Words (Drink to Me)', 'Refuge of the Roads' seems to mimic and complete the overarching gestural arc of *Hejira*. In an interview recorded for the documentary film *Jaco* (2014), Mitchell shared her insights on this unique collaboration: 'I set up this architecture ... and he just kind of instinctively played, figuratively. You're inviting another painter to join you on your canvas. It's very conversational'.[51]

Thrillington

As mentioned, John Lennon's retirement from the music business meant that Paul McCartney no longer had an equal partner to bounce off of, either directly or in remote fashion. The immediate result was that the kind of conversation that Joni Mitchell described with regard to her own collaboration with Jaco Pastorius was temporarily on hold. Lennon would no longer be a friendly competitor. He would now focus his attention and his energies on his wife and his infant son. Paul would now have to do it all, and he started the process by revisiting the *Ram* sessions with a new release.

Following the conclusion of the *Ram* project, McCartney had enlisted the services of Richard Hewson on what would become one of the most eccentric episodes of his solo career. The plan was to record the entire album again, but this time as a series of exotic instrumentals. Ranging from rock to jazz to easy listening, the collection took on a decidedly experimental tone. Curiously, Paul chose not to play or sing on any of the tracks, and instead employed the services of some of the best session musicians in the business. The title of this unusual collection was *Thrillington*.[52]

Thrillington showed McCartney revisiting his conceptual idea for *Sgt. Pepper's Lonely Hearts Club Band* in that he fashioned a fictional alter-ego for the project called Percy 'Thrills' Thrillington. Percy was a musician and bandleader who had evidently been active for many years but had somehow remained largely unknown to the general public. This fluid approach to personal identity was certainly whimsical, but also reflected something more organic. Author Ian Peel described how Paul's approach in this regard suggests a continuing interest in expanding his work to include 'words, images, personae, and contexts which, far more than just music alone, shape the modern world'.[53]

Sidewalk Galleries

Over the next three years, Paul McCartney and Wings would record two ambitious albums of new material. Each would include songs/tracks that sought to extend the notion of musical diptych. Each would also attempt to further the notion of LP as gallery by bridging to other art forms and media. The first of these LPs, entitled *London Town*, was issued in early 1978. In the manner adopted for earlier albums, some of the material for *London Town* would be recorded in an exotic location. Following a series of productive sessions at EMI Studios, the band headed west for the Virgin Islands. There, they rented three yachts for the project: two would be for the members of the Wings entourage to live on during the trip; the other, called the *Fair Carol*, would be outfitted with recording equipment so as to allow the band to record tracks for the album. The working title for the project was *Water Wings* and the idea seemed to be that the sounds and rhythms of the sea would enhance the creation of the music. As it turned out, water would become a central theme of the new album.[54]

London Town

Co-written by Paul McCartney and Denny Laine, the title track begins with a rising pattern on electric piano that emphasizes Paul's aforementioned geo-metric approach to music composition. It would become the basis for a transi-tional device that would link up the song's two main sections. The first of these featured an assertive melody that managed to sustain itself on spare harmonic changes in E major. The contrasting section is similar but with a more complex melodic line. It also features a more varied harmonic progression, now in the key of A major.

The LP's title track was among those recorded at Abbey Road Studios in London between February and March 1977. Additional parts were overdubbed the following August at Paul's Spirit of Ranachan Studio in Campbeltown, Scotland. He provided vocals, piano, bass, and synthesizer, and may also have added electric and acoustic guitars. Linda played keyboards and sang backing vocals, while Denny Laine added electric piano and electric and acoustic guitars, and also sang backing vocals. Jimmy McCulloch was featured on electric guitar and slide guitar, and Joe English played drums.[55]

The space created in the title track of *London Town* sets the tone for the entire LP as gallery. It seems to resemble the kind of pictures created by Bert, another character from P.L. Travers' *Mary Poppins* who, when the weather was fair, made his living as a screever:

> If it was wet, he sold matches because the rain would have washed away his pictures if he had painted them. If it was fine, he was on his knees all day, making pictures in coloured chalks on the side-walks, and doing them so quickly that often you would find he had painted up one side of a street and down the other almost before you'd had time to come round the corner.[56]

Intrinsic to Bert's artistry was the notion that no matter how much he might wish to preserve the enchanting imagery he creates, sooner or later the rain will fall and wash it all away.

This fluid sensibility seems to spread through the entirety of the *London Town* LP. Here, McCartney presents us with a collection of colourful sketches that bring out the magical qualities of everyday experience. Through these images, one might travel from the sidewalks of London, through Epping Forest, to the cafés of Paris, and beyond. Along the way, one might encounter tiny waterfalls, oceans made of snow, and songs that sail merrily on the moon. However, just as with the pavement drawings of *Mary Poppins*, these musical images are fleeting. Eventually, they must yield to the waters of change and be washed away.

'Backwards Traveller/Cuff Link'

Here, we have the latest in a series of two-panel works by McCartney. Panel One offers a remarkably effective update on a pop-folk song. The infectious energy created here suggests that an urgent message is on its way. Panel Two is an instrumental that creates a remarkable sense of texture through the layering of keyboards. It is less compressed than the music on Panel One, yet more expansive in scope.

'Backwards Traveller' was recorded at Abbey Road Studios during the autumn of 1977. The musicians were Paul McCartney on vocals, drums, bass, guitars, and synthesizer; Linda McCartney on keyboards and backing vocals; and Denny Laine on guitar and backing vocals. 'Cuff Link' was recorded during the same series of Abbey Road sessions as 'Backwards Traveller'. Paul played synthesizer and drums and may also have added bass. Linda could be heard on keyboards, while Denny Laine added synthesizer, and possibly bass as well.[57]

The space created for 'Backwards Traveller/Cuff Link' seems rooted in the text of the first panel. There, Paul describes his artistic process in a relatively clear manner. Referencing a theme from his first solo album, he describes how he goes back in time in order to retrieve the artefacts of human experience that have been either lost or discarded. The journey he describes is one that is both mystical and mythic in scope. The instrumental that constitutes Panel Two ('Cuff Link') can thus be seen as a rendering in sound of the spaces his mind travels in Panel One.

'With a Little Luck'

As the opening track for side two of the original LP, 'With a Little Luck' brightens the mood of *London Town* considerably. Here, McCartney gives listeners a reason to carry on by encouraging them to trust in the rhythms of natural process. His control over the momentum of the piece is masterful. He takes advantage of the song's extended length by subtly manipulating the groove as the track unfolds. The resulting effect recalls the moulding of clay or the blending of colours on a painter's palette.

The initial sessions for 'With a Little Luck' took place in early May 1977 using a mobile recording studio on the yacht *Fair Carol* in the Virgin Islands. Subsequent recording took place at Abbey Road Studios the following November. Paul evidently recorded the electric piano first using a drum machine to guide him. Linda McCartney and Denny Laine's involvement appears to have been limited to backing vocals alone. Thus, the final version may actually have been a near solo recording in a manner similar to *McCartney* (1970).[58]

The sounds of 'With a Little Luck' seem to exist in an aquatic world. They often seem to be moving like ripples on the water. This quality is intensified during a curious contrasting section towards the end of the track, which prominently features the sounds of a synthesizer. There, the tonic harmony is sustained for over twenty seconds, an eternity in popular music. At that point, one becomes increasingly aware of the overall depth of the track, as if one is looking down past the surface of a mysterious lake or pond.

Galleries-on-the-Air

Towards the end of the *London Town* project, Wings had another shift in personnel. Guitarist Jimmy McCulloch left to join the Small Faces, and drummer Joe English, who'd been homesick for America, decided to return to his native land. And so Wings once again became a trio consisting of Paul, Linda, and Denny.[59] Soon they would reform again by adding Lawrence Juber on guitar and Steve Holley on drums. Nevertheless, the band's energy was waning, and their next LP would become the final entry in the Wings catalogue.[60]

Having scored a massive hit the previous year with their 45-rpm single release 'Mull of Kintyre', Wings could afford to experiment some more. Their follow-up to *London Town* was another ambitious LP called *Back to the Egg*. The intention here seems to have been to employ the metaphor of broadcast to create what might be described as a gallery-on-the-air. In order to realize this idea, Paul structured the entire album as if it were a radio broadcast. Author Ian Peel described the precedents for this approach:

> The roots of radio-as-music can be traced back over 30 years before *Back to the Egg* to the composers McCartney was getting into in the late 1960s. In 1951, John Cage's 'Imaginary Landscapes, No. 4' was the sound of 12 radio sets being simultaneously tuned and retuned. In France in the late 1940s composers Pierre Schaeffer and Pierre Henry wrote the groundbreaking 'Symphonie pour un homme seul', which was made up of noise from many electronic sources.[61]

'Reception'

The opening track begins with the electronic sounds of a radio receiver in the process of tuning in a series of voices from an unspecified broadcast. The sounds heard are a combination of voiceovers and musical excerpts. Soon, the band appears playing a funk groove underneath the various broadcast sounds. Led by the bass, the groove recalls one used on 'Everybody's Got Something to Hide Except Me and My Monkey' from *The Beatles* (1968). 'Reception' continues with a succession of riffs on guitar and synth that move in alternation with the various broadcast sounds throughout.

Some of the recording sessions for *Back to the Egg* took place in another exotic location. Following an initial stay at Paul's Spirit of Ranachan Studio in Campbeltown, Scotland, Wings travelled to Kent to work at Lympne Castle using a mobile studio system to record their music in the great hall. 'Reception', the first song recorded after the band's arrival at the castle, featured Paul on bass; Linda on keyboards; Denny Laine and Lawrence Juber on electric guitars; and Steve Holley on drums.[62] Among the elements heard throughout the track were vocal sounds especially recorded by Deirdre, one of the owners of Lympne Castle. There was also a narration derived from a Norwegian radio programme called *The Lutheran Hour*.[63]

The space of 'Reception' is tight and compressed. In this regard, the bass and drums seem pushed to their very limit. They are soon joined by an electric guitar that displays the same kind of intensity and urgency. By comparison, the broadcast voices heard throughout lend a soft and comforting regularity to the proceedings by recalling the pleasant sounds of a kitchen radio. At one point, this warmth is enhanced by the sounds of an orchestra playing a rising line that suggests a cadence. Finally, the various sounds begin to fade away as someone spins the tuner towards a new station, suggesting that the focus all along has been on what might be called 'radio space'.

'Arrow Through Me'

The closing track from side one of the original *Back to the Egg* LP was a remarkable composition entitled 'Arrow Through Me'. The song combines Paul's geometric melodic skills with what seems to be a new harmonic sophistication. The primary section displays a blend of smooth voice-leading within the context of a progression that helps push pop into the realm of jazz. The contrasting section features a series of floating major seventh chords that, as Wings guitarist Lawrence Juber pointed out, suggests a continental influence:

> Those major sevenths, all that stuff, you know, those major seventh chords. It's a European, almost impressionistic kind of sensibility. Rather than, let's say, with the Carpenters, with Paul Williams, where the major sevenths have a different kind of role. It's that intervallic thing; it's playing with this light and shade thing. You know, that's what you want out of high-level composition, and 'Arrow Through Me' is a great example of Paul, compositionally, at a very high level.[64]

The song also contains an instrumental passage in which Paul revisits the rhythmic play of songs like 'Another Day'. Here, he presents an extended riff played with terrific zeal by the horn section. It dances merrily across alternating groups of fours and threes in which the bass drum and snare exchange places as the pattern unfolds. When this section returns just before the song's coda, Paul adds another remarkable feature. Against the repeating riff, he adds a vocal improvisation that, when considered in relation to the song's various elements, results in what might be described as mathematical frenzy.

Initial sessions for 'Arrow Through Me' took place at Paul's Spirit of Ranachan Studio in June 1978. Overdubs were recorded the following October at Abbey Road Studios. The song is unusual in that it only features two members of the band.

McCartney played electric piano and also added vocals, while Steve Holley played drums and a vintage instrument called a Flexatone. Brass and woodwinds on the track were provided by Howie Casey, Tony Dorsey, Steve Howard, and Thaddeus Richard.[65]

'Arrow Through Me' seems to have a curious double function in the gallery of *Back to the Egg*. Outside of the conceptual space of a gallery-on-the-air, the song demonstrates Paul's abilities as a composer and as a practitioner of the kind of soulful pop music then a part of the contemporary scene. Stevie Wonder was the acknowledged master of the form. At the same time, the song/track brings that scene into the album's concept of radio broadcast as a gallery-on-the-air. Thus, the concept, while fancifully creative, is also grounded firmly in the cultural reality of its time.

'Winter Rose/Love Awake'

London Town had featured an interesting song/track called 'Backwards Traveller/ Cuff Link', another in a series of two-panel works by Paul. On *Back to the Egg*, we find two more examples of this form. 'After the Ball/Million Miles' connects its panels with a rhythmic rise and fall that suggests the process of breathing. Panel One ('After the Ball') portrays a ballroom in which the singer feels isolated, alone, and ultimately overwhelmed in a crowd until he is found and rescued by his loved one. Panel Two ('Million Miles') suggests a street singer outside the same party who may be in dire straits, but nevertheless offers up a song/prayer for everyone, no matter what their station in life may be.

The LP features another fascinating two-panel work entitled 'Winter Rose/ Love Awake'. There, Panel One ('Winter Rose') is a meditation on the changing seasons, which mimics that natural process through a deft alternation of major and minor keys. It ends in the depths of winter when spirits are at their lowest ebb. Suddenly, Panel Two ('Love Awake') appears, suggesting the emergence of spring and the return of hope. The panel then concludes with a brief coda that blends elements of both panels in a comforting message of hope concerning the inevitability of the cycle of the seasons.

'Winter Rose' was recorded at Paul's Spirit of Ranachan Studio during July 1978. The track featured McCartney on piano, bass, vocals, and perhaps a harpsichord; Linda on keyboards and backing vocals; Denny Laine on backing vocals and perhaps an acoustic guitar; Lawrence Juber on electric guitar; and Steve Holley on drums and percussion.[66] 'Love Awake' was begun during the sessions at Lympne Castle in September 1978 and was completed with additional overdubs at EMI Studios in April 1979. The track featured Paul on acoustic guitar and vocals; Linda on keyboards and backing vocals; Denny Laine on acoustic guitar and backing vocals; Lawrence Juber on acoustic guitar and bass; Steve Holley on drums and percussion; and finally, The Black Dyke Mills Band conducted by Martyn Ford.[67] Although recorded separately, the two songs were edited together to become part of the final sequence for *Back to the Egg*.

'Winter Rose/Love Awake' offers a musical rendering of the seasons and their respective spaces. Only three are mentioned here directly: summer, winter, and spring. However, the bleak portrayal of winter carries with it the memory of the anxiety of autumn in terms of the inevitable departure of summer. The portrayal of the seasons here recalls a memorable sequence from the film *A Man for All Seasons* (1966). There, as Sir Thomas More languishes in confinement, we are shown his view from the narrow window of his cell in which the seasons slowly dissolve from summer, on through the bleak winter, and into the bright promise of spring.[68]

'The Broadcast'

Although it appears three songs before the end of *Back to the Egg*, 'The Broadcast' feels like a concluding statement. As a companion piece to 'Reception', it reasserts the gallery-on-the-air idea mentioned earlier, and also brings it to a decisive close. Built on a repeating series of arpeggiated chords played on piano, the focus of 'The Broadcast' is an elaborate spoken-word passage. The spoken elements presented here seem to suggest an interesting development from the album's opening track. There, they were used more like added effects; here, they have become part of the basic work materials of the piece.

'The Broadcast' was recorded at Lympne Castle in September 1978. Reaching back to the spirit of his first solo album, all of the instruments heard on the track (piano, electric guitar with effects, and mellotron) were provided by Paul McCartney himself.[69] The orchestral effects heard throughout the track were actually created with guitar played through a Gizmotron, an effects device invented by Kevin Godley and Lol Creme of 10cc.[70] The spoken-word elements were provided by Harold Margary, the owner of Lympne Castle. He read excerpts from two plays chosen at random from the castle's library: Ian Hay's *The Sport of Kings* (1924)[71] and *The Little Man* by John Galsworthy (1915).[72] In *Conversations with McCartney* (2016), the composer described how his collaboration with Harold and Deirdre Margary was based on like-mindedness:

> The two people who owned the castle we were recording at [Harold and Deirdre Margary at Lympne] … We set up a little mobile unit and they used to invite us in for a drink every evening. Me and Linda would sit in their sitting room and they were [gently upper-class accent] 'very lovely people, very far back'. We got a great relationship with them. Even though we were different generations and classes, we just had a lot in common.[73]

As mentioned above, the musical sounds moving through the virtual space of 'The Broadcast' were created using a blend of modern and classical instrumentation. As a result, they provide an appropriate underscore for the spoken-word passages read by Harold Margary. In another connection with 'The Man Who Found God on the Moon', these passages evoke a sense of human feeling and cooperation as the impetus for the kind of technological progress that made sound recording and radio broadcasts possible. In the process, they seem to reach back for the best of the past, while also looking ahead towards a promising future.

Notes

1 Chip Madinger and Mark Easter, *Eight Arms to Hold You: The Solo Beatles Compendium* (Chesterfield, MO: 44.1 Productions, 2000), 192.
2 'Mike McGear McCartney'. The Strange Brew Podcast, 9 January 2019. https://thestra ngebrew.co.uk/interviews/mike-mcgear-mccartney.
3 Geoffrey Giuliano, *Blackbird: The Life and Times of Paul McCartney* (New York: Plume, 1992), 264.
4 Chip Madinger and Mark Easter, *Eight Arms to Hold You: The Solo Beatles Compendium* (Chesterfield, MO: 44.1 Productions, 2000), 192.
5 Luca Perasi, *Paul McCartney: Recording Sessions (1969–2013)* (Milan: L.I.L.Y. Publishing, 2014), 117.
6 PodBean. 'Consequences 10cc Podcast 76 – The Great Alcester Bake-off #3: Hello from Mike, Paul and Linda'. 23 August 2021. https://consequences.podbean. com/e/consequences-10cc-podcast-76-the-great-alcester-bake-off-3-hello-from-mike-paul-and-linda.
7 'Video, Photography and Audio Services: Sean Macreavy Media: Alcester'. seanmacreavy. Accessed 20 March 2022. www.seanmacreavy.com.
8 Sean Macreavy, 'Paul McCartney – Unreleased "Effects Tape" for McGear'. Strawberry Studios, 1974. 24 August 2021. www.youtube.com/watch?v=SRKyIJbCexk%3Fhd%3D1.
9 David Buckley, *Elton: The Biography* (Chicago, IL: Chicago Review Press, 2007), 178–179.
10 Philip Norman, *Elton John* (New York: Fireside, 1991), 25.
11 David Buckley, *Elton: The Biography* (Chicago, IL: Chicago Review Press, 2007), 29.
12 Philip Norman, *Elton John* (New York: Fireside, 1991), 51–52.
13 David Buckley, *Elton: The Biography* (Chicago, IL: Chicago Review Press, 2007), 45.
14 'Spectacle: Elvis Costello with Elton John (Elton Interview and Performance)'. YouTube. Spectacle Elvis Costello, 27 December 2019. https://youtu.be/tc_MI4jdbJs.
15 Philip Norman, *Elton John* (New York: Fireside, 1991), 63.
16 David Buckley, *Elton: The Biography* (Chicago, IL: Chicago Review Press, 2007), 178–179.
17 Philip Norman, *Elton John* (New York: Fireside, 1991), 503.
18 John Blaney, *John Lennon: Listen to This Book* (Guildford: Paper Jukebox, 2005), 138.
19 David Buckley, *Elton: The Biography* (Chicago, IL: Chicago Review Press, 2007), 180.
20 The song/track mentioned here was called 'Funeral for a Friend/Love Lies Bleeding'. Actually, the latter part of 'Love Lies Bleeding' features an instrumental section that might qualify as an additional panel. That discussion, however, will have to wait for another day….
21 David Buckley, *Elton: The Biography* (Chicago, IL: Chicago Review Press, 2007), 184.
22 David Buckley, *Elton: The Biography* (Chicago, IL: Chicago Review Press, 2007), 179.
23 Philip Norman, *Elton John* (New York: Fireside, 1991), 280.
24 John Blaney, *John Lennon: Listen to This Book* (Guildford: Paper Jukebox, 2005), 147.
25 Philip Norman, *John Lennon: The Life* (Toronto: Anchor Canada, 2009), 738–739.
26 Philip Norman, *Elton John* (New York: Fireside, 1991), 287–289.
27 Philip Norman, *John Lennon: The Life* (Toronto: Anchor Canada, 2009), 718–719.
28 John Blaney, *John Lennon: Listen to This Book* (Guildford: Paper Jukebox, 2005), 160.

29 Paul Du Noyer, *Conversations with McCartney* (New York: The Overlook Press, 2016), 114.

30 Bruce Spizer, *The Beatles Solo on Apple Records* (New Orleans, LA: 498 Productions, 2005), 195.

31 Chip Madinger and Mark Easter, *Eight Arms to Hold You: The Solo Beatles Compendium* (Chesterfield, MO: 44.1 Productions, 2000), 203.

32 'Venus and Mars (Album)'. The Paul McCartney project, 19 April 2016. www.the-paulmccartney-project.com/album/venus-and-mars.

33 Luca Perasi, *Paul McCartney: Recording Sessions (1969–2013)* (Milan: L.I.L.Y. Publishing, 2014), 123.

34 Luca Perasi, *Paul McCartney: Recording Sessions (1969–2013)* (Milan: L.I.L.Y. Publishing, 2014), 129.

35 'Venus and Mars (Album)'. The Paul McCartney project, 19 April 2016. www.the-paulmccartney-project.com/album/venus-and-mars.

36 Luca Perasi, *Paul McCartney: Recording Sessions (1969–2013)* (Milan: L.I.L.Y. Publishing, 2014), 132–135.

37 'Listen to What the Man Said (Song)'. The Paul McCartney project, 26 March 2020. www.the-paulmccartney-project.com/song/listen-to-what-the-man-said.

38 Philip Norman, *John Lennon: The Life* (Toronto: Anchor Canada, 2009), 750.

39 Chip Madinger and Mark Easter, *Eight Arms to Hold You: The Solo Beatles Compendium* (Chesterfield, MO: 44.1 Productions, 2000), 216–221.

40 Chip Madinger and Mark Easter, *Eight Arms to Hold You: The Solo Beatles Compendium* (Chesterfield, MO: 44.1 Productions, 2000), 211–213.

41 Luca Perasi, *Paul McCartney: Recording Sessions (1969–2013)* (Milan: L.I.L.Y. Publishing, 2014), 145.

42 Luca Perasi, *Paul McCartney: Recording Sessions (1969–2013)* (Milan: L.I.L.Y. Publishing, 2014), 143–145.

43 Chip Madinger and Mark Easter, *Eight Arms to Hold You: The Solo Beatles Compendium* (Chesterfield, MO: 44.1 Productions, 2000), 214.

44 This part may have been played by Denny Laine. See Luca Perasi, *Paul McCartney: Recording Sessions (1969–2013)* (Milan: L.I.L.Y. Publishing, 2014), 143–145.

45 Robert Rodriguez, *Fab Four FAQ 2.0: The Beatles' Solo Years, 1970–1980* (Milwaukee, WI: Backbeat Books, 2010), 370.

46 Luca Perasi, *Paul McCartney: Recording Sessions (1969–2013)* (Milan: L.I.L.Y. Publishing, 2014), 147.

47 Howard Sounes, *Fab: An Intimate Life of Paul McCartney* (Cambridge, MA: Da Capo Press, 2010), 308–309.

48 '"The Ocean View" Book Published'. The Paul McCartney project, 4 May 2020. www.the-paulmccartney-project.com/1982/12/the-ocean-view-book-published.

49 *Jaco*, directed by Paul Marchand (2015; Los Angeles, CA: Slang East/West, 2015), DVD.

50 'Joni Mitchell Library – Biography: 1976–1977 Refuge of the Roads: Jonimitchell.com, January 1998'. 28 March 2009. https://jonimitchell.com/library/view.cfm?id=2035.

51 *Jaco*, directed by Paul Marchand (2015; Los Angeles, CA: Slang East/West, 2015), DVD.

52 Chip Madinger and Mark Easter, *Eight Arms to Hold You: The Solo Beatles Compendium* (Chesterfield, MO: 44.1 Productions, 2000), 161–163.

53 Ian Peel, *The Unknown Paul McCartney: McCartney and the Avant-Garde* (London and Richmond, Surrey: Reynolds & Hearn, 2002), 93.

54 Peter Ames Carlin, *Paul McCartney: A Life* (New York: Touchstone, 2009), 247.

55 Luca Perasi, *Paul McCartney: Recording Sessions (1969–2013)* (Milan: L.I.L.Y. Publishing, 2014), 151–152.

56 P.L. Travers, *Mary Poppins: 80th Anniversary Collection* (New York: Houghton Mifflin Harcourt, 2014), 32–33.

57 Luca Perasi, *Paul McCartney: Recording Sessions (1969–2013)* (Milan: L.I.L.Y. Publishing, 2014), 165–167.

58 Luca Perasi, *Paul McCartney: Recording Sessions (1969–2013)* (Milan: L.I.L.Y. Publishing, 2014), 157–158.

59 Peter Ames Carlin, *Paul McCartney: A Life* (New York: Touchstone, 2009), 248.

60 Howard Sounes, *Fab: An Intimate Life of Paul McCartney* (Cambridge, MA: Da Capo Press, 2010), 321.

61 Ian Peel, *The Unknown Paul McCartney: McCartney and the Avant-Garde* (London and Richmond, Surrey: Reynolds & Hearn, 2002), 96.

62 Luca Perasi, *Paul McCartney: Recording Sessions (1969–2013)* (Milan: L.I.L.Y. Publishing, 2014), 171–178.

63 Ian Peel, *The Unknown Paul McCartney: McCartney and the Avant-Garde* (London and Richmond, Surrey: Reynolds & Hearn, 2002), 96.

64 'Understanding McCartney. Ep 2: CULT HERO'. YouTube. breathless345, 14 March 2021. https://youtu.be/m7q0D7lFTIs?t=2970.

65 Luca Perasi, *Paul McCartney: Recording Sessions (1969–2013)* (Milan: L.I.L.Y. Publishing, 2014), 174–175.

66 Luca Perasi, *Paul McCartney: Recording Sessions (1969–2013)* (Milan: L.I.L.Y. Publishing, 2014), 176–177.

67 Luca Perasi, *Paul McCartney: Recording Sessions (1969–2013)* (Milan: L.I.L.Y. Publishing, 2014), 179–180.

68 *A Man for All Seasons*, directed by Fred Zinnemann (1966; Culver City, CA: Sony Pictures Home Entertainment, 2007), DVD.

69 Luca Perasi, *Paul McCartney: Recording Sessions (1969–2013)* (Milan: L.I.L.Y. Publishing, 2014), 181–182.

70 Ian Peel, *The Unknown Paul McCartney: McCartney and the Avant-Garde* (London and Richmond, Surrey: Reynolds & Hearn, 2002), 97.

71 Chip Madinger and Mark Easter, *Eight Arms to Hold You: The Solo Beatles Compendium* (Chesterfield, MO: 44.1 Productions, 2000), 245.

72 James Gindin, *Galsworthy's Life and Art: An Alien's Fortress* (Houndmills, Basingstoke: The Macmillan Press Ltd., 1987), 337.

73 Paul Du Noyer, *Conversations with McCartney* (New York: The Overlook Press, 2016), 121–122.

PART III
New Colours

7

A HEART PLAY

In the years since he'd gracefully left the stage, John Lennon had settled into a pleasant domestic life with Yoko and Sean. Seeking stability for his family as well as for himself, he took on the role of househusband. Thus, while Yoko looked after the business, John looked after her and Sean.[1,2] In the process, he learned how to bake bread.[3]

John was unique among his peers in that during the early stages of his career, he had published two books. However, he had put his literary aspirations aside to focus on music. Now that The Beatles were finished and his solo career was on hold, he finally had time to concentrate on his writing. His new pieces were more adventurous in tone, with an openness that suggested the influence of Yoko. A selection of these writings were later published as *Skywriting by Word of Mouth* (1987), thereby completing his literary trilogy.

Despite the fact that he was 'retired' from the business, John still composed music. He demoed a number of new songs that reflected his still-evolving musical approach as well as his changing perspective on society. Several of these songs would find a place on John and Yoko's *Double Fantasy* (1980),[4] and on The Beatles' *Anthology* during the 1990s.[5] All of this music-making remained largely a private matter until one day, his curiosity was piqued by something he heard on the radio. It was an interesting new record from his old friend Paul.

McCartney II

McCartney and Wings had once again scored big in early 1979 with their 45-rpm single release 'Goodnight Tonight'. Unfortunately, the success of this record would not offset the negative reaction that was awaiting *Back to the Egg*. That ambitious LP was widely seen as a disappointment by fans and critics alike. Even the all-star line-up that Paul had assembled for 'Rockestra', a driving instrumental that opened side

DOI: 10.4324/9781003300212-11

two, could not seem to affect the album's fortunes. Years later, however, it would be seen as an important entry in the band's catalogue, as Lawrence Juber says:

> *Back to the Egg* went from being a two-star album to a four-star album over the course of a generation. It's a very, very eclectic album – so, perhaps not so consistent and coherent as would be typical of an American rock record from that era. But the English have always been able to be somewhat more eccentric.[6]

In the summer of 1979, Paul McCartney returned to his home studio to engage once again in the recording process as refuge. As on his first solo album, he hired a multi-track recorder, and once again opted to play all the instruments himself. Now, however, it was sixteen tracks he'd be working with rather than four. In spite of the additional tracks, he continued to use the machine in the same way – that is, as a kind of sketchbook – as he explained in an interview with Tim Rice in 1980:

> I just had a machine and the 16-track machine was like a glorified cassette recorder, but it's a professional machine. Microphone right into the back of it and then I would record let's say a drum kit and I'd just listen to it back and if I didn't like it I'd just move the microphone because I didn't have all the technical eq's and echoes and all the gimmicks. So, I just had to move the mic. So, it wasn't exactly engineering, you know, it was more like moving mics really.[7]

'Secret Friend'

As with *Red Rose Speedway*, Paul's new solo album was originally planned as a double LP. Also, as before, that version never actually materialized, which meant that a number of the more experimental tracks recorded during the sessions, such as 'Secret Friend', were cut from the final running order. In conversation with Paul Du Noyer, Paul commented on this particular song/track and his deliberate efforts to explore variety in his work:

> It's very dismissable: 'A ten-minute track, called "Secret Friend"? Leave it out! It's not "Hey Jude". So shut up'. Well, it isn't 'Hey Jude' but I knew what I was doing. I wasn't trying to write 'Hey Jude'. It's like Picasso – dare I compare myself? Ha! No, you daren't! But whenever he got a groove going, his Blue Period or his Cubist Period, he kicked it over. He never did any more, and the people would go, 'I loved your Blue Period'. 'Yeah, well, I'm fed up with that, I'm doing cubist now'.[8]

The track in question was built on a repeating pattern played on electric keyboard. High vari-speeded vocals effectively matched the exotic colour of the keyboard part throughout.[9] The opening section of the song initially seems to be continually looping without a clear sense of direction. Soon, however, a brief descending motive appears, providing suitable contrast as well as a sense of renewal. Finally, we are treated to a full cadence with an unexpected resolution, and the entire process begins again, and again, and again…

All the instruments heard on 'Secret Friend' are played by Paul himself. These included drums, percussion, bass, electric guitar, mellotron, and synthesizer.[10] A fascinating quality of this particular track is its playing time, which was ten minutes and thirty-one seconds. Paul had always been known for his conciseness as a composer, but here he challenges himself to explore a much larger temporal landscape. As a testament to the artist's creative instincts, 'Secret Friend' succeeds beautifully and points the way towards the more experimental works he would create in the 1990s with The Fireman.

In keeping with its extreme length, the virtual space created for 'Secret Friend' is vast and inviting. The electronic effects generated by the keyboard in combination with the processed vocals creates an expansive quality that contrasts nicely with the topic of the text. It suggests that the friendship need not be secretive given the wide-open spaces that provide room enough for all. It might also be an indication that given the vast space of the universe, it's useless to try to hide. The reason is that on a certain level, nothing is hidden; everything is open to view.

The techno-driven quality of many of the tracks on *McCartney II* is nicely contrasted by several songs that are based on a more traditional approach. One of these, entitled 'On the Way', is built on a blues pattern in the classic style. However, the song also displays broad gestures derived from the larger rock forms of the 1970s. An especially noteworthy moment is when the electric guitar creates its own brief section with a repeating power chord before slipping back into the basic progression. The song's lead vocal, which is drenched in echo, gently reminds listeners of McCartney's early influences (Example 11).

EXAMPLE 11 MULTI-TRACK OUTLINE FOR 'ON THE WAY'[11]

Track 1	Bass drum
Track 2	'Top kit' (presumably hi-hat, snare, small tom)
Track 3	Bass
Track 4	Vocal
Track 5	Electric guitar 1
Track 6	Electric guitar 2

'On the Way' was one of the most straightforward recordings of the sessions. Evidently, the entire process only required six of the sixteen tracks available on the master tape. The drum kit seems to have been divided between Track 1 (bass drum) and Track 2 ('top kit'), with the bass guitar then being added to Track 3. Lead vocals were added to Track 4, while Tracks 5 and 6 each featured electric guitar.[12]

The space created for 'On the Way' comprises an interesting blend of 'wet' and 'dry' sounds. The vocals and the guitars are heavily treated with reverb, or wet, while the drums and bass are noticeably lacking in effects, or dry. This is not an unusual approach to take in the recording and mixing process. Here, however, it seems to have been employed in order to create a marked contrast between the two elements. As a result, the vocals and guitars seem to hover like smoke above the drums and bass, which seem decidedly grounded by comparison. A further contrast is created within the space, this time between vocals and guitar. Of the two, the vocals seem to be more reverberant, suggesting that they may be at a higher level than the guitar parts just below.

'Coming Up'

Now we come to the song/track that piqued John Lennon's curiosity regarding exactly what his ex-partner was getting up to. Seemingly a development on the assertive rhythmic play of earlier tracks like 'Arrow Through Me' and 'Goodnight Tonight', 'Coming Up' opens with an infectious repeating riff on electric guitar that becomes the foundation for the entire piece. The riff is answered during the song's contrasting section by a rising bass line in octaves that support the song's melodic vocal hook. Despite the fact that the recording seems to have been made using a 'click' track, the rhythmic groove feels human rather than mechanical. During the coda, the entire song slows down convincingly in a manner that suggests the expressive play of a full ensemble.

The recording of 'Coming Up' filled the entirety of the sixteen-track master tape. This seems to be the result of a generous amount of layering of overdubs. Six tracks of synthesizer as well as four tracks of vocals were recorded. However, special care seems to have been taken to ensure the cohesion of the various parts. The overall groove on the track was evidently guided using a rhythm machine placed at the beginning of the process on Track 1 (Example 12).[13]

EXAMPLE 12 MULTI-TRACK OUTLINE FOR 'COMING UP'[14]

Track 1	Rhythm box
Track 2	Bass drum
Track 3	Snare
Track 4	Electric guitar 1
Track 5	Electric guitar 2
Track 6	Synth
Track 7	Vocals, handclaps
Track 8	Vocals, handclaps
Track 9	Vocals, handclaps
Track 10	Vocals, handclaps

Track 11	Bass
Track 12	Synth
Track 13	Synth
Track 14	Synth, tambourine
Track 15	Synth
Track 16	Synth

'Coming Up' seems to inhabit a similar soundspace as the one that had been created for 'Secret Friend'. However, while that song/track sounds broad and expansive, the virtual space of 'Coming Up' is decidedly compressed. This lends the piece a sense of urgency that may have led to its being chosen as the single. This compressed quality also creates an effective setting for the song's lyric, which is optimistic and encouraging throughout. In that sense, the space created for the recording might suggest a seed that is ready to burst open and grow, or a flower that is about to bloom.

Four months after completing his home studio sessions, McCartney and Wings went on a short tour of Britain. During those shows, they performed an impressive version of 'Coming Up', which was yet to be released. Everything looked bright and promising for the coming year. Then, on 16 January 1980, at the start of a two-week tour of Japan, McCartney was arrested at Tokyo's Narita International Airport for possession of marijuana. The tour was cancelled and he spent the next nine nights in a Japanese prison before being released.[15] Although it would not generally become known until the following year, the incident in Japan would turn out to be the beginning of the end for Wings.[16] In conversation with author Paul Du Noyer, McCartney described his state of mind before going to Tokyo:

> I think the Japanese 'episode' as we can call it, was the end of Wings. It's strange, that period for me. I didn't want to go to Japan with this band. I felt under-rehearsed. And I don't like that feeling at all. I will normally rehearse so I feel, We've got a great show. Then I'm happy to go. We were going to rehearse in Tokyo, and I thought, Oh, a bit last minute … So I was panicking about it all.[17]

Double Fantasy

The tracks Paul had recorded at home the previous summer would be released to the public in May 1980 as a sequel to his first solo LP. That album, *McCartney* (1970), had lately been rediscovered by a new generation of listeners who seemed better able to appreciate its underlying concept. The cultural mood, it seemed, was more receptive to an approach in which the studio could be viewed as a kind of gallery/

workshop for the presentation of various works in progress. Thus, *McCartney II* was considered a success. More importantly, there was an old friend across the Atlantic who was very impressed.

As mentioned, John Lennon, though retired, was still composing. Based on an assessment of his home recordings from this period, he was still developing elements of his work that had been in progress since the late 1960s. During that time, he was also aware of his former partner's progress. On occasion, he had even been quite complimentary and encouraging. But Paul's latest LP did more than elicit a comment; it actually generated a full musical response.

Lennon had been so struck by *McCartney II* and its 45-rpm single 'Coming Up' that it inspired him to come out of retirement and record a new LP entitled *Double Fantasy* (1980). This new album would constitute an attempt to unify many of his earlier creative threads within the context of a renewed collaboration with Yoko. During an interview conducted while he was preparing the album, John spoke about comparisons between himself and his former partner with what sounded like an art-school sensibility: 'I think it's like comparing, I don't know, Magritte and, uh Picasso if you want to put it on that level, or whatever. How can you compare it? It's like comparing Gauguin and Van Gogh'.[18]

'Dear Yoko'

In many ways, Lennon's side of *Double Fantasy* picks up where *Walls and Bridges* had left off. A good example of this is 'Dear Yoko', a lively song that blends the sentiments of 'Oh Yoko!' with the assertive sound of his New York-based albums of the early to mid-1970s. Hugh McCracken makes a remarkable musical contribution by playing multiple harmonicas that were doubled with his slide guitar.[19] There is also a trace of Buddy Holly evident in Lennon's hiccupping vocal interjections. As in many songs, the musical materials are conventional but the rhythmic activation of those materials by the ingenuity of the composer generates considerable interest throughout.

The session for the basic tracks of 'Dear Yoko' took place on 14 August 1980. Lennon returned on 22 September to add his lead vocal.[20] A key difference between these sessions and the ones Lennon led in the early to mid-1970s was the conspicuous absence of drugs and alcohol. A mood of wellness pervaded the process, as author Philip Norman points out:

> The complement of top session musicians did not include any old crony of John's who might lead him astray again. Indeed, the studio atmosphere suggested a health spa more than a rock album. Yoko created a special 'quiet room' for the two of them, softly lit, with palm trees and a white piano. Instead of cocaine and Cognac, the band were served tea and sushi ('dead fish', John called it); a plate of sunflower seeds and raisins stood beside every microphone, and shiatsu massages were available on request.[21]

As his ex-partner had done on 'Coming Up', Lennon compresses the sounds of 'Dear Yoko' almost to breaking point. The resulting space is one in which an urgent message needs to be delivered and heard by the listener. Here, Lennon creates a fascinating 1970s update on the imperative power of early rock and roll. The references to the sounds of Buddy Holly greatly enhance this effect. At the same time, he also generates a compelling metaphor for the intensity of his feelings for the mother of his young son.

Yoko's side of *Double Fantasy* is interesting to reconsider. On each of her solo albums following *Plastic Ono Band*, she embraced conventional rock and ballad forms from a new perspective, one which allowed her to appreciate those elements that had become obscured from overuse. Now, her approach was completely in step with the popular music of the time.

'Kiss Kiss Kiss'

Double Fantasy was structured as a dialogue in which each partner would speak from their own perspective. This was reflected on the first single issued from the sessions, Lennon's 'Starting Over' and Yoko's 'Kiss Kiss Kiss'. Responding to the optimistic sense of renewal expressed by John on the A-side, Yoko's song/track attempts to break down barriers regarding female sexuality, as she herself pointed out:

> On the other side of the record is my song, 'Kiss Kiss Kiss', which is the other side of the same question. There is the sound of a woman coming to a climax on it, and she is crying out to be held, to be touched. It will be controversial, because people still feel it's less natural to hear the sounds of a woman's lovemaking than, say, the sound of a Concorde, killing the atmosphere and polluting nature.[22]

The final version of 'Kiss Kiss Kiss' featured Andy Newmark on drums; Tony Levin on bass; Earl Slick and Hugh McCracken on guitars; George Small on keyboards; Arthur Jenkins on percussion; and Yoko herself on vocals.[23] Given the personal nature of the song's content, every effort was made to give Yoko privacy while recording her vocals for the song. A rug was placed on the floor and the microphone was positioned so that she could sing while lying down. The lights were dimmed, and studio baffles were positioned to block any view of her as she sang. As the vocal was being recorded, John Lennon cheered her on from the control room.[24]

The space created for 'Kiss Kiss Kiss' might be described as an invisible landscape. The changes made to the recording studio effectively minimized visual space. In keeping with the lyric of the song, which explores sound and touch, the goal here may have been to bring tactile and auditory space into prominence. This would conceivably enable one to consider and better understand those aspects of human experience that lie beyond the limits of the visual sense. This process would potentially lead to a more unified human sensorium.

'Watching the Wheels'

'Watching the Wheels' was Lennon's final entry in what might be described as his tetralogy in the key of C major. The first three instalments, 'Imagine', 'Mind Games', and '#9 Dream', had each demonstrated a mastery of composition and recording as a mode for engaging complex ideas: 'Imagine' had proposed connections between sanctuary, creative thought, and positive change; 'Mind Games' took listeners on a perilous yet hopeful journey through the inner spaces of the human mind; and '#9 Dream' described a similar journey, but one that seemed steady and more controlled.

'Watching the Wheels' finds the composer calmly sharing his observations regarding the games being played by those around him, and the calamities that ensue when one indulges freely in that process. Having let go of the situation, he makes no recommendations. However, in the final moments of the song/track, his sense of relief is palpable, and thereby suggests the kind of peace one can attain simply by letting go.

Anyone who happened to be in New York City on 8 December 1980 would have noticed a peculiar quality in the air. It's difficult to explain, but something about the day didn't feel quite right. For one thing, it had been unusually warm for the time of year, reaching, by late afternoon, into the low sixties.[25] There was also a curious breeze stirring the branches of the trees in Central Park. In retrospect, it was the kind of weather that provokes expectations for an early spring.

Towards the end of that year, John and Yoko had been promoting their *Double Fantasy* LP and also preparing a projected follow-up album. Late that afternoon, they left their apartment at the Dakota to attend a session for the song 'Walking on Thin Ice'. Getting into the car, they were approached by a young man asking for an autograph. John obliged him by signing his copy of *Double Fantasy*. The studio session ended at 10:30 pm, after which John and Yoko returned to the Dakota. When they arrived, the young man who had asked for an autograph was waiting for them.[26]

'Rainclouds'

Across the Atlantic, Paul McCartney was scheduled to attend a recording session at AIR Studios in London. He had received a call from his office early that morning telling him about what had happened to his friend.[27] Devastated by the news, he decided that rather than cancel the session, it would be better to go in and try to work. His friend and bandmate Denny Laine was in attendance and remembered the mood of the session:

> The really strange thing was that I went to work that morning somehow knowing Paul would ultimately show up – despite what had happened. Of course, from the point of view of his Liverpool upbringing, the best way to deal with something like that is to keep right on doing what you'd normally

do. It helps to take your mind off it ... I remember the first thing he said to me was, 'I just don't know what to think'.[28]

The song that was being recorded during the session on 9 December 1980 was a collaboration between McCartney and Laine entitled 'Rainclouds'. This was a Celtic-folk-styled ballad that featured Paddy Moloney of the Chieftains on Uilleann pipes. Although the song initially seems simple in form, it gradually reveals a clever strategy for shifting into different key areas. The abruptness of these shifts suggests that the composers are thinking of the various keys as regions existing in parallel space. This quality is especially enhanced by the set of harmonic changes that are unique to Paddy Moloney's solo section.

As noted above, the basic tracks of 'Rainclouds' were recorded at George Martin's AIR Studios in London. The initial sessions took place on 8 and 9 December 1980, while overdubs were completed between May and December of the following year. Paul McCartney played lead and backing vocals, twelve-string acoustic guitar, and bass drum. Denny Laine added backing vocals and possibly a second twelve-string acoustic guitar. Finally, Paddy Moloney played the Uilleann pipes, while Linda McCartney and Eric Stewart added vocal harmonies.[29]

The space created for 'Rainclouds', as suggested by the lyric, sets two environmental elements in opposition. The poet's desire to be washed in sunlight is repeatedly hampered by clouds that arrive to block out the light. Soon, however, the rain that comes with the clouds is acknowledged to be in balance with the sunlight that the singer seeks. The water they produce is essential to life in all its forms and also facilitates travel and discovery. Thus, the expansiveness of the space created for the song is impressive, inclusive, and ultimately inspiring,

'No, No, No'

In early 1981, Yoko Ono plotted a course similar to the one taken by Paul McCartney in December 1980 – she went back to work.[30] In June, she released *Season of Glass*, an album that was initially controversial because of a cover that contained a photo of the glasses her husband had worn on the night he died. Record company executives tried to dissuade her from using the photo, but she insisted.[31] In a manner similar to Jacqueline Kennedy's refusal to change the dress she had been wearing the day that her husband was killed, Yoko evidently wanted the public to see what had been done.[32] She made this point even more clearly with a powerful track entitled 'No, No, No'.

The song opens with sound effects that portray the tragic event of 8 December 1980. Accessing the sounds of contemporary New Wave, Yoko then creates an appropriately dissonant sound field that grounds the song's powerful text. In the liner notes for *ONOBOX* (1992), she described how she approached the musical setting:

> When I wrote the song, I juxtaposed the atonal and minor chords. Which suited the woman who felt like she was wearing a pair of mismatched shoes.

In the recording, I used real gun shots and sirens ... A musician came to me and said he could make a siren effect with the guitar, using two of my atonal chords ... He played the chords. I didn't like it. It was too beautiful. It lacked the urgency I was feeling. No, it had to be the real siren.[33]

Yoko chose to work with an old collaborator by co-producing the album with Phil Spector. For 'No, No, No', they created a sound field that recalled their work on the *Plastic Ono Band* albums of 1970. The sonic elements at the base of the track are blended together into an indeterminate sound mass in which individual details seem lost or obscured. The colours of this sound mass suggest faded newsprint in that they seem drained of all life and feeling. The most remarkable brushstrokes here are the recurring spoken-word elements ('Help me', 'Touch me', 'Hold me', etc.) that counter the lyric in a manner that reveals the singer's true feelings.

The space of 'No, No, No' is a landscape of urban life at its most harsh and unforgiving. Here, human tragedy becomes recycled as vulgar spectacle. The siren effect calls attention to the crisis but paralyzes onlookers by turning them into an audience that cannot affect the action of the drama they are witnessing. At the centre of this landscape is the narrator, directly affected by the events, but ultimately isolated by the role she is obliged to play. In lieu of resolution, the best that she, and we, can hope for is that all of the unbearable pain will gradually recede.

'Here Today'

The recording of 'Rainclouds' was part of the initial phase of what ultimately became a new Paul McCartney solo album. After a series of recording sessions at AIR Studios, and a side project with Wings at Abbey Road, the McCartneys and Denny Laine relocated to AIR Studios, Montserrat to continue the process.[34] Guest musicians on the project included Stanley Clarke, Steve Gadd, Carl Perkins, Ringo Starr, and Stevie Wonder.[35] Later in the spring, work resumed at AIR Studios, London. It was there that Paul recorded his response to the tragic events of the previous year.

'Here Today' is a gentle ballad in the style of 'Yesterday'. In keeping with its subject matter, which recounts the story of the friendship between John and Paul, the song has a curious winding structure throughout. Some of the transitions between the various sections are abrupt. However, they always manage to find their way back to the song's graceful opening line. This, of course, is an apt metaphor for the relationship itself, which, in spite of its occasional heated moments, would inevitably return to the ease of process that had characterized the Lennon and McCartney collaboration from its earliest days.

As on 'Yesterday', McCartney provided vocals and acoustic guitar for the track. He was backed by a tasteful string quartet arranged by producer George Martin. The quartet consisted of Jack Rothstein and Bernard Partridge on violins, Ian Jewell on viola, and Keith Harvey on cello. The violinist Jack Rothstein was no stranger to Beatles sessions. Back in 1967, he had played on both George Harrison's 'Within You Without You' and John Lennon's 'I Am the Walrus'.[36]

In keeping with the song's subject matter and the quartet setting, the space created for 'Here Today' is a decidedly intimate one. As such, it creates a curious inversion of the original Beatles process. On 'Yesterday', The Beatles had presented a play or mini movie concerning the loss of a loved one or love relationship. As was generally the case with their songs, the subject matter was universal, and its presentation was all. Here, however, The Beatles dynamic itself has become the focus of the text, as Paul himself pointed out:

> I wrote 'Here Today' about John. It's just a song saying, you know, 'If you were here today you'd probably say what I'm doing is a load of crap. But you wouldn't mean it, cos you like me really, I know'. It's one of those 'Come out from behind your glasses, look at me', things. It was a love song, really, not to John but a love song about John, about my relationship with him. I was trying to exorcise the demons in my own head.[37]

'It's Alright'

In November 1982, Yoko returned with her sixth album, *It's Alright (I See Rainbows)*. In a manner that would have been inconceivable to listeners and critics only ten years earlier, she had now landed firmly in the musical mainstream. The unorthodox ideas she'd been exploring on her own and with John Lennon had become a part of popular music parlance. Yoko had initially anticipated some resistance to her ideas, but as she herself pointed out, there was none to be found: 'Surprisingly, no one was upset this time. It was '82 and it seemed as though I was finally in sync with the world. I love it'.[38]

The near-title track of the LP began with the sound of Sean Lennon telling his mother that it was time to wake up. The soft reassurance of his voice triggered a larger significance for Yoko. The framing device she employs here has a different function from the one heard on 'No, No, No'. There, the opening sounds focused the listener on what had occurred on 8 December 1980. Here, they help us consider the gradual process of acceptance that followed the event and how a family had found a way to reconnect with the world.

One of the interesting things to take note of about *It's Alright (I See Rainbows)* is that Yoko is working with a new group of musical collaborators. On the liner notes for the original release, there don't appear to be any holdovers from recent projects.[39] Since a theme of the album and its near-title track concerns letting go of the past and embracing the present, this may have been a conscious decision on her part. In that regard, she succeeded beautifully. As mentioned above, she was now completely in step with the musical sounds of her time.

The space of 'It's Alright' shows Yoko letting in the light just as she'd done on the video for 'Imagine'. This time she uses sound rather than light. With a sense of ease that seems rooted in resolution and acceptance, she encourages everyone to do the same. The spaces that she helps reveal are wide and spacious. As had been suggested on Paul's 'Rainclouds', they inevitably lead to a sense of renewal and hope.

'Pipes of Peace'

In an interview with Lesley Ash for *The Tube* in 1983, Paul mentioned that *Tug of War* was originally conceived as a double LP. That plan never materialized because of resistance from the record company. As a result, songs that had been recorded for but not included on the original album were combined with newly recorded material for a semi-sequel entitled *Pipes of Peace*.[40] The title track was one of McCartney's most accomplished and inspired musical creations since Wings. Produced by George Martin, it incorporates a diverse array of musical elements within the familiar McCartney style. It also featured an elaborate music video that connected with the original song/track in a manner similar to the title track from *A Hard Day's Night* (1964).

'Pipes of Peace' opens with a cacophony of orchestral instruments suggesting a distant battle. This is followed by an ascending pattern that is nuanced with subtle touches of harmonic colour. Next comes the main section, which is more harmonically and rhythmically active than the introduction. It is also more diverse in its cultural sources. The somewhat unorthodox return of the introduction at the end of the song lends a sense of completion to the entire piece, a quality that is further enhanced by the final cadence, which skilfully blends elements that are derived from both sections.

The track was recorded at AIR Studios, London in October 1982. McCartney provided vocals, piano, and bass, but may also have added keyboards and percussion. The other musicians heard on the track are Linda McCartney and Eric Stewart on backing vocals; Adrian Brett on pan flute; and James Kippen on tabla. The choir was the Pestalozzi Children's Choir, and the orchestration was provided by producer George Martin.[41] Martin's orchestration skills seem to have been a factor in the final mix, which features a particularly rich field of musical colour.

'Pipes of Peace' attempts to create a landscape that is international in scope. Following the chromatic touches of the introduction, the materials become very basic. This seems to have been intended so that the song/track could conceivably play across as many musical traditions as possible. The international quality is greatly enhanced by the music video, which dramatizes the Christmas truce of 1914 in which troops on both sides of the conflict put down their weapons and met on the battlefield to celebrate the holiday. In terms of historical accuracy, the clip seems to have compressed the actual events of the truce in order to create a unity of time and place, as Terri Blom Crocker says:

> The separate truces that occurred on 25 December 1914 and for a few days afterward were not prearranged, centrally coordinated, or consistent, but rather were composed of individually negotiated armistices, entered into at

different times, ranging from early Christmas Eve through Christmas afternoon, and widely divergent in nature.[42]

'Grow Old with Me'

During the *Double Fantasy* sessions of 1980, John and Yoko had recorded a considerable number of songs/tracks. Their plan at the time was to follow the album with a new collection to be released the following year. Continuing with that idea, Yoko released *Milk and Honey* in early 1984. Despite the fact that the various Lennon tracks included on the LP had an unfinished quality, one of them entitled 'Nobody Told Me' ultimately reached the top ten. And although it wasn't recorded during the studio sessions of 1980, Yoko chose to include John's home demo of a song that was meaningful for both of them, and which would continue to resonate on a number of levels for years to come.[43]

'Grow Old with Me' is a gentle ballad that ultimately attains an almost hymn-like status. The lyric was adapted from the first stanza of Robert Browning's poem, 'Rabbi Ben Ezra'.[44] As he'd done on earlier ballads, Lennon pares down his ideas for maximum effect. In the process, he creates a unified gesture of melody, harmony, and text. As the song unfolds, it becomes difficult to tell where any of these elements begin or end.

As mentioned, the released version of 'Grow Old with Me' included on *Milk and Honey* (1984) was an enhanced version of a demo recorded at home. One might be inclined to think it rather unfortunate that John was never able to create a fully realized version of the track. The sound quality is limited and could certainly be an obstacle to anyone approaching the song/track for the first time. However, the original demo version does have a certain charm that warrants serious consideration.

The recording of 'Grow Old with Me' seems to have taken place sometime during August to September 1980.[45] John recorded the song on his home recorder which picked up both his vocal and his piano simultaneously. He was also using a drum machine that, when heard in combination with the left hand of the piano part, created a kind of instant rhythm section for the track. Listening to the demo decades after its creation, it seems clear that the recording has the qualities of a preliminary sketch or perhaps a work in progress. The fact that a fully realized version never actually emerged only enhances this remarkable quality.

'Grow Old with Me' was one of the songs under consideration for The Beatles' *Anthology* in the 1990s. When it wasn't chosen for the project, Yoko contacted George Martin and asked if he would consider creating an orchestration for the track. Martin agreed, recorded the parts at Abbey Road, and then mixed the track at AIR Studios.[46] This reworking of the demo take has been controversial in that some have suggested that the composer would likely have rejected the idea outright.[47] However, a careful review of the two versions suggests that Martin was on the same page regarding John's original intentions, and, in the final analysis, he extended and enhanced the composition beautifully.

The ambience of both versions of 'Grow Old with Me' suggests the space of the Lennon and Ono relationship itself. The couple seemed to view their collaboration in historical terms and the facts surrounding their time together tend to bear this out. In addition to being one of the most successful musicians in modern times, John had received early training as a graphic artist and later became a published author. Yoko was a renowned conceptual artist and a member of Fluxus, who brought experimental ideas from the fine arts into the mainstream of popular music. In retrospect, their creative union arguably helped reify the connection between The Beatles and the artworld as envisioned by Stuart Sutcliffe, John Lennon, and Paul McCartney all those years ago.

Notes

1 'Paul McCartney Paintings – Pinchukartcentre'. Paul McCartney paintings. pinchukartcentre. Accessed 20 March 2022. https://pinchukartcentre.org/files/exhibiti ons/pdf/pm_catalogue_preview.pdf.

2 David Sheff, *All We Are Saying: The Last Major Interview with John Lennon and Yoko Ono* (New York: St. Martin's Griffin, 2000), ix.

3 Paul Du Noyer, *Conversations with McCartney* (New York: The Overlook Press, 2016), 164–165.

4 John Blaney, *John Lennon: Listen to This Book* (Guildford: Paper Jukebox, 2005), 192.

5 Howard Sounes, *Fab: An Intimate Life of Paul McCartney* (Cambridge, MA: Da Capo Press, 2010), 423.

6 Nick DeRiso, 'Laurence Juber, Formerly of Wings: Something Else! Interview'. Something Else!, 18 March 2017. https://somethingelsereviews.com/2012/02/08/ something-else-interview-laurence-juber-formerly-of-wings.

7 'Paul McCartney Interview Tim Rice 1980 "Meet Paul McCartney"'. YouTube. Graham72, 2 December 2020. https://youtu.be/qQzdAsjWGPg?t=192.

8 Paul Du Noyer, *Conversations with McCartney* (New York: The Overlook Press, 2016), 293–294.

9 Ian Peel, *The Unknown Paul McCartney: McCartney and the Avant-Garde* (London and Richmond, Surrey: Reynolds & Hearn, 2002), 104.

10 Luca Perasi, *Paul McCartney: Recording Sessions (1969–2013)* (Milan: L.I.L.Y. Publishing, 2014), 197.

11 Luca Perasi, *Paul McCartney: Recording Sessions (1969–2013)* (Milan: L.I.L.Y. Publishing, 2014), 194.

12 Luca Perasi, *Paul McCartney: Recording Sessions (1969–2013)* (Milan: L.I.L.Y. Publishing, 2014), 194.

13 Luca Perasi, *Paul McCartney: Recording Sessions (1969–2013)* (Milan: L.I.L.Y. Publishing, 2014), 200–202.

14 Luca Perasi, *Paul McCartney: Recording Sessions (1969–2013)* (Milan: L.I.L.Y. Publishing, 2014), 200–201.

15 Howard Sounes, *Fab: An Intimate Life of Paul McCartney* (Cambridge, MA: Da Capo Press, 2010), 335–339.

16 Luca Perasi, *Paul McCartney: Recording Sessions (1969–2013)* (Milan: L.I.L.Y. Publishing, 2014), 225.

17 Paul Du Noyer, *Conversations with McCartney* (New York: The Overlook Press, 2016), 124.

18 'Scotland Outside New York'. YouTube. breathless345, 22 May 2018. https://youtu.be/Dslrn6mJpxs?t=4456.

19 Ken Sharp, *Starting Over: The Making of John Lennon and Yoko Ono's Double Fantasy* (New York: Gallery Books, 2010), 169.

20 Chip Madinger and Mark Easter, *Eight Arms to Hold You: The Solo Beatles Compendium* (Chesterfield, MO: 44.1 Productions, 2000), 140.

21 Philip Norman, *John Lennon: The Life* (Toronto: Anchor Canada, 2009), 795.

22 David Sheff, *All We Are Saying: The Last Major Interview with John Lennon and Yoko Ono* (New York: St. Martin's Griffin, 2000), 130.

23 John Blaney, *John Lennon: Listen to This Book* (Guildford: Paper Jukebox, 2005), 188.

24 Ken Sharp, *Starting Over: The Making of John Lennon and Yoko Ono's Double Fantasy* (New York: Gallery Books, 2010), 150–151.

25 'December 8, 1980 Weather History at New York City, Central Park, New York, United States'. Weather Spark. Accessed 20 March 2022. https://weatherspark.com/h/d/147190/1980/12/8/Historical-Weather-on-Monday-December-8-1980-at-New-York-City-Central-Park;-New-York;-United-States#Figures-Temperature.

26 Philip Norman, *John Lennon: The Life* (Toronto: Anchor Canada, 2009), 805–806.

27 Howard Sounes, *Fab: An Intimate Life of Paul McCartney* (Cambridge, MA: Da Capo Press, 2010), 343–344.

28 Geoffrey Giuliano, *Blackbird: The Life and Times of Paul McCartney* (New York: Plume, 1992), 3–4.

29 Luca Perasi, *Paul McCartney: Recording Sessions (1969–2013)* (Milan: L.I.L.Y. Publishing, 2014), 208–209.

30 Alan Clayson, *Woman: The Incredible Life of Yoko Ono* (New Malden: Chrome Dreams, 2004), 168.

31 'Onobox by Yoko Ono'. IMAGINE PEACE, 9 May 2011. http://imaginepeace.com/archives/6364.

32 Larry J. Sabato, *The Kennedy Half-Century: The Presidency, Assassination, and Lasting Legacy of John F. Kennedy* (New York: Bloomsbury, 2013), 17.

33 'Onobox by Yoko Ono'. IMAGINE PEACE, 9 May 2011. http://imaginepeace.com/archives/6364.

34 Luca Perasi, *Paul McCartney: Recording Sessions (1969–2013)* (Milan: L.I.L.Y. Publishing, 2014), 213.

35 Howard Sounes, *Fab: An Intimate Life of Paul McCartney* (Cambridge, MA: Da Capo Press, 2010), 350.

36 Luca Perasi, *Paul McCartney: Recording Sessions (1969–2013)* (Milan: L.I.L.Y. Publishing, 2014), 225–227.

37 Paul Du Noyer, *Conversations with McCartney* (New York: The Overlook Press, 2016), 160.

38 'Onobox by Yoko Ono'. IMAGINE PEACE, 9 May 2011. http://imaginepeace.com/archives/6364.

39 *It's Alright (I See Rainbows)*, liner notes, 1982.

40 'Onobox by Yoko Ono'. IMAGINE PEACE, 9 May 2011. http://imaginepeace.com/archives/6364.

41 Luca Perasi, *Paul McCartney: Recording Sessions (1969–2013)* (Milan: L.I.L.Y. Publishing, 2014), 231–233.

42 Terri Blom Crocker, *The Christmas Truce: Myth, Memory, and the First World War* (Lexington, KY: The University Press of Kentucky, 2015), 45–46.

43 John Blaney, *John Lennon: Listen to This Book* (Guildford: Paper Jukebox, 2005), 222.

44 Robert Browning, *The Poetical Works of Robert Browning with Portraits in Two Volumes, Volume 1* (London: Smith Elder and Co., 1897), 580–581.
45 John Blaney, *John Lennon: Listen to This Book* (Guildford: Paper Jukebox, 2005), 222.
46 John Blaney, *John Lennon: Listen to This Book* (Guildford: Paper Jukebox, 2005), 287.
47 John Blaney, *John Lennon: Listen to This Book* (Guildford: Paper Jukebox, 2005), 222.

8

ONCE UPON A LONG AGO

During the late 1970s, Paul McCartney had been developing a film project for Wings. In an effort to get the project going, he contracted Willy Russell and Mike Ockrent to develop a screenplay. The script they produced was called *Band on the Run*. In it, McCartney would play an established pop music star who would take up with a new band to be played by Wings.[1] The film never got to the production stage, but Paul was still keen on making a movie. By the early 1980s, the idea had transformed into a new project called *Give My Regards to Broad Street*.

Returning to a strategy that The Beatles had employed for *Magical Mystery Tour* (1967), McCartney attempted to take on much of the creative work himself. Thus, for *Give My Regards to Broad Street* he served as screenwriter, composer, and star. The idea was originally conceived as a television special, but gradually morphed into a full-length feature film.[2] In addition, Paul wanted to perform the music live rather than mime to pre-recorded tracks. In an interview for the *South Bank Show* in 1984, producer George Martin explained how they proceeded:

> So, I said, 'Well, in that case, let's cover ourselves. Let's first of all do the tracks in the ordinary way, the way films are normally made'. You normally do your music first, and then you've set it up and film once the music's done. But then also let us record live on top. And we wanted to record in twenty-four track form. So, we actually were playing back twenty-four tracks into the film studio, recording twenty-four tracks, and locking to camera. And those three things together I don't think have ever been done before.[3]

If you recall, *Magical Mystery Tour* (1967) had been an attempt to bring together music and film in a manner that gave The Beatles complete control over music and image. For *Let It Be* (1970), they continued the process by becoming the content. The live recording of the songs they had composed for the project became the

DOI: 10.4324/9781003300212-12

subject matter. There, however, they had specified that there would be no over-dubbing. Here, on *Give My Regards to Broad Street*, Paul and George Martin tried to bring together both ideas so that the filming of the movie and the recording (tracking) of the music were a unified process.

The soundtrack of *Give My Regards to Broad Street* featured new material along with remakes of songs from McCartney's career with The Beatles and his solo career as well. The new material ranged from rough-hewn rockers in the style of late-period Wings to the meticulous ballad 'No More Lonely Nights', which featured the guitar work of David Gilmour. Produced by George Martin, the remakes were given interesting arrangements. These could also be viewed conceptually as an example of an artist somehow managing to 'cover' his own material. Amidst the songs on hand, there was also a curious new track in a much earlier style.

'Goodnight Princess'

Here, Paul creates a perfect rendering of an earlier musical era. 'Goodnight Princess' effectively reaches back to of the kind of pop made famous during the 1930s by Ray Noble on songs such as 'Goodnight, Sweetheart' and 'The Very Thought of You'.[4] McCartney's version of the style features a clever modulation that is authentic to the period in that it creates an effective shape for the entire piece. The only thing missing is the singer, which is a pity, since Paul had already demonstrated his vocal abilities with this style on 'You Gave Me the Answer' from *Venus and Mars* (1975) and 'Baby's Request' from *Back to the Egg* (1979). It would have been nice to hear him attempt a lead vocal here in the style of Al Bowlly.[5]

'Goodnight Princess' was recorded at AIR Studios in December 1983.[6] As mentioned, Paul does not play on the track but opts instead to take the role of an announcer who seems to be speaking to radio listeners from a live ballroom feed. The rhythm section was John Dean (drums, percussion); Russ Stableford (double bass); Gerry Butler (piano); and Eric Ford (guitar). Brass and woodwinds were provided by Ronnie Hughes (trumpet); Bobby Haughey (trumpet); Chris Smith (trombone); Vic Ash (tenor sax); Eddie Mordue (tenor sax and clarinet); and Derek Grossmith (tenor sax and clarinet). Violins were played by Tony Gilbert, Pat Halling, Raymond Keenlyside, and Laurie Lewis.[7]

The space of 'Goodnight Princess' works on a variety of levels. As noted, the musical materials recreate the approach of an earlier era. This is enhanced by the production, which tries to accent the qualities of early recording technology. However, the real magic is revealed in the way in which Paul himself emulates a radio announcer for a live radio feed. This lends the entire piece a conceptual quality since it is clearly Paul McCartney who is addressing the listener. Lest things become too precious, though, he takes the concept a step further by imitating an audience member who unpretentiously cheers the musicians on.

In the final film, 'Goodnight Princess' was featured in the scene that took place upstairs from a pub called the Old Justice. In that scene, Paul asks the proprietor, played by Sir Ralph Richardson, if he knows anything about the missing master tape that is the focus of the plot. As the two men chat, 'Goodnight Princess' plays gently in the background, presumably on an old radio set. In retrospect, the song seems worthy of its own separate concept. Perhaps it could become the centrepiece of a new album by Percy 'Thrills' Thrillington...

As a narrative film, *Give My Regards to Broad Street* never quite seems to take hold. There is, however, one interesting dramatic sequence that highlighted Paul's talents as a sketch artist. At the outset of the story, his character is informed that the master tapes of his new album have gone missing. Later, he attends a meeting with a character named Mr Rath, an unsavoury businessman who has designs on his company. During the meeting, Paul surreptitiously creates a perfect rendering of the man while otherwise seeming to doodle casually on a notepad.[8]

'Stranglehold'

After completing the promotional duties for *Give My Regards to Broad Street*, Paul went to work on a new album. While his last few projects had been recorded mainly at AIR Studios, London, this new LP would be recorded closer to home at the newly completed Hog Hill Studio in Sussex. Paul also invited his old friend Eric Stewart from 10cc along to help co-write the LP. In an interview about the album, he described how they approached writing together:

> We started off with 'Stranglehold', putting rhythmic words in, using lyrics like a bongo, accenting the words. We both enjoyed the experience, then went on together to write the six songs that are featured on the album. I remembered the old way I'd written songs with John, the two acoustic guitars facing each other, like a mirror, but better! Like an objective mirror, you're looking at the person playing chords, but it's not you.[9]

As the opening song/track of *Press to Play*, 'Stranglehold' starts things off very nicely. An acoustic guitar provides the basis for the infectious rhythmic groove, which is subsequently distributed around the ensemble. As Paul himself described, the melody and lyrics of the opening section seem to emulate the percussive pattern of a bongo. This generates a peculiar tension that soon finds its release in the contrasting section where the bass plays a repeating descending line against the song's title line and hook. The groove never lets up and seems to gain intensity as the song unfolds.

'Stranglehold' was the first song committed to tape during the *Press to Play* sessions. The basic tracks were recorded at Hog Hill Studio in the spring of 1985. Overdubs were then completed that autumn during sessions at the same location. On the finished track, Paul provided lead and backing vocals, electric and acoustic guitars, and bass; Eric Stewart sang backing vocals and played electric and acoustic guitars; and Jerry Marotta played the drums. The horns were likely added by Gary Barnacle and Dick Morrisey.[10]

One of the most fascinating aspects of the *Press to Play* LP was its sleeve design. There, one could find a series of colour sketches created by Paul himself that depicted the final mixes for each of the ten tracks featured on the album. Although these were not widely discussed at the time of the LP's release, they did catch the attention of his friend and colleague Brian Wilson, who was greatly impressed with the idea: 'Paul McCartney did colorful drawings showing where all the instruments should go in the mix; some of them were published in the liner notes to one of his albums, and I thought they were amazing'.[11]

The outer region of McCartney's sketch for 'Stranglehold' is framed by his own guitar accompaniment on the far right and Eric Stewart's on the far left. Horns span the distance that completes the arc between them. In the centre between the horns is the lead vocal, and directly above that, sitting atop the entire mix, is the solo sax line. Below the vocal is the bass drum, which sits between the backing vocals on either side, with electric guitars (left) and electric guitar answers (right). Further left is a guitar played by Eric Stewart through a Rockman amplifier.

In the centre below the bass drum is the snare drum, and below that, Paul's bass. Next come the remaining drums, which occupy much of the centre of the image. Below the drums are 'eerie' keyboards, which take up much of the space in the sketch. Two additional details are included: on the left below the keyboards is a swell that seems to move towards Eric Stewart's guitar accompaniment; and on the far right is a sax swell that seems directed towards Paul's guitar accompaniment.[12]

The space created for 'Stranglehold' seems almost elastic in quality. The various bends and turns of the riff line and melody open up gaps and crevices that somehow invite further and deeper exploration. The motion downward in the song's contrasting section seems to relieve the mystery inherent in these auditory spaces. Soon, the entire process begins again with the return of the opening section. Once again, the charm is wound up and will soon be ready for release.

'Footprints'

Reaching back to the folk sounds of 'Don't Let It Bring You Down' from *London Town*, 'Footprints' is arguably the best of the McCartney/Stewart collaborations. A delicate ballad that tells the story of a lonely drifter, it slowly sketches in the details of the man's life and the events that led him to his current situation. What particularly stands out here is the pacing. McCartney and Stewart seem completely comfortable taking their time with the form. This allows them to deepen the effect of the material via the arrangement and the production.

The basic tracks of 'Footprints' were recorded at Hog Hill Studio during spring 1985. Overdubs were added the following December. Paul played acoustic guitars, bass, vocals, piano, and keyboards. Eric Stewart was featured on acoustic guitar and may have also played electric guitar and keyboards. Jerry Marotta provided LinnDrum programming and percussion.[13]

Paul's sketch of the mix for 'Footprints' indicates that his acoustic guitar was placed on the far left of the sonic image, while Eric Stewart's acoustic guitar was on the far right. In the top centre of the image, just below an array of spinet and electric guitars, is McCartney's lead vocal. The vocal is also in the centre of an arch in which we find hi-guitars and a Spanish guitar during the chorus. Directly below the vocal is Paul's bass, a pipe solo, which may have been played on a keyboard, and finally a bass drum. Below the arch is a series of percussion instruments. On the left are hi-triangle, lo-conga, clave, and hi-hat, with woodblocks placed directly below the bass drum. On the right are conga and tom, tambourine, hi-conga, and lo-triangle. In the front of the image are an array of effects followed by the song's title, which is partly framed by images of footprints.[14]

The ambience of 'Footprints' works on the order of filmic space. The snowy scene that is described here seems to be viewed from above. The character of an old man moves deliberately and slowly through the scene. The image created for the song has a decidedly tactile quality. The various effects suggest the falling of snow. In an interview with *Sound-on-Sound* magazine in October 1986, Paul discussed the origin of the imagery:

> The song was written on a snowy day. It came from an image of a magpie looking for food out in the snow. Eric and I changed the magpie to an old man, although the magpie came back for the third verse. The old man is out there looking for Yule logs or something, like the character in Good King Wenceslas. He's lonely. Does he live on his own? What do we know about him? The song goes into what his story might have been, the heartaches there might have been, the girl he might have left behind, the paths he didn't take, the moves he didn't make, etcetera.[15]

Despite the compositional chemistry between Paul and Eric, a problem emerged as the sessions began. Stewart had been under the impression that he would co-produce the LP, but at some point McCartney had invited producer Hugh Padgham to man the boards.[16] Padgham had famously crafted hits for contemporary artists such as Phil Collins, Peter Gabriel, and The Police. Why then couldn't he do the same for Paul? Confusion over who was actually in charge seems to have intensified as the process wore on. Finally, Eric Stewart decided to bow out gracefully and leave the production duties to Hugh Padgham and Paul McCartney.[17] In the end, he co-wrote six of the album's ten tracks, and also added guitar, keyboards, and backing vocals to the mix.

'Only Love Remains'

Reaching back to his trademark piano ballad style, Paul concluded side one of *Press to Play* with 'Only Love Remains'. The composition is among the more interesting pieces he had produced since the dissolution of Wings. The opening is distinctive and innovative, recalling the melodic and harmonic ingenuity of 'Arrow Through Me'. Its use of an arpeggiated tonic major seventh chord followed by a diminished seventh chord built on the tonic pitch is impressive and appealing. Paul's contrasting section builds on a descending bass pattern that effectively releases the tension created by the song's rather complex opening.

Sessions for 'Only Love Remains' took place at Hog Hill Studio during the autumn of 1985. The players on the track were Paul on vocals, classical guitar, piano, and possibly a synthesizer; Eric Stewart on backing vocals and possibly guitar; Simon Chamberlain on synth bass; Graham Ward on drums; Ray Cooper on marimba and percussion; and John Bradley on violin. Backing vocals were provided by Linda McCartney, Kate Robbins, and Ruby James.[18] The orchestration was created by Tony Visconti. The session was unusual, however, in that Paul wanted to record everything live, as Visconti himself described:

> The plan was to try and record a rhythm track in the morning, to be safe, and overdub the orchestral instruments in the afternoon. Once that was achieved we had a go recording the entire ensemble with Paul singing and playing live … We managed the overdub, then set up for the live performance. I stood next to him as he played piano and sang, while I conducted the orchestra; it was like having my own private McCartney concert. I would look over to Paul for a cue and he would smile and continue to sing to me. He never made a mistake and each take was a 'keeper'.[19]

The sketch for 'Only Love Remains' places a synthesizer and marimba from left to right across the outer rim of the image. An additional synthesizer is indicated in the centre of this arch. Directly below is the synth bass that sits between the outer arch and an array of toms with a drum kit, miked from overhead. Beneath this array is the vocal, which sits neatly in the centre between the toms, the drum kit, and various percussion: shakers (left), tam-tam (left), bell tree (centre), wine glass (right), hi-hat (right), and triangle (right). The bass drum sits below the vocal, next to the backing vocals on the left, with guitar and harpsichord on the right. Below the bass drum is the snare, rim shot, and tambourine, with guitars appearing to the left and right of the snare. Next is the piano, which takes up the lion's share of space within the sonic image. Finally, we have the orchestra, which is placed prominently at the front of the track.[20]

The space of 'Only Love Remains' is dreamlike, but somehow ominously thick. The deftness of the song's opening melodic dance, which is born out of love, seems to be yielding inevitably to a cloudy sky over a stormy sea. The storm that begins to emerge continues to build as the track unfolds. Gradually, it becomes more ominous than it had originally seemed. The suggestion is that it might grow to proportions that overwhelm everything – except love.

'Good Times Coming/Feel the Sun'

Another one of the new songs that Paul brought to the sessions on his own was a two-panelled work called 'Good Times Coming/Feel the Sun'. Panel One ('Good Times Coming'), the larger of the two, begins with the main melodic hook sung acapella, apparently on location at the seaside. This leads into the song's main section, which returns to the familiar McCartney theme of seasonal change. Finally, we get the complete hook, now fully developed with a connecting melodic line built on Paul's trademark geometric phrasing. The lyrics present descriptions of three golden summers of the past. The description provided in the last of these is particularly worrying, as Paul himself pointed out: 'I remember I heard there were a couple of really cracking summers in 1936 and 1937, or whenever, but Hitler was just round the corner … That's the twist in the tail of that song'.[21]

Panel Two ('Feel the Sun') is more conventional and suggests a resolution of the tensions generated by the geometric motions of Panel One. There is a sense of relaxation in the extended chord progression. Novelty now gives way to the natural creative processes that can seem to be writing themselves. Ultimately, human creativity must yield to the tidal energies that carry us all along. The golden summer emerges all on its own.

The basic tracks of 'Good Times Coming/Feel the Sun' were recorded at Hog Hill Studio during the spring of 1985. Overdubs were then added during the autumn. In the final mix, McCartney added vocals, guitars, and bass, and may have played percussion and electric keyboards as well; Eric Stewart and Carlos Alomar added electric guitars; and Jerry Marotta played the drums. Backing vocals were provided by Kate Robbins and Ruby James.[22]

The outer arch of the sketch for 'Good Times Coming' features 'Girls BV' (backing vocals) to the left and 'Boys BV' (backing vocals) to the right. These are described directly below as 'Outside' vocals. In the centre of this arch and between the backing vocals is 'Eddies guitar'. This seems to refer to an acoustic guitar played by Paul McCartney's maintenance man during the recording of the 'Outside' vocals.[23] Directly below this is the lead vocal, and below that, electric bass, bass drum, and snare. On an arch between the bass and the bass drum, we find guitar (left) and piano (right). Below and behind these are a cabasa on the left and a tambourine on the right. Between the bass drum and snare, there is another arch that contains lin toms and toms on the left and right. The next layer down features overhead miking on the drum kit from left to right, and directly below that are keyboards, which appear across the entire arch. Finally, we come to the guitar solo by Carlos Alomar and a 'flute solo' that was presumably played on keyboards.[24]

The outer arch of McCartney's sketch of the mix for 'Feel the Sun' depicts toms on the left, overhead mikes on the drums centre-left, and 'ambience' on the right. In the centre, directly above the overheads, are maracas. Below the overheads are bass, vocoder, and lead vocals. The vocals are surrounded by Emu keyboard arpeggiations that are in the process of being panned left and right. There is also a piano placed to the left of the bass drum and snare, and a Baldwin piano on the right. Additional guitar was added just to the right of the Baldwin piano. Backing vocals are placed below the snare from left to right and in front of these, more guitar.[25]

The space created on Panel One ('Good Times Coming') seems to be driven by the expectation of the summer season coming in. The sounds are compressed as if ready to burst with anticipation. Finally, we enter a transition containing rhythmic groupings of three. These then change into a duple pattern that signals the arrival of Panel Two ('Feel the Sun'). The anticipation has now been dissipated as we bask in the soothing sunlight of a summer day.

The various observations outlined above seem clearer when one places the sketches for the two panels side by side. Panel One ('Good Times Coming') seems more concentrated in that the various elements are gathered together in the centre of the image. In contrast, Panel Two ('Feel the Sun') seems more open and spacious. There, the image of the sun at the bottom of the sketch takes up considerable space, keeping the various instrumental sounds at bay. At the same time, however, it seems to be energizing them with its soothing rays.

An interesting observation might be made here regarding The Beatles' work in the multi-panel form. If one considers the idea all the way back to its origins as the double-A-sided 45-rpm record, it now seemed to be yielding diminishing returns. This may have had something to do with the move towards placing the panels next to one another on the same side of a vinyl record. Although this was arguably closer to the way in which visual art works are perceived, the results never seemed to surpass the impact of the original form. In the final analysis, it may well be that the double-A-sided 45-rpm single will never be surpassed.

At this point, the various sketches included on the foldout cover of the *Press to Play* LP are interesting to reconsider. On one level, they function as an informal tutorial on the mixing process. Their study can offer insights into the narrative power generated through the placement of instruments within an audio image. On another, their presence effectively turns the LP cover into a gallery space. Moreover, as portraits of the various track designs contained on the vinyl record within, they remind listeners of the notion of the LP itself as a kind of gallery of recorded sound.[26]

It's also interesting to consider these sketches in connection with Paul's own notes for the recording process of his first solo album, *McCartney* (1970).[27] There, he outlined a series of steps through the creative process. Here, he portrays that process as a kind of creative space in which all of the various steps seem to happen at once.

De Kooning

The visual arts were now becoming an increasingly important part of Paul McCartney's creative output. He had already published a collection of his sketches as part of the songbook *Paul McCartney: Composer/Artist* (1981), where each of the songs was accompanied by a McCartney sketch. In point of fact, Paul had been very involved with the arts community dating all the way back to the 1960s, as Barry Miles points out:

> Though it was Lennon who was art school trained, it was McCartney who engaged the most with the art-related side of The Beatles: the sleeves of Sgt.

Pepper and Abbey Road were both based upon his sketched ideas, and it was Paul who arranged the minimalist white sleeve for The Beatles (the 'white album') with Richard Hamilton.[28]

In the mid-1970s, McCartney became friendly with the painter Willem de Kooning.[29] While vacationing on Long Island, Paul and Linda would often visit him in his studio. Watching the artist at work seems to have encouraged Paul to give the process a try for himself. He began creating canvases to hang on the walls of the house that they'd rented in East Hampton: 'There were these painting hooks all around the walls. I thought, "A big red painting would look really good there" … They were abstract. You have to paint abstract after you've been seeing Bill de Kooning'.[30]

McCartney's work as a painter seemed to audibly influence his next single release, 'Once Upon a Long Ago'. This particular track was one of the most adventurous created by Paul so far. The chord progression was still guided by his renowned tonal logic, but he now seemed equally interested in the sonic qualities of the various chord clusters featured throughout. Each of his chord voicings work within a colour field as well as a key area. This was well suited to the lyric with its focus on memories of youthful innocence and acceptance.

The basic tracks of 'Once Upon a Long Ago' were recorded at Hog Hill Studio in March 1987. Overdubs were completed at Abbey Road the following July. The musicians were Paul McCartney (vocals, piano, bass, acoustic guitars, electric lead guitar, and keyboards); Henry Spinetti (drums); Linda McCartney (backing vocals, percussion); Tim Renwick (acoustic guitar); and Nick Glennie-Smith (keyboards). Nigel Kennedy played the electric violin, Stan Sulzman added saxophone, and Adrian Brett played the flute. The sweeping orchestration was prepared and conducted by George Martin.[31]

The space here is broad and inviting. The instrumental passages pick up on the issue of chordal colour mentioned above and pursue varied melodic lines that often seem to veer outside the key area. Thus, questions begin to emerge regarding the nature of tonal space itself and how one might at times yearn to break free and wander beyond its boundaries. Nevertheless, in spite of the rather dissonant musical gestures that appear throughout the track, 'Once Upon a Long Ago' ultimately serves to soothe and reassure. The overarching quality of the soundspace that Paul and his collaborators create works to blanket the listener within its soft textures.

'Once Upon a Long Ago' was released as a single in the UK in November 1987.[32] As mentioned above, it suggested a departure for Paul in that he seemed to be thinking differently about tone and colour. He and his collaborators seemed to be blending the various sound colours across a much larger canvas. In that regard, the more complex harmonic elements arguably gave them more to work with. He would continue this process on the B-side with a song that was begun on his own but was completed with the help of a new collaborator, and friend.

McCartney/McManus

Paul McCartney had always seemed to work exceptionally well within a col-laborative musical relationship. In each of the bands he'd been associated with there existed a dynamic that tended to feed his creative instincts. In recent years, the absence of that kind of challenge seemed to be having a negative effect on his work. Following the lukewarm response to both *Give My Regards to Broad Street* and *Press to Play*, it was felt that he needed someone who might be able to challenge him. The most logical candidate at the time was a pop singer with a very unlikely name.[33]

Elvis Costello, born Declan Patrick McManus, had come to prominence during the era of punk rock. Although he seemed to personify the angry young man typical of the time, his skill set was actually more in keeping with the singer-songwriters that had preceded him. The songs on his first few albums had demonstrated an encyclopaedic knowledge that stretched back beyond the rock era. His music was driving, melodic, and innovative. At the same time, his lyrics echoed the wit and energy of Bob Dylan, Ray Davies, and John Lennon.

Paul McCartney and Elvis Costello initially agreed to meet to get a sense of how they might proceed. At that meeting, they worked on a Costello song in pro-gress called 'Veronica'. It explored the challenges facing the elderly as their sens-ibilities decline. They also worked on a piece that McCartney had recently been developing called 'Back on My Feet'. The music for the song was consistent with Paul's works during this period in that it incorporated colourful chord clusters in the accompaniment. It was also built on three distinct sections, one of which doubled as an extended coda. In *Unfaithful Music and Disappearing Ink* (2015), Costello described his contribution to the song: 'I added just a few details to the lyrics, mostly cinematic directions to change the point of view, and a counter-melody, in which the words of an unsympathetic chorus of onlookers could be heard'.[34]

'Back on My Feet' was recorded at Hog Hill Studio on 9 March 1987. The track was among those produced by Phil Ramone and featured Paul on vocals, piano, bass, and electric guitar. Linda McCartney provided backing vocals and Charlie Morgan played the drums. The remaining players on the track were Tim Renwick on electric guitar and Nick Glennie-Smith on keyboards.[35,36] Elvis Costello is not listed as having contributed vocally or instrumentally to the recording.

A fascinating aspect of 'Back on My Feet' is the way in which the track incorporates characteristics of cinematic space. 'Footprints' had begun to go in this direction, but 'Back on My Feet' takes the process even further with direct references to elements of film grammar. In the process, it allows for an ironic distance from the medium and also raises interesting questions regarding how we have begun to think through cinema. In that regard, a shift from one thought to another might be said to correspond to a filmic 'cut'. Likewise, a detailed memory from one's own life experience could be described as being gloriously cinematic.

Снóва в СССР

In 1988, Paul McCartney released an LP that explored the curation of influence that had characterized Lennon's *Rock 'n' Roll* album. Over the previous year, he had been rehearsing and recording songs that were among his favourites while growing up. Classic works by Fats Domino, Lloyd Price, Little Richard, Elvis Presley, Sam Cooke, Bo Diddley, and Duke Ellington were all on offer. There was also one particular selection that held a special significance. This was Eddie Cochran's 'Twenty Flight Rock', the song he played for John Lennon way back on 6 July 1957, the day they first met.

Снóва в *CCCP* was recorded live in McCartney's Hog Hill Studio during a two-day session in July 1987.[37] The players for the 20 July session were Paul McCartney on bass and vocals; Mick Green on guitar; Mick Gallagher on piano; and Chris Whitten on drums. The players for the 21 July session were Paul on guitar and vocals; Nick Garvey on bass and backing vocals; Henry Spinetti on drums; and Mick Gallagher on the keyboards. A considerable number of songs were recorded, with eleven ultimately chosen for the LP release. The sessions were produced by McCartney and engineered by Peter Henderson.[38]

An interesting idea soon began to emerge for the project. In the age of Gorbachev and *Glasnost*, Paul wondered if he might somehow be able to pirate his own album. The plan he developed involved licensing the release of a limited number of vinyl pressings exclusively in the Soviet Union. Thus, listeners in the West who wanted to obtain a copy of the album would have to buy it as a Soviet import.[39] And so, on 31 October 1988, Снóва в *CCCP* was released on the Melodiya (Мелодия) label exclusively in the USSR. The liner notes on the original LP contained a message from McCartney:

> When I was young I asked my dad if people wanted peace. He said to me, 'Yes, people everywhere want peace – it's usually politicians that cause trouble'. It always seemed to me that the way The Beatles' music was admired in the USSR tended to prove his point that people in the world over have a great deal in common … In releasing this record exclusively in the Soviet Union, I extend the hand of peace and friendship to the people of the U.S.S.R.[40]

'My Brave Face'

The parallels between John Lennon and Elvis Costello had been duly noted – so much so that it caused resistance on McCartney's part when it was suggested that the two men might lean on some of those similarities as they worked on new material. However, following assurances that it would be okay, Paul agreed to explore the idea.

The opening track of *Flowers in the Dirt* shows Paul and Elvis incorporating various Beatles-esque elements into their lyrical and musical structures. For instance, the song opens with its chorus hook melody, as did 'Can't Buy Me Love' from *A Hard Day's Night*. It also features a number of melodic passages reminiscent of early Beatles songs like 'I'll Get You' and 'Thank You Girl'. The lyric concerns a young man in the aftermath of a breakup who is confronted with the daily realities of living alone. However, despite the sorrow and loneliness that has ensued following the departure of his loved one, he is determined to put on his brave face, if only he can find it.

'My Brave Face' was recorded at Olympic Studios in London during September and October 1988. The players on the track were McCartney on lead and backing vocals, Hofner bass, twelve-string acoustic guitar, and percussion; Mitchell Froom on keyboards; Chris Witten on drums; Hamish Stuart on backing vocals, acoustic guitar, and electric guitar; Robbie McIntosh on acoustic guitar and electric guitar; David Rhodes on Ebow guitar; and Dave Bishop, Chris Davis, and Chris White on saxophones.[41] In January 1988, Elvis Costello was involved in the recording of an early version of 'My Brave Face'. During one of those sessions, he encouraged McCartney to play his Hofner violin bass. This suggestion led Paul to The Beatles-esque bass guitar riffs that can be heard prominently throughout the track.[42]

In keeping with The Beatles references described above, the space of 'My Brave Face' is decidedly compressed. As such, it references early Beatles songs like 'She Loves You' in which the upbeat content was contrasted by the urgency conveyed through its intense production. Here, the narrative is a relatively calm report on the glum realities of living alone. Beneath the surface, however, there is the suggestion that the singer may be cracking under the pressure of his own loneliness. This fragility finds expression through the intensity of the soundscape as the singer searches for his own 'brave face' as a mask.

'You Want Her Too'

Flowers in the Dirt featured another piece of songcraft that referenced The Beatles and their interest in identity and voice. In terms of its narrative structure, 'You Want Her Too' was one of the most ambitious song/tracks Paul had ever recorded. The song's design presents the singer sharing his feelings for a woman he loves. As he tells us, and himself, what he feels about the situation, an ethereal voice chimes in, countering and correcting some of the claims he is making. Thus, we have a dialogue between a man and himself. As on 'Back on My Feet', the two composers develop a strategy that seems connected with cinema as well as with sound recording.

The basic tracks of 'You Want Her Too' were recorded between January and February 1988 at Hog Hill Studio. Overdubs were completed the following autumn in two parts: the first at Olympic Studios in London and the second at Sunset Sound Factory in Los Angeles. Paul sang lead and backing vocals, and also added guitars, bass, and percussion. Elvis Costello played keyboards and sang lead vocals. Hamish Stuart added electric guitar and sang backing vocals, and Robbie McIntosh played electric guitar. Drums and percussion were provided by Chris

Witten, while Mitchell Froom played additional keyboards and Chris Davis added saxophone. The arrangement for big band that could be heard during the song's coda was created by Richard Niles.[43]

The space of 'You Want Her Too' adroitly combines inner and outer worlds. The contrast here is between what the singer outwardly tells us and what his inner voice knows to be the truth. As previously noted, this kind of effect seems to be rooted in the language of cinema. Here, the voices are required to carry much of the narrative weight. They manage to do so very effectively, and the final results suggest that the composers are reaching towards a translation of cinematic gestures into song.

As was the case for McCartney's previous album, Flowers in the Dirt was originally conceived as a collaborative project. The idea was that Elvis Costello would be co-writer for various tracks, and also co-producer of the LP. Soon, however, problems began to emerge.[44] Specifically, they could never seem to successfully blend their ideas on production. Costello's approach could be rather experimental, and this seems to have clashed with Paul's renowned perfectionism in the studio. Ultimately, Elvis left the project.[45]

'Distractions'

The break with Elvis Costello was probably inevitable given the eclectic nature of Paul's own vision for his recorded works. As previously mentioned, he tended to move across a variety of styles with relative ease and this would not likely have been the case if the LP was completed as a McCartney/Costello collaboration, as Paul himself pointed out: 'Thinking back to the time, I didn't just want to just make an Elvis Costello album. There were other things I was interested in'.[46] Left on his own once again, he produced a remarkable song/track that reached ahead to the kind of music he would explore in the 1990s and beyond. 'Distractions' is a mellow ballad that skilfully incorporates elements of both folk and jazz. The song's opening melodic phrase seems to be an homage to Noël Coward's 'World Weary', which was written for the revue This Year of Grace! (1928).[47] There is also the suggestion of a subtle Burt Bacharach influence in some of the musical gestures, particularly during the coda.

'Distractions' was recorded at Hog Hill Studio between April and July 1987. The players were Paul on vocals, acoustic guitar, bass, and percussion; Linda McCartney sang backing vocals; Hamish Stuart sang backing vocals and played acoustic guitar; and Chris Witten added drums and percussion.[48] Instrumental overdubs were recorded at Mad Hatter Studios in Los Feliz, Los Angeles, California during an afternoon session that took place on 1 November 1987. The orchestration for that session was created by Clare Fischer and consisted of fourteen violins, four violas, two cellos, and an acoustic bass.[49]

The space created for 'Distractions' seems to be a daydream space, or daydream-scape. In a daydream, one is wide awake and can drift beyond the present back towards what was, and also towards what might be. This quality is intensified by Clare Fischer's orchestration, in which the sliding gestures suggest that time itself is being curved. Here, the singer might be wondering wishfully about what lies ahead. In the coming years, many seemingly impossible dreams would begin to be fulfilled.

Notes

1 Howard Sounes, *Fab: An Intimate Life of Paul McCartney* (Cambridge, MA: Da Capo Press, 2010), 324.

2 Paul Du Noyer, *Conversations with McCartney* (New York: The Overlook Press, 2016), 298.

3 'South Bank Show – Paul McCartney 1984'. YouTube. ommadawnfan, 30 September 2019. https://youtu.be/87i6WQ8k6yA?t=925.

4 John Chilton, *Who's Who in British Jazz*, 2nd edition (London: Continuum, 2004), 264–265.

5 'Record Research 30: Dinosaur Discs: Free Download, Borrow, and Streaming'. Internet Archive, 4 September 2013. https://archive.org/details/RecordResearch30.

6 Luca Perasi, *Paul McCartney: Recording Sessions (1969–2013)* (Milan: L.I.L.Y. Publishing, 2014), 240.

7 Chip Madinger and Mark Easter, *Eight Arms to Hold You: The Solo Beatles Compendium* (Chesterfield, MO: 44.1 Productions, 2000), 279.

8 Linda Hrochova, *Sir Paul McCartney: His Life's Work and Its Contribution to British Culture* (2012. BA Thesis. University of West Bohemia), 11.

9 Humphries, Patrick. 'Press to Play (Sound on Sound, Oct 1986)'. Sound on Sound. Accessed 20 March 2022. www.muzines.co.uk/articles/press-to-play/1668#.

10 Luca Perasi, *Paul McCartney: Recording Sessions (1969–2013)* (Milan: L.I.L.Y. Publishing, 2014), 246–248.

11 Brian Wilson with Ben Greenman, *I Am Brian Wilson: A Memoir* (Boston, MA: Da Capo Press, 2016), 249.

12 *Press to Play*, liner notes, 1986.

13 Luca Perasi, *Paul McCartney: Recording Sessions (1969–2013)* (Milan: L.I.L.Y. Publishing, 2014), 248.

14 *Press to Play*, liner notes, 1986.

15 Humphries, Patrick. 'Press to Play (Sound on Sound, Oct 1986)'. Sound on Sound. Accessed 20 March 2022. www.muzines.co.uk/articles/press-to-play/1668#.

16 Howard Sounes, *Fab: An Intimate Life of Paul McCartney* (Cambridge, MA: Da Capo Press, 2010), 374.

17 Howard Sounes, *Fab: An Intimate Life of Paul McCartney* (Cambridge, MA: Da Capo Press, 2010), 375.

18 Luca Perasi, *Paul McCartney: Recording Sessions (1969–2013)* (Milan: L.I.L.Y. Publishing, 2014), 257–258.

19 Tony Visconti, *Bowie, Bolan, and the Brooklyn Boy* (New York: HarperCollins, 2007), 327.

20 *Press to Play*, liner notes, 1986.

21 Humphries, Patrick. 'Press to Play (Sound on Sound, Oct 1986)'. Sound on Sound. Accessed 29 March 2022. www.muzines.co.uk/articles/press-to-play/1668#.

22 Luca Perasi, *Paul McCartney: Recording Sessions (1969–2013)* (Milan: L.I.L.Y. Publishing, 2014), 248.

23 Chip Madinger and Mark Easter, *Eight Arms to Hold You: The Solo Beatles Compendium* (Chesterfield, MO: 44.1 Productions, 2000), 282.

24 *Press to Play*, liner notes, 1986.

25 'Good Times Coming / Feel the Sun (Song)'. The Paul McCartney project, 2 May 2020. www.the-paulmccartney-project.com/song/good-times-coming.

26 Eric Iozzi, 'Another Day (Paul McCartney Song)'. Wikipedia. Wikimedia Foundation, 28 January 2022. https://en.wikipedia.org/wiki/Another_Day_(Paul_McCartney_s ong)#/media/File:Record_Sheet_01.jpg. (A close examination of the printing on the various mix sketches provided with the *Press to Play* album seems to match the printing on the sixteen-track CBS Records tape box that listed the track layouts for 'Another Day', 'Get on the Right Thing', and 'Eat at Home'.)

27 'McCartney (Album)'. McCartney Times, 3 May 2017. www.mccartney.com/?p=8656.

28 Brian Clarke, *Paul McCartney: Paintings* (Boston, MA: Bulfinch Press, 2000), 16.

29 Mark Stevens and Annalyn Swan, *De Kooning: An American Master* (New York: Alfred A. Knopf, 2004), 556.

30 Brian Clarke, *Paul McCartney: Paintings* (Boston, MA: Bulfinch Press, 2000), 16–17.

31 Luca Perasi, *Paul McCartney: Recording Sessions (1969–2013)* (Milan: L.I.L.Y. Publishing, 2014), 265–267.

32 Luca Perasi, *Paul McCartney: Recording Sessions (1969–2013)* (Milan: L.I.L.Y. Publishing, 2014), 265.

33 Howard Sounes, *Fab: An Intimate Life of Paul McCartney* (Cambridge, MA: Da Capo Press, 2010), 388.

34 Elvis Costello, *Unfaithful Music and Disappearing Ink* (New York: Blue Rider Press, 2015), 487.

35 Luca Perasi, *Paul McCartney: Recording Sessions (1969–2013)* (Milan: L.I.L.Y. Publishing, 2014), 263–264.

36 Снова в СССР, liner notes, 1991.

37 Luca Perasi, *Paul McCartney: Recording Sessions (1969–2013)* (Milan: L.I.L.Y. Publishing, 2014), 268.

38 Снова в СССР, liner notes, 1991.

39 Howard Sounes, *Fab: An Intimate Life of Paul McCartney* (Cambridge, MA: Da Capo Press, 2010), 387.

40 Снова в СССР, liner notes, 1991.

41 Luca Perasi, *Paul McCartney: Recording Sessions (1969–2013)* (Milan: L.I.L.Y. Publishing, 2014), 286–288.

42 Elvis Costello, *Unfaithful Music and Disappearing Ink* (New York: Blue Rider Press, 2015), 493–494.

43 Luca Perasi, *Paul McCartney: Recording Sessions (1969–2013)* (Milan: L.I.L.Y. Publishing, 2014), 275–276.

44 Howard Sounes, *Fab: An Intimate Life of Paul McCartney* (Cambridge, MA: Da Capo Press, 2010), 389.

45 Elvis Costello, *Unfaithful Music and Disappearing Ink* (New York: Blue Rider Press, 2015), 495.

46 'Chicago Tribune, March 16, 2017'. The Elvis Costello Wiki. Accessed 20 March 2022. www.elviscostello.info/wiki/index.php/Chicago_Tribune,_March_16,_2017.

47 Philip Hoare, *Noël Coward: A Biography* (London: Sinclair-Stevenson, 1998), 198–199.

48 Luca Perasi, *Paul McCartney: Recording Sessions (1969–2013)* (Milan: L.I.L.Y. Publishing, 2014), 279–280.

49 Chip Madinger and Mark Easter, *Eight Arms to Hold You: The Solo Beatles Compendium* (Chesterfield, MO: 44.1 Productions, 2000), 302.

9
CIRCLES

Following the completion of *Flowers in the Dirt*, Paul McCartney decided to embark on his first extended tour in a decade. Many of the players featured on the album were now a part of the band. In addition to Paul himself on vocals, guitars, and keyboards, the band featured Hamish Stuart on guitar and vocals, Robbie McIntosh on guitar, Chris Witten on drums, Paul Wickens on keyboards, and Linda McCartney on backing vocals and keyboards. The songs they performed spanned his entire recording career to date. Thus, works by The Beatles, Wings, and McCartney on his own were all included.

The Paul McCartney World Tour would last from 1989 to 1990. Early in 1991, the band (with Blair Cunningham replacing Chris Witten on drums) recorded a performance for MTV's popular *Unplugged* series. A number of obscure gems from his catalogue were brought out for the performance, including his first composition, 'I Lost My Little Girl'. The programme became the springboard for a series of live dates throughout Europe that combined both acoustic and electric performances in the set. And if all this wasn't enough, a few months later came the premiere of a classical work by Paul entitled *Liverpool Oratorio*.[1]

The origins of the *Liverpool Oratorio* date back to the sessions for *Flowers in the Dirt*.[2] Paul was originally approached by composer Carl Davis to consider writing a piece for the 150th anniversary of the Liverpool Philharmonic. In addition to his work in the concert hall, Davis had worked extensively in music for film. Anticipating a standard pop artist/trained composer kind of relationship, Davis was delighted by the way in which the two sparked each other creatively. He was also impressed by the distinctive nature of McCartney's process:

> I would say this about Paul, that is fascinating for me: words and music come at the same time. Maybe the lyrics wouldn't be absolutely complete, but the concept for the vocal line was there together, it was conceived at the same

DOI: 10.4324/9781003300212-13

time. And I thought this is fantastic, this is what popular songs is about, very different from a classical idea where a composer would say, 'I need to have a song and I will look in a book of poetry or I'll look in the Bible, or I'll look for a source'.[3]

The *Liverpool Oratorio* was conceived autobiographically in that it would access Paul's own life experiences as a way of presenting a story about growing up in Liverpool. During the writing process, he visited his alma mater, the Liverpool Institute. The school was now closed, and the building was in a state of disrepair. Thus, Paul began to wonder if it might be possible to somehow revive the 'Inny'.[4] In an effort to generate interest in the idea, he made a short film entitled *Echoes*. It showed him touring the building and reminiscing about his time there. At one point in the film, Paul described how the painting he'd done to win the Coronation prize in 1953 was hung prominently in the main hall of the school, indicating that it was still a source of pride after so many years.[5]

Paul found support for his idea to revive the Institute from George Martin. The producer had recently been working with Mark Featherstone-Witty, an actor, journalist, and educator who was trying to create a school for the performing arts in London.[6] Perhaps the same idea could be used to revive the 'Inny'. Thus began the long and arduous process of creating the Liverpool Institute for Performing Arts (LIPA). The school opened its doors in 1996 and later incorporated the adjacent building that originally housed the Liverpool College of Art, thereby reunifying the alma maters of both John Lennon and Paul McCartney.[7]

In 1993, Paul released a follow-up to *Flowers in the Dirt* entitled *Off the Ground*. The album featured a fresh batch of songs, two of which were co-written with Elvis Costello. That same year he began a collaboration with Martin Glover of the band Killing Joke, who went by the stage name Youth. Originally thinking that they were creating a collection of remixes for *Off the Ground*, the two opted instead to take the project in a fascinating direction. Working in what might be described as an ambient or techno style, the two released *Strawberries Oceans Ships Forest*. The album was credited to The Fireman, a pseudonym the two would continue to use on subsequent collaborations.[8]

Anthology

In the early 1990s, the long-planned documentary project on The Beatles' career was picking up steam. The collection created for the project would include archival recordings and films that would, in effect, allow the surviving members to tell their own story. In addition to opening up a window on The Beatles' creative process, the *Anthology* served to foreground the impressive scale of the band's recorded catalogue. What became clear was that this body of work had a shape, or a contour. This shape seems connected to the ways in which the band helped transform our understanding of music and musical process.

This naturally leads to comparisons with the visual arts. Returning to two artists who were mentioned earlier in this text, we can now consider The Beatles' recorded works in what is perhaps a new light. In his book *Andy Warhol* (2009), Arthur C. Danto described the importance of Warhol's works in relation to those of Pablo Picasso:

> Picasso, it must be said, was the most important artist of the first half of the twentieth century, inasmuch as he revolutionized painting and sculpture in deep and liberating ways. Warhol revolutionized art as such. His decisions were always surprising, and if they did not especially make his work popular, they seem, in retrospect, to have been precisely in harmony with the spirit of his era. Which makes it natural to think of ours as the Age of Warhol, to the degree that he set his stamp on what was allowable.[9]

As Picasso and Warhol did for the visual arts, The Beatles helped revolutionize popular musical process in their time by furthering the unification of music composition and recording. They first gained notoriety as a live band, but quickly remade themselves into studio artists. The recording studio became their musical workshop in which they could explore and create freely. With each new technological advancement they expanded the parameters of their work in order to enhance its expressive power. In the final analysis, they produced a catalogue of recordings that transformed the way we think about music.

In keeping with the flexibility afforded by the new technologies, Yoko Ono gave Paul a tape that contained various John Lennon demos. The idea was that the surviving Beatles could add additional instrumentation in order to complete the track for possible release.[10] The sessions were supervised by Jeff Lynne, whose work with the Electric Light Orchestra, and more recently with George Harrison on *Cloud Nine* (1989), made him an ideal choice. The recording engineer was another old friend, Geoff Emerick. The first John Lennon demo they worked on in February 1994 was 'Free as a Bird'.[11]

The following year the team met once again to continue the process. Now they would work on the demo of another John Lennon song called 'Real Love'. The difference here was that, while 'Free as a Bird' required additional material composed by Paul and George, this new track did not require any new material added. Thus, they returned to the process they'd employed for *The Beatles* (1968) in which three Beatles tended to act as session men for whomever had written the song. Although 'Real Love' was beautifully realized, the lack of creative synergy may have led them to abandon the third track scheduled for completion.

'Now and Then'

The Beatles briefly began to work on another Lennon demo entitled 'Now and Then'. However, as in each of the previous tracks, a tremendous amount of work would have been required to remove noise and clarify the various musical elements on the original recording. That, combined with the fact that George Harrison was not enamoured with the song, led to The Beatles abandoning work on 'Now and Then'. Of course, that means that there is no finished version of the song to review.[12] However, using John's original demo and the two completed tracks as a guide, it seems possible to speculate on how The Beatles might have proceeded had they chosen to finish the track. So, with the reader's permission, what follows is a speculative Songscape for the uncompleted 'Now and Then'.

The basic progression of Lennon's demo version shifts between A minor and E minor chords, seemingly referencing the opening section/panel of 'Happiness Is a Warm Gun'. In this case, however, the key is firmly established as A minor rather than E minor – for the moment, anyway. Soon, a new section appears with a remarkable shift to E major through the supertonic chord (F sharp minor), a common chord of the parallel major of the key area of the first section. The previous idea might be considered transitional in that it leads to a more settled progression in G major. Although the description above may suggest that the song is exceedingly complex, it actually unfolds quite gently in performance.

'Now and Then' was begun at Paul McCartney's Hog Hill Studio. Speculating on what might have been, the distinctive snare drum sound associated with Jeff Lynne and used to great effect on both 'Real Love' and 'Free as a Bird' might have worked very well here. This could have served to further extend the direction Lennon was going in with some of the tracks from *Imagine* (1971). It would also have further demonstrated the timbral and tactile brilliance of Ringo Starr. The use of acoustic guitars could have created a gentle yet firm support for the drum kit. Finally, one might consider a soothing string section in the manner of the one created by Torrie Zito for 'Imagine' or George Martin for 'Grow Old With Me'.

It's challenging to attempt to imagine the space created for a track that has yet to be completed. However, given what we know about this composer's approach, it seems reasonable to speculate. A completed version of 'Now and Then' might have continued to expand on the kind of dream imagery that characterized various Lennon recordings with The Beatles and on his own. Songs such as 'Love', '#9 Dream', and 'Strawberry Fields Forever' all involved painterly portrayals of such experiences. Thus, the unfinished song/track could well have continued what seems to have been an ongoing effort by the composer to create a vivid musical rendering of his inner life. At the time of this writing, an officially completed version of 'Now and Then' has yet to be released. And so, until a finished version of the song/track appears, it will have to remain, like an unobserved subatomic particle/wave, only as a set of probabilities.[13]

'Hiroshima Sky Is Always Blue'

In January 1995, Paul collaborated with Yoko Ono and her son Sean on 'Hiroshima Sky Is Always Blue'. The recording was intended as a remembrance for victims of the atomic blast at Hiroshima. In creating the piece, Ono drew on memories from her childhood in which she had been evacuated to the countryside during the war. Originally conceived for a play by Ron Destro, the piece was built around the image of a young girl engaged in the Japanese custom of folding 1,000 paper cranes in order to make a wish. Before she is able to complete the process, she is killed by the detonation of the atomic bomb.[14]

'Hiroshima Sky Is Always Blue' was recorded at Paul McCartney's Hog Hill Studio in January 1995.[15] The main musicians on the track were Yoko on vocals and Paul on backing vocals and double bass. Linda McCartney played keyboard, while Sean Lennon and James McCartney played guitars. Backing vocals and assorted percussion were provided by Heather McCartney, Mary McCartney, and Stella McCartney. An excerpt of the completed track was broadcast on Japanese radio on 6 August 1995, the fiftieth anniversary of the event.[16]

The track begins with a series of bells ringing through the image. This is followed by Yoko saying: 'John, we're here now together. Bless you, peace on earth, and Strawberry fields forever'. Paul sustains a low note on the bass, which establishes a tonal centre, and then becomes the foundation for the rest of the ensemble as they improvise under and around Yoko's voice. She makes a series of sounds and sings phrases in Japanese but soon switches to English for several lines including 'Hiroshima sky is always beautiful' and 'Hiroshima sky is always blue'. After seven minutes and forty-five seconds, the piece ends with an exhale.

'Hiroshima Sky Is Always Blue' creates an effective soundscape of the tragic event alluded to in the song's title. The balance between the supporting instruments and the various vocal parts suggests the composition of a painting in which the background is the environment and the foreground is a human figure expressing how it felt to be present at the event. The title creates an intriguing ambiguity through the use of the word blue. On one level, it suggests the promise of a bright, clear day. However, it might also be heard to imply a lingering sadness that was born in the wake of the event.

'The Ballad of the Skeletons'

In 1995, Paul collaborated with poet Allen Ginsberg on a new poem entitled 'The Ballad of the Skeletons'. In preparation for a live performance of the work, Ginsberg asked McCartney to recommend guitarists who might accompany him on stage. After coming up with several big names, McCartney offered his own services for the gig. Ginsberg agreed and the two met at the Royal Albert Hall on 16 October 1995 during a presentation entitled 'Return of the Forgotten'.[17] In a touching act of camaraderie, McCartney touches Ginsberg on the shoulder before they begin the poem/song. Following the performance, Paul offered to help with a recording if one ever came about. Ginsberg described the process that followed:

> He said if I ever got around to recording it, let him know. So he volunteered, and we made a basic track, and sent it to him, on 24 tracks, and he added maracas and drums, which it needed. It gave it a skeleton, gave it a shape. And also organ, he was trying to get that effect of Al Kooper on the early Dylan.

And guitar, so he put a lot of work in on that. And then we got it back just in time for Philip Glass to fill in his arpeggios on piano.[18]

As it turned out, Allen Ginsberg's weathered cynicism was perfect for the times. 'The Ballad of the Skeletons' caught the wave of 1990s alternative pop culture and was a surprise hit. In the spirit of the times, a video was made for airplay on MTV. Directed by Gus van Sant, the film shows Ginsberg, initially wearing an 'Uncle Sam' top hat, reciting the poem.[19] Around him was shown a series of images from contemporary and vintage sources that connected with the critical tone of the text.[20]

Flaming Pie

During the *Anthology* project, Paul began planning a new solo album that would be called *Flaming Pie*. Co-produced by McCartney, Jeff Lynne, and George Martin, it was something of a return to form in that it featured many of the strengths of his eclectic approach with Wings, along with elements of *McCartney* (1970) and *McCartney II* (1980) thrown in for good measure. The title track grew out of a studio jam between Paul and Jeff Lynne during the recording of another song from *Flaming Pie* called 'Souvenir'.[21] The lyric was based on an article written by Lennon in 1961 for Bill Harry's *Mersey Beat* called 'Being A Short Diversion On The Dubious Origins Of Beatles (Translated From The John Lennon)'. In the article, John describes how The Beatles got their distinctive name: 'It came in a vision – a man appeared on a flaming pie and said unto them "From this day on you are Beatles with an 'A'"'. "Thank you, mister man", they said, thanking him'.[22] In Paul's adaptation, the singer takes on the role of 'mister man'.

On the surface, 'Flaming Pie' is fairly conventional in that it consists of two main sections: the primary section which builds towards an iteration of the title line, thereby creating a solid foundation for the story; and a contrasting section that is built on a series of unusual lyrical assertions supported by a clever elaboration of the dominant harmony. Next comes a brief piano interlude that recalls the coda of 'Rock Show' from *Venus and Mars* (1975). Here, however, the part has the quality of an intro that is somehow appearing in the middle rather than at the beginning of the song. In comparison with some of his earlier works, Paul seems to be shifting the weight between various sections at will. In the process, he frees himself from the format while at the same time lending the piece a sense of organic growth.

'Flaming Pie' was recorded at Hog Hill Studio on 27 February 1996. In a seeming return to the aesthetic of *McCartney* (1970) and *McCartney II* (1980), the main player on the track was Paul himself. Here, he provided lead and backing vocals, piano, bass, drums, and electric guitar. Additional backing vocals and electric guitar were added by producer Jeff Lynne.[23] In what seems to have a self-imposed compositional exercise, the recording of the track was done in a hurry, as pointed out in the album liner notes:

Paul suggested that the song be taped with the speed that The Beatles often worked, cutting three songs in a day. Setting themselves a four hour deadline, Paul singing live to his own piano accompaniment with Jeff on guitar before adding drums and bass, and then, guitars and harmony vocals.[24]

The space of 'Flaming Pie' is decidedly tight and compressed. This is contrasted by the lyrical content, which consists largely of exclamations of the joy of being. Normally, one might associate such sentiments with a relaxed attitude. Here, however, they are intoned by a voice that seems squeezed like the space around it. Thus, 'Flaming Pie' suggests that getting in touch with one's own sense of self is a very urgent matter indeed.

'Beautiful Night'

The song that would become the penultimate track on *Flaming Pie* had been kicking around in the McCartney catalogue for over a decade. 'Beautiful Night' had first been attempted during sessions produced by Phil Ramone in August 1986. That version is very impressive, but for some reason Paul felt it needed more. The song was then tried again during sessions for *Off the Ground* (1993), but once again it was abandoned. Finally, it was revised, completed, and released on *Flaming Pie* in 1997.[25]

'Beautiful Night' is a ballad that consists of two main sections. These are distinguished by being in two different key areas: A major and C major. There is also a standalone section in F sharp minor that creates an effective sense of balance throughout. The revised version adds a coda that serves to transform the song from a wistful ballad into a rocking piece with full orchestra. If that were not enough, Ringo appears on lead vocals during this section, repeating the title line to tremendous effect, as Paul himself pointed out in the album's liner notes:

I unearthed this old song for when Ringo was coming, changed a few lyrics and it was really like the old days, I realized that we hadn't done this for so long, but it was very comfortable. And it was still there.[26]

The basic tracks of 'Beautiful Night' were recorded over two days (13 and 14 May) in 1996. Paul provided lead and backing vocals, bass, piano, electric piano, organ, acoustic guitar, electric guitar, and percussion. Linda sang backing vocals along with Jeff Lynne, who also added guitars to the track. Finally, Ringo Starr played drums and percussion, and also sang lead vocals during the song's extended coda.[27] An orchestration created by George Martin and conducted by David Snell was recorded on 14 February 1997 at EMI Studios, Studio One, Abbey Road.[28]

Initially, the space of 'Beautiful Night' seems sedate and rather contained. Then, during the contrasting section, there is a sense of expansion seemingly generated by the change of key. Things seem to narrow down further during the brief section in F sharp minor. The coda, which was added to the song for the *Flaming Pie* sessions, changes thing considerably. There, the chord progression is pared down as the groove intensifies and the texture thickens. The addition of Ringo on lead vocals is irresistible and adds to the overall effect of the track. Finally, when it seems like we can go no further, the song crashes down to earth, revealing the space in which it had been moving all along.

'Great Day'

The concluding track of *Flaming Pie* is another song with a long history. Tracking back to the early 1970s, 'Great Day' was a folk song that Paul and Linda would perform with the children as a bit of family fun.[29] The primary section is built on a descending chromatic pattern over a D bass, which then resolves upward to an E major chord. This ingenious contrary motion pattern is then followed by a contrasting section that features a rising pattern alternating between A and E chords. The energy generated between these two patterns is such that no other sections are required.

The space of 'Great Day' recalls the days of *McCartney* (1970) in that it blends the close aesthetics of a home studio with the ambience of a professional recording space. This is evident in the song's two sections. The first suggests the home environment that was a feature of Paul's first solo album. The second section, however, evokes the larger soundspaces one would find at a studio like Abbey Road. As was the case in the song's structure, the energy generated by the contrasting production approaches helps propel the song forward with ease.

'Great Day' was recorded at Hog Hill Studio on 3 September 1992 during a session that was co-produced by McCartney and George Martin. That same session produced another track that appeared on *Flaming Pie* entitled 'Calico Skies'. The musicians on the track were Paul on vocals, guitar, and knee slap percussion and Linda on backing vocals. Although it wasn't clear at the time, this would be the last Paul McCartney album on which Linda would appear.[30]

'Wide Prairie'

On 17 April 1998, Linda McCartney succumbed to cancer at the age of fifty-six.[31] She had been struggling with the illness for several years and the family had worked hard to make her comfortable, whatever the outcome.[32] A project that followed in the wake of her passing was a collection of Linda's own original compositions recorded with Wings and on her own since the early 1970s. The scope of the album is impressive and suggests a unique musical vision. The recordings also highlight the way in which she was an integral part of the distinctive Wings sound.

The title track achieves a remarkably eclectic quality through the fluid use of multiple musical styles. The opening is an expressionistic passage in which Linda delivers a short, sultry description of a chance encounter with a man in a Parisian setting. This is followed by the main section of the song, which is a blend of reggae and country and western. Next comes Paul with a spirited jazz/rock response, which leads back into Linda's restatement of the main section. The opening passage recurs, this time as a coda that features increased vocal and instrumental improvisation as the scene fades slowly into the distance.

The basic tracks of 'Wide Prairie' were recorded at EMI Pathé Marconi Studios in Paris, France on 20 November 1973. Further recording took place at Soundshop Recording Studios in Nashville, Tennessee on 8 and 11 July 1974. The players were Linda McCartney on vocals and mellotron; Paul McCartney on piano, organ, Rhodes, bass, and vocals; Denny Laine on acoustic guitar; Jimmy McCulloch on electric guitar; and Davey Lutton on drums. Additional instrumentation was provided by Thaddeus Richard on alto saxophone; Johnny Gimble and Vassar Clements on fiddle; George Tidwell and Barry McDonald on trumpet; Norman Ray on baritone sax; Hewlett Quillen on trombone; and William Puett on tenor sax.[33]

The conceptual space of 'Wide Prairie' is decidedly cinematic. The opening section seems to quote the ambience of a classic film that is equal parts New Wave and film noir. The setting then shifts to a fascinating blend of the Caribbean and the American Southwest. Paul then takes us to Vegas for a horn-driven and jazz-influenced idea that never loses its rock and roll edge. Finally, we return to the original scene, suggesting perhaps that the journey we have been taking may have been occurring entirely within the minds of the two main characters.

The Art of Paul McCartney

For the better part of two decades, Paul McCartney's work as a painter had been growing by leaps and bounds. During the production of a television film about the making of *Flaming Pie* (1997) entitled *Paul McCartney: In the World Tonight*, he invited a camera crew into his private painting studio. There, he described part of the process he used to create the paintings *Celtic Eloquence* (1994) and *Yellow Celt* (1994): 'I tell you, actually, the most fun about this for me was playing with charcoal. I'd draw the charcoal away from the line, see, and you'd get that, and try and leave the line'.[34]

McCartney had produced a remarkable amount of work in a distinctive style. It seemed clear that he'd found his feet as a visual artist. It was also clear that he'd been able to overcome inhibitions he'd been harbouring for years about the painting process itself. He described the problem to his friend Barry Miles: 'I felt in John's shadow because I hadn't been to art college. This was one of my biggest blocks. I felt that only people who'd gone to art college were allowed to paint'.[35] In 2002, he would completely transcend those feelings with an exhibition of his work at the Walker Gallery in Liverpool.

The exhibition took place between 24 May and 4 August 2002 and consisted of over sixty paintings that McCartney had created since 1982. In a press release for the exhibit, he credited Willem de Kooning as a major inspiration for his style and process. He also described the sense of accomplishment he felt at having an exhibition in his hometown: 'John and I spent many a pleasant afternoon wandering around Walker Art Gallery when we were young, so going back to the 'Pool with my paintings will complete some kind of circle for me'.[36]

One of the paintings featured in the Walker Gallery exhibition was a delightful piece entitled *Yellow Linda with Piano*. The work was painted in 1988, and the materials are oil on canvas. Considering Paul's previous experience as a sketch artist and caricaturist, the painting seems to be somewhat transitional. His sketch captures Linda's character and mood perfectly, but he also tells the viewer a great deal more with pure colour. McCartney later described how this particular strategy emerged:

> This is Linda relaxing in my room at home where I have the piano, and she is sitting on the couch and she was in yellow. So I made everything yellow. The piano isn't really yellow, but I just thought it would be nice. Her hair was yellow, her blouse was yellow, so I made them all yellow. So it became a very yellow picture. It didn't need brown or any of their real colors.[37]

Here, Linda's relaxed mood and personal charm, as represented by the colour yellow, seem to be suffusing the space around her like bright morning sunlight.

Painting about Music

Several years later, Paul produced a trio of paintings that focused on music. One of the most interesting aspects of the *Press to Play* LP was its sleeve design, which contained a series of colour sketches created by Paul that depicted the final mixes for each of the ten tracks featured on the album. In this trio of paintings, he seemed to be trying to further that idea by translating musical effects into a purely visual language.

C Minor (1993) was described by the artist as 'a rather lonely-looking picture because it can be a bit of a sad chord'.[38] His description leads one to think back to the song/track 'Dear Friend' from *Wild Life* (1971), in which C minor is the tonic chord. In that song, he was reaching out to Lennon to try to end the loneliness and re-establish healthy communication. The painting uses the figure of a human face against a light-green background. The face seems to be cloaked with linen or gauze. Beneath, there is evidence of injury, perhaps indicating that the sadness of C minor has now manifested itself physically. What is particularly interesting here is that the figure aspect (the face) seems to be receding into the background. Dynamic backgrounds seemed to be taking on an increasingly important role in Paul's work as a painter.

Key of F (1993) consists of abstract shapes on the canvas that seem formed out of colour as the primary material. These shapes are asymmetrical in their design. The title and the curious formation of the figures suggests a connection with 'Yesterday', Paul McCartney's most famous song. There, it was noted earlier that a seeming asymmetry was employed by the composer as the means for sustaining listener interest in the musical structure. In *Key of F*, a sense of balance is achieved by the suggestion that colour could be thought of as a fundamental musical element rather than a mere attribute.

Unfinished Symphony (1993) is a more complex work that, nevertheless, builds from the paintings mentioned above. It consists of various shapes cluttered together into a central mass. These shapes feature a variety of colours bursting outwards towards the viewer. The colours are pleasing but complex, suggesting that the music being portrayed here might be dealing with issues not so easily resolved. McCartney himself described the work as being an attempt 'to try and paint a whole symphony. The whole thing rather than one chord, a musical explosion, an orchestra playing something'.[39]

Looking back on the creative dialogue of John Lennon and Paul McCartney, both with The Beatles and on their own, one may conclude that it was driven by the notion that art forms were viable tools of aesthetic inquiry. Throughout their careers, they often seemed to be using music to ask questions about the art of painting. Key examples of this include the development of the double-A-sided single as a kind of musical diptych, the studio-as-gallery approach of the *McCartney* LP (1970), and the Jackson Pollock-inspired action painting of 'Revolution 9'. In that regard, McCartney's work in *C Minor*, *Key of F*, and *Unfinished Symphony* seems particularly significant. In effect, he goes through the looking glass and begins to use painting as a means of asking questions about the art of music.

Notes

1 Howard Sounes, *Fab: An Intimate Life of Paul McCartney* (Cambridge, MA: Da Capo Press, 2010), 403–405.
2 Chip Madinger and Mark Easter, *Eight Arms to Hold You: The Solo Beatles Compendium* (Chesterfield, MO: 44.1 Productions, 2000), 345.
3 Luca Perasi, *Paul McCartney: Recording Sessions (1969–2013)* (Milan: L.I.L.Y. Publishing, 2014), 297–298.
4 Howard Sounes, *Fab: An Intimate Life of Paul McCartney* (Cambridge, MA: Da Capo Press, 2010), 391–392.
5 'Liverpool Institute High School for Boys'. V4 Files. Libyans.org. Accessed 20 March 2022. www.liobians.org/files/Echoes.mp4.
6 Howard Sounes, *Fab: An Intimate Life of Paul McCartney* (Cambridge, MA: Da Capo Press, 2010), 391–392.
7 Paul Du Noyer, *Conversations with McCartney* (New York: The Overlook Press, 2016), 23.
8 Paul Du Noyer, *Conversations with McCartney* (New York: The Overlook Press, 2016), 132.
9 Arthur C. Danto, *Andy Warhol* (New Haven, CT: Yale University Press, 2010), 48.
10 Chip Madinger and Mark Easter, *Eight Arms to Hold You: The Solo Beatles Compendium* (Chesterfield, MO: 44.1 Productions, 2000), 278.
11 Ian MacDonald, *Revolution in the Head: The Beatles' Records and the Sixties* (London: Vintage, 2008), 376.
12 Ian MacDonald, *Revolution in the Head: The Beatles' Records and the Sixties* (London: Vintage, 2008), 380.
13 Robert Lanza with Bob Berman, *Biocentrism: How Life and Consciousness Are the Keys to Understanding the True Nature of the Universe* (Dallas, TX: BenBella Books, Inc., 2009), 50.
14 Ian Peel, *The Unknown Paul McCartney: McCartney and the Avant-Garde* (London and Richmond, Surrey: Reynolds & Hearn, 2002), 144.

15 Luca Perasi, *Paul McCartney: Recording Sessions (1969–2013)* (Milan: L.I.L.Y. Publishing, 2014), 324.

16 Chip Madinger and Mark Easter, *Eight Arms to Hold You: The Solo Beatles Compendium* (Chesterfield, MO: 44.1 Productions, 2000), 378–379.

17 'Return of the Forgotten – Allen Ginsberg Live at the Royal Albert Hall (Concert)'. The Paul McCartney project, 26 September 2020. www.the-paulmccartney-project.com/concert/1995-10-16.

18 '"The Ballad of the Skeletons": Allen Ginsberg's 1996 Collaboration with Philip Glass and Paul McCartney'. Open Culture. Accessed 20 March 2022. www.openculture.com/2012/04/the_ballad_of_the_skeletons_allen_ginsbergs_1996_collaboration_with_philip_glass_and_paul_mccartney.html.

19 Ian Peel, *The Unknown Paul McCartney: McCartney and the Avant-Garde* (London and Richmond, Surrey: Reynolds & Hearn, 2002), 155.

20 'Allen Ginsberg with Paul McCartney "Ballad of …" – Youtube'. YouTube. BVMTValternative. Accessed 21 March 2022. www.youtube.com/watch?v=ZdvM0IB5Sbs.

21 Chip Madinger and Mark Easter, *Eight Arms to Hold You: The Solo Beatles Compendium* (Chesterfield, MO: 44.1 Productions, 2000), 388.

22 Mark Lewisohn, *Tune In: The Beatles All These Years, Volume 1* (New York: Crown Archetype, 2013), 422–424.

23 Luca Perasi, *Paul McCartney: Recording Sessions (1969–2013)* (Milan: L.I.L.Y. Publishing, 2014), 332–333.

24 *Flaming Pie*, liner notes, 1997.

25 Chip Madinger and Mark Easter, *Eight Arms to Hold You: The Solo Beatles Compendium* (Chesterfield, MO: 44.1 Productions, 2000), 389.

26 *Flaming Pie*, liner notes, 1997.

27 Luca Perasi, *Paul McCartney: Recording Sessions (1969–2013)* (Milan: L.I.L.Y. Publishing, 2014), 333–334.

28 'Orchestral Overdubs for "Beautiful Night" (Feb 14, 1997)'. The Paul McCartney project, 17 June 2020. www.the-paulmccartney-project.com/session/orchestral-overdubs-for-beautiful-night.

29 *Flaming Pie*, liner notes, 1997.

30 Luca Perasi, *Paul McCartney: Recording Sessions (1969–2013)* (Milan: L.I.L.Y. Publishing, 2014), 318–319.

31 Howard Sounes, *Fab: An Intimate Life of Paul McCartney* (Cambridge, MA: Da Capo Press, 2010), 451.

32 Howard Sounes, *Fab: An Intimate Life of Paul McCartney* (Cambridge, MA: Da Capo Press, 2010), 435–436.

33 'Wide Prairie (Album)'. The Paul McCartney project, 16 March 2022. www.the-paulmccartney-project.com/album/wide-prairie.

34 'Paul McCartney – In The World Tonight (Full Documentary in Full HD, 1997)'. YouTube. Kitsu Beatles, 20 May 2021. https://youtu.be/-BhnIClthqQ?t=136.

35 Brian Clarke, *Paul McCartney: Paintings* (Boston, MA: Bulfinch Press, 2000), 15.

36 'The Art of Paul McCartney'. National Museums Liverpool. Accessed 20 March 2022. www.liverpoolmuseums.org.uk/whatson/walker-art-gallery/exhibition/art-of-paul-mccartney#section--the-exhibition.

37 Brian Clarke, *Paul McCartney: Paintings* (Boston, MA: Bulfinch Press, 2000), 42.

38 Brian Clarke, *Paul McCartney: Paintings* (Boston, MA: Bulfinch Press, 2000), 54.

39 Brian Clarke, *Paul McCartney: Paintings* (Boston, MA: Bulfinch Press, 2000), 54.

CODA

Chaos and Creation

Over the next two decades, the art of painting continued to resonate through McCartney's work. He collaborated on a new album with Nigel Godrich, the talented young producer who had worked extensively with progressive artists like Beck and Radiohead. That album was released in 2005 with the curious title *Chaos and Creation in the Backyard*. At the time of its recording, Paul had been touring and recording with his own band and assumed that they would all play together on the sessions. Godrich, however, had a different idea:

> [T]he second week he said, 'I'd like to try something different. I want you to play a lot of instruments'. So, he got me drumming a bit, which I love to do. Thinking about it afterwards, possibly what happened was that I write the songs, I bring them to the studio and then the drummer kinda takes over and he writes the drum part. Whereas, if I play it, I'm still sort of composing.[1]

Earlier, it was asserted that The Beatles had helped change the way we hear and think about music. Here, Godrich seemed to be encouraging McCartney to carry on in that process. He evidently wanted him to continue unifying the compositional and recording process as he'd done with The Beatles and on LPs like *McCartney* (1970) and *McCartney II* (1980). As a result, Paul would also revisit the idea of the recording studio as a workshop and gallery.

On 28 July 2005, Paul gave a live presentation entitled *Chaos and Creation at Abbey Road*. On that evening, an audience was invited into Studio Two, the room that The Beatles had transformed into their own creative workshop all those years ago. During the presentation, which was supervised by Godrich, Paul performed a variety of songs from his back catalogue, including several from *Chaos and Creation in the Backyard*.[2] He also involved the audience members in a demonstration of some of the recording techniques that The Beatles and their collaborators had

DOI: 10.4324/9781003300212-14

helped pioneer.[3] In that regard, his presentation effectively unified the idea of the recording studio as workshop, gallery, and now performance space.

'Fine Line'

The opening track contains a lyric that is the source of the album's title. The key idea here seems to concern oppositions that yield desired results. Sensing the listener's expectation for balance, McCartney sets up a structure that seems decidedly out of balance. Gradually, he arrives at a rich, colourful passage that effectively transforms the asperity that preceded it. The coda then creates a layering effect, suggesting that the earlier oppositions are in fact interrelated.

The studio version of 'Fine Line' was recorded in September 2004 at AIR Studios in London. Here, Paul provides vocals, grand piano, spinet, drums, bass, acoustic guitar, electric guitar, and percussion. The strings were performed by the Millennia Ensemble conducted by Joby Talbot from his own arrangement.[4] The lyrical content explores a theme that dominates the project; that is, the connection between chaos and creativity. There are also intriguing references to a situation not described in detail regarding someone being driven away. In an interview with Kevin O'Hare, McCartney commented on these references, suggesting that they were likely an unconscious aspect of the creative process. He goes on to connect this with the idea of varied interpretations of his work:

> It's strange. I hadn't meant that, but that's one of the things I think is very interesting about writing songs. Because you can write one way with one meaning, and suddenly they can become applicable in other ways. But I like that. I want people to be able to draw their own meanings from songs. I would never say 'No it must mean this'.[5]

The recording of 'Fine Line' seems decidedly modern in that it appears compressed yet somehow spacious as well. This quality works well in terms of the seeming opposition between chaos and creation that the song explores. As the rhythm section turns up the pressure, the subtle orchestration continues to creep through the transom like a welcome breeze that suggests new possibilities. During an interlude, the pressure subsides and the rhythm section seems to yield to this new mood. The expanded space depicted here might then be considered to be the end result of the oppositions heard earlier in the track, and a welcome respite before a crowded coda makes the composer's final point.

'Jenny Wren'

Another standout from the album was an acoustic track called 'Jenny Wren'. Here, Paul revisited the kind of musical scaffolding between lines that was a feature of 'Blackbird'. The new song was harmonically complex and also featured a solo section with its own unique chord progression, which is then blended into a restatement of the melody and chords of the contrasting section. The song's harmonic complexity creates a great deal of tonal colour. These patches of colour are further enhanced on the sound recording through the use of a duduk, a double-reed woodwind instrument of Armenian origin. During this live performance in Studio Two, Paul sings the line for the solo section.

The studio version of 'Jenny Wren' was recorded at Ocean Way Recording Studio in Los Angeles, California in October 2004. There, McCartney recorded vocals, acoustic guitar, and floor tom on the track. The duduk was played by Pedro Eustache.[6] The accent seemed to be on proximity as the song suggests the tone of a lullaby. If one were to create a sketch of the mix in the manner of Paul's sketches on *Press to Play* (1986), acoustic guitars would be placed on the far left and right. Paul's vocal would be in the centre with the floor tom underneath. During the solo, the duduk would occupy the same space as Paul's vocal.

The live performance at Abbey Road mentioned above features only the composer on acoustic guitar and vocals. Bear in mind, though, that this performance took place in Studio Two. Earlier, it was noted how that soundspace can seem soft (a good thing) and the effect of the room on Paul's performance seems tangible.[7] It was also noted how this soundspace had become as familiar to him as his own home studio. Once again, we might reference Bachelard's comments regarding the connections between our own stored memories and the spaces we inhabit: 'Now everything becomes clear, the house images move in both directions: they are in us as much as we are in them'.[8]

'Opening Station'

In 1988, the same year he had created *Yellow Linda with Piano*, Paul painted a work called *Egypt Station*. Here, he worked in a deliberately elemental style. Nevertheless, parts of the painting began to resemble familiar images.[9] Nearly two decades later, Paul revisited the painting in relation to a new album he was planning. In an interview with musician Jarvis Cocker that took place at the Liverpool Institute for Performing Arts (LIPA) on 25 July 2018, Paul described how the original painting suggested a concept for the entire project:

> I was looking at it one day and I thought it's quite a nice title that, *Egypt Station*, so that could be the new album's title. And then I thought, you know, that the painting could be the cover. That's where it started and then we got some really good art directors who took it, but yeah that's cool, and so, you know, we start off like with a station noise.[10]

'Opening Station' begins the album with a clever soundscape that is based on the image created in the painting. This is then followed by a choir that floats around the space freely. There is a sense of realism at work in that the sounds correspond to those one would expect to hear in such a location. In effect, McCartney has created a sound score for *Egypt Station* by using Foley techniques

typically associated with the cinema. In the process, he continues The Beatles practice of building bridges between seemingly disparate art forms: from painting to
recording to music to film.

McCartney III

In December 2020, Paul released an album that would complete the trilogy he'd
begun with *McCartney* (1970) and then continued with *McCartney II* (1980). The
appropriately titled *McCartney III* is an album that is unified by process. Once again,
Paul plays the majority of the instruments himself. It continues the LP-as-gallery
idea that was a feature of the first two instalments in his trilogy, and also revisits
the notion of studio space as a creative sanctuary during challenging times. The
opening track is particularly interesting in that it suggests the quality of an abstract
painting.

'Long Tailed Winter Bird' opens with a repeated riff on acoustic guitar. The
groove under this riff suggests the sound of scraping on a washboard. In that sense, it
recalls the march-like rhythms of 'Famous Groupies' from *London Town* (1978). The
song also features a chanted series of questions. The lyric here is vague but seems
to indicate that the singer has now become estranged from a former loved one.
Nothing here is finely tuned in the manner that listeners have come to expect in
a Paul McCartney song/track. Instead, the sounds seem deliberately broad in how
they evoke bold primary colours.

Elements of the song return at the conclusion of the album. Now called 'Winter
Bird', the guitar riff described above acts as the prelude to 'When Winter Comes'.[11]
This song/track dates back to 1992 and was recorded during the sessions that
produced 'Calico Skies' and 'Great Day', each of which were featured on *Flaming
Pie* (1997). The lyric describes the kind of comfort one derives from following the
rhythms of the natural world. It mainly concerns the preparations one must make
in order to keep up with the change of seasons.

Paul McCartney repeatedly returns to nature for creative insights regarding
his artistic process. This certainly applies to his music, as can be heard in songs/
tracks such as 'Mother Nature's Son', 'Winter Rose/Love Awake', and 'Good Times
Coming/Feel the Sun'. However, it also applies to his work as a painter. In a conversation with Wolfgang Suttner, he was asked about the green colours featured in
his 1993 painting *Unfinished Symphony*. His response, which reaches across music
and the visual arts, is worth considering:

> Well, you know, one of my big inspirations is nature. I love nature and I love
> what it does. If you go down on the seashore and watch the water, see what
> it does to the sand, it bubbles up and goes back – what you could call chaos.
> And yet it's so beautiful, it leaves beautiful marks on the sand. I kind of trust to
> that, and that is a large part of painting abstracts – to try and think of myself
> as nature itself, without a mind, a sophisticated mind that knows how to play
> a piano.[12]

Notes

1 'Understanding McCartney. Ep 5: SIR PAUL'. YouTube. breathless345, 18 June 2020. https://youtu.be/AqS2z2Rbx2Y?t=1851.
2 'Paul McCartney – Creating Chaos at Abbey Road (Full Documentary in Full HD/ 60fps, 2007)'. YouTube. Kitsu Beatles, 4 June 2021. www.youtube.com/watch?v=IRNd _KKqJMI.
3 'Paul McCartney: Chaos and Creation at Abbey Road – YouTube'. YouTube. JimmyMcCullochFan, 21 January 2011. https://youtu.be/9elQeVfrLOo.
4 'Chaos and Creation in the Backyard (Album)'. The Paul McCartney project, 8 December 2014. www.the-paulmccartney-project.com/album/chaos-and-creation-in-the-backyard.
5 'Yesterday and Today – Rock's Renaissance Man Is Back on the Road'. The Paul McCartney project. Accessed 20 March 2022. www.the-paulmccartney-project.com/ interview/yesterday-and-today-rocks-renaissance-man-is-back-on-the-road.
6 'Chaos and Creation in the Backyard (Album)'. The Paul McCartney project, 8 December 2014. www.the-paulmccartney-project.com/album/chaos-and-creation-in-the-backyard.
7 Author's notes from The Abbey Road Lectures 2018 (3 August 2018).
8 Gaston Bachelard, *The Poetics of Space* (Boston, MA: Beacon Press, 1994), xxxvii.
9 Brian Clarke, *Paul McCartney: Paintings* (Boston, MA: Bulfinch Press, 2000), 56.
10 'Paul McCartney in Casual Conversation with Jarvis Cocker at LIPA'. YouTube. PAUL McCARTNEY, 15 August 2018. https://youtu.be/-gxdrjRqcZQ?t=1724.
11 'Recording "Great Day", "Calico Skies", "When Winter Comes" (Sep 03, 1992)'. The Paul McCartney project, 18 December 2020. www.the-paulmccartney-project.com/sess ion/flaming-pie-session-1.
12 Brian Clarke, *Paul McCartney: Paintings* (Boston, MA: Bulfinch Press, 2000), 54.

BIBLIOGRAPHY

Avedon, Elizabeth. *Rauschenberg*. New York: Random Hose, 1987.

Bachelard, Gaston. *The Poetics of Space*. Boston, MA: Beacon Press, 1994.

Beatles, The. *Anthology*. San Francisco, CA: Chronicle Books, 2000.

Bernstein, Leonard, *The Unanswered Question: Six Talks at Harvard*. Cambridge, MA: Harvard University Press, 1976.

Blaney, John. *John Lennon: Listen to This Book*. Paper Jukebox, 2005.

Bockris, Victor. *The Life and Death of Andy Warhol*. New York: Bantam Books, 1989.

Bockris, Victor. *Warhol: The Biography*. New York: Hachette Books, 2009.

Borja-Villel, Manuel, *Constant: New Babylon*. Amsterdam: MNCARS, 2015.

Browning, Robert. *The Poetical Works of Robert Browning with Portraits in Two Volumes, Volume I*. London: Smith Elder and Co., 1897.

Buckley, David. *Elton: The Biography*. Chicago, IL: Chicago Review Press, 2007.

Carlin, Peter Ames. *Paul McCartney: A Life*. New York: Touchstone, 2009.

Carroll, Lewis. *Alice in Wonderland and Through the Looking Glass*. Kingsport, TN: Kingsport Press (Grosset & Dunlap), 1946.

Carroll, Lewis. *The Unknown Lewis Carroll: 8 Major Works in Humor, Children's Material, Mathematical Recreations*. New York: Dover Publications, 1961.

Cavallaro, Dani. *Synesthesia and the Arts*. Jefferson, NC and London: McFarland & Company, Inc., 2013.

Chilton, John. *Who's Who in British Jazz*, 2nd edition. London: Continuum, 2004.

Chilvers, Ian, and Harold Osborne (eds.). *The Oxford Dictionary of Art*. Oxford: Oxford University Press, 1994.

Clarke, Brian. *Paul McCartney: Paintings*. Boston, MA: Bulfinch Press, 2000.

Clayson, Alan. *Woman: The Incredible Life of Yoko Ono*. New Malden: Chrome Dreams, 2004.

Clough, Matthew H., and Colin Fallows (eds.). *Stuart Sutcliffe: A Retrospective*. Liverpool: Victoria Gallery & Museum, Liverpool University Press, 2008.

Costello, Elvis. *Unfaithful Music and Disappearing Ink*. New York: Blue Rider Press, 2015.

Crocker, Terri Blom. *The Christmas Truce: Myth, Memory, and the First World War*. Lexington, KY: The University Press of Kentucky, 2015.

Danto, Arthur, C. *Andy Warhol*. New Haven, CT: Yale University Press, 2010.

Davis, Richard Brian. *Alice in Wonderland and Philosophy: Curiouser and Curiouser.* Hoboken, NJ: John Wiley & Sons, 2010.

Du Noyer, Paul. *Conversations with McCartney.* New York: The Overlook Press, 2016.

Emerick, Geoff, and Howard Massey. *Here, There, and Everywhere: My Life Recording the Music of The Beatles.* New York: Gotham Books, 2006.

Epstein, Michael, dir. *John and Yoko: Above Us Only Sky.* Wandsworth, London: Eagle Vision, 2019.

Eyre, Richard, and Nicholas Wright. *Changing Stages: A View of British and American Theatre in the Twentieth Century.* New York: Alfred A. Knopf, 2001.

Finneran, Richard J. (ed.). *The Collected Poems of W B. Yeats.* New York: Scribner Paperback Poetry, 1996.

Gambaccini, Paul (ed.). *Paul McCartney: In His Own Words.* London: Omnibus Press, 1976.

Gindin, James. *Galsworthy's Life and Art: An Alien's Fortress.* Houndmills, Basingstoke: The Macmillan Press Ltd., 1987.

Gingeras, Alison M. *The Avant-Garde Won't Give Up: Cobra and Its Legacy.* New York: Blum & Poe, 2017.

Gioia, Ted. *The Jazz Standards: A Guide to the Repertoire.* New York: Oxford University Press, 2012.

Giuliano, Geoffrey. *Blackbird: The Life and Times of Paul McCartney.* New York: Plume, 1992.

Glynn, Stephen. *A Hard Day's Night.* London: I.B. Taurus, 2005.

Granata, Charles L. *Wouldn't It Be Nice: Brian Wilson and the Making of The Beach Boys' Pet Sounds.* Chicago, IL: Chicago Review Press, 2003.

Haddix, Chuck. *Bird: The Life and Music of Charlie Parker.* Urbana, Chicago, and Springfield, IL: University of Chicago Press. 2013.

Hale, C.W. *A Short History of the Origins of Art and Design Further Education in Liverpool* (pamphlet). 1977 (courtesy of the archives of John Moores University).

Hamilton, Paul, Peter Gordon, and Dan Kieran (eds.). *How Very Interesting: Peter Cook's Universe and All That Surrounds It.* London: Snowbooks, 2006.

Harris, Jonathan. *Art History: The Key Concepts.* New York: Routledge, 2006.

Hess, Thomas. *Willem de Kooning.* New York: The Museum of Modern Art, 1968.

Higgins, Hannah. *Fluxus Experience.* Stanford, CA: University of California Press, 2002.

Hilton, Simon (ed.). *Imagine: John Lennon.* London: Universal Music Ltd., 2018.

Hilton, Simon (ed.). *John Lennon/Plastic Ono Band.* London: Universal Music Ltd., 2021.

Hoare, Philip. *Noël Coward: A Biography.* London: Sinclair-Stevenson, 1998.

Holdsworth, Nadine. *Joan Littlewood.* New York: Routledge, 2006.

Hrochova, Linda. *Sir Paul McCartney: His Life's Work and Its Contribution to British Culture.* 2012. BA Thesis. University of West Bohemia.

Hughes, Robert. *The Shock of the New.* London: Thames & Hudson, Ltd., 1991.

Jaffe, Hans L.C. *Picasso.* New York: Harry N. Abrams, Inc., 1983.

Johnstone, Nick. *Yoko Ono 'Talking'.* London: Omnibus Press, 2005.

Kandinsky, Wassily. *Concerning the Spiritual in Art.* Mineola, NY: Dover Publications, 2021.

Kennedy, Michael, and Joyce Bourne (eds.). *The Concise Oxford Dictionary of Music.* Oxford: Oxford University Press, 2004.

Kleiner, Fred S. *Gardner's Art Through the Ages: A Global History.* Boston, MA: Thompson Wadsworth, 2013.

Koestenbaum, Wayne. *Andy Warhol.* New York: Penguin Putnam, Inc., 2001.

Kurczynski, Karen. *The Cobra Movement in Postwar Europe: Reanimating Art.* New York and London: Routledge, 2021.

Kuspit, Donald. *The End of Art.* New York: Cambridge University Press, 2004.

Lanza, Robert, with Bob Berman. *Biocentrism: How Life and Consciousness Are the Keys to Understanding the True Nature of the Universe.* Dallas, TX: BenBella Books, Inc., 2009.

Lennon, John. *In His Own Write.* London: Jonathan Cape, 1964.

Lennon, John. *Skywriting by Word of Mouth.* New York: Harper Perennial, 1987.

Lennon, John. *Lennon Remembers.* London and New York: Verso, 2000.

Lennon, John. *A Spaniard in the Works.* London: Canongate Books, 2014.

Lennon, John, with Adrienne Kennedy and Victor Spinetti. *The Lennon Play: In His Own Write.* New York: Simon & Schuster, 1968.

Lennon, John, and Yoko Ono. *The Lennon Tapes: John Lennon and Yoko Ono in Conversation with Andy Peebles, 6 December 1980.* London: Jolly and Barber Ltd., 1981.

Lennon, John, and Yoko Ono. *Imagine John Yoko.* London: Thames & Hudson, Ltd., 2018.

Lester, Richard, dir. *A Hard Day's Night.* 1964. New York: The Criterion Collection, 2014, DVD.

Lester, Richard, dir. *Help!* 1965. Hollywood, CA: Capitol Records/Apple, 2007, DVD.

Lewisohn, Mark. *The Beatles Recording Sessions.* New York: Harmony Books, 1988.

Lewisohn, Mark. *The Complete Beatles Chronicle.* New York: Harmony Books, 1992.

Lewisohn, Mark. *Tune In: The Beatles All These Years, Volume 1.* New York: Crown Archetype, 2013.

Lindsay-Hogg, Michael, dir. *Let It Be.* 1970. Burbank, CA: Warner Home Video, 1984, VHS.

Lorca, Gabriel Garcia. *In Search of Duende.* New York: New Direction Books, 1998.

MacDonald, Ian, *Revolution in the Head: The Beatles' Records and the Sixties.* London: Vintage, 2008.

Madinger, Chip, and Mark Easter. *Eight Arms to Hold You: The Solo Beatles Compendium.* Chesterfield, MO: 44.1 Productions, 2000.

Marchand, Paul, dir. *Jaco.* 2015. Los Angeles, CA: Slang East/West, 2015, DVD.

Marom, Malka. *Joni Mitchell: In Her Own Words.* Toronto: ECW Press, 2014.

Martin, Henry. *Charlie Parker, Composer.* New York: Oxford University Press, 2020.

Masters, Robert E., and Jean Houston. *Mind Games.* New York: Dell, 1972.

McCartney, Paul. *Paul McCartney: Composer/Artist.* New York: MPL Communications, 1981.

McCartney, Paul. *Play Piano with … Paul McCartney.* London: Wise Publications, 2006.

McCartney, Paul. *The Lyrics: 1956 to the Present.* New York: Liveright, 2021.

Mellers, Wilfrid. *The Twilight of the Gods: The Music of The Beatles.* New York: Viking Press, 1973.

Miles, Barry, and Paul McCartney. *Many Years from Now.* New York: H. Holt, 1997.

Miller, Arthur I. *Einstein, Picasso: Space, Time, and the Beauty That Causes Havoc.* New York: Basic Books, 2001.

Mitchell, Joni. *Hejira.* New York: Warner Bros. Publications, 1977.

Morris, Catherine. *The Essential Willem de Kooning.* New York: The Wonderland Press, 1999.

Morris, Colin. *History of Liverpool Regional College of Art, 1825–1970.* 1985. MPhil thesis. Housed in Special Collection (courtesy of the archives of John Moores University).

Norman, Philip. *Elton John.* New York: Fireside, 1991.

Norman, Philip. *Shout! The Beatles in Their Generation.* New York: Simon & Schuster, 2005.

Norman, Philip. *John Lennon: The Life.* Toronto: Anchor Canada, 2009.

Norman, Philip. *Sir Elton.* London: Pan Macmillan, 2019.

O'Brien, Karen. *Shadows and Light: Joni Mitchell, the Definitive Biography.* London: Virgin Books, 2001.

O'Grady, Terence J. *The Beatles: A Musical Evolution.* Boston, MA: Twayne Publishers, 1983.

Orland, Ted. *The View from the Studio Door: How Artists Find Their Way in an Uncertain World.* Santa Cruz, CA and Eugene, OR: The Image Continuum Press, 2006.

Osborne, Harold (ed.). *The Oxford Companion to Twentieth-Century Art.* New York: Oxford University Press, 1981.

Peel, Ian. *The Unknown Paul McCartney: McCartney and the Avant-Garde.* London and Richmond, Surrey: Reynolds & Hearn, 2002.

Perasi, Luca. *Paul McCartney: Recording Sessions (1969–2013).* Milan: L.I.L.Y. Publishing, 2014.

Prendergast, Mark. *The Ambient Century: From Mahler to Moby.* London: Bloomsbury, 2003.

Priestly, Brian. *Chasin' the Bird: The Life and Legacy of Charlie Parker.* London: Equinox, 2005.

Randel, Don Michael (ed.). *The Harvard Concise Dictionary of Music and Musicians.* Cambridge, MA: Belknap Press, 1999.

Riley, Tim. *Tell Me Why: A Beatles Commentary.* New York: Alfred A. Knopf, 1988.

Rodriguez, Robert. *Fab Four FAQ 2.0: The Beatles' Solo Years, 1970–1980.* Milwaukee, WI: Backbeat Books, 2010.

Rothko, Mark. *The Artist's Reality: Philosophies of Art.* New Haven, CT: Yale University Press, 2012.

Ryan, Kevin, and Brian Kehew. *Recording The Beatles: The Studio Equipment and Techniques Used to Create Their Classic Albums.* Houston, TX: Curvebender Publishers, 2006.

Sabato, Larry J. *The Kennedy Half-Century: The Presidency, Assassination, and Lasting Legacy of John F. Kennedy.* New York: Bloomsbury, 2013.

Scott, Ken. *From Abbey Road to Ziggy Stardust.* Los Angeles, CA: Alfred Music Publishing, 2012.

Seuphor, Michel. *Abstract Painting: 50 Years of Accomplishment, from Kandinsky to the Present.* New York: Dell Publishing, 1964.

Sharp, Ken. *Starting Over: The Making of John Lennon and Yoko Ono's Double Fantasy.* New York: Gallery Books, 2010.

Sheff, David. *All We Are Saying: The Last Major Interview with John Lennon and Yoko Ono.* New York: St. Martin's Griffin, 2000.

Sounes, Howard. *Fab: An Intimate Life of Paul McCartney.* Cambridge, MA: Da Capo Press, 2010.

Southall, Brian. *Abbey Road: The Story of the World's Most Famous Recording Studios.* Cambridge: P. Stephens, 1982.

Spizer, Bruce. *The Beatles Solo on Apple Records.* New Orleans, LA: 498 Productions, 2005.

Stevens, Carolyn S. *The Beatles in Japan.* London and New York: Routledge, 2018.

Stevens, Mark, and Annalyn Swan. *De Kooning: An American Master.* New York: Alfred A. Knopf, 2004.

Stoker, Wessel. *Where Heaven and Earth Meet: The Spiritual in the Art of Kandinsky, Rothko, Warhol, and Kiefer.* New York: Rodopi, 2012.

Stokvis, Willemijn. *Cobra: The Last Avant-Garde Movement of the Twentieth Century.* Aldershot: Lund Humphries, 2004.

Sulpy, Doug, and Ray Schweighardt. *Get Back: The Unauthorized Chronicle of The Beatles' 'Let It Be' Disaster.* New York: St. Martin's Press, 1997.

Thomson, Elizabeth, and David Gutman (eds.). *The Lennon Companion: Twenty-Five Years of Comment.* Cambridge, MA: DaCapo Press, 2004.

Travers, P.L. *Mary Poppins: 80th Anniversary Collection.* New York: Houghton Mifflin Harcourt, 2014.

Tiffen, H.J. *A History of the Liverpool Institute Schools, 1825–1935.* Liverpool Institute Old Boys Association, 1935 (courtesy of the archives of John Moores University).

Visconti, Tony. *Bowie, Bolan, and the Brooklyn Boy.* New York: HarperCollins, 2007.

Webster, Roger, and Shonagh Wilkie. *The Making of a Modern University: Liverpool John Moores University.* London: Third Millennium Publishing, 2017 (courtesy of the archives of John Moores University).

Wilson, Brian, with Ben Greenman. *I Am Brian Wilson: A Memoir*. Boston, MA: Da Capo Press, 2016.

Wukovits, John. *Admiral 'Bull' Halsey: The Life and Wars of the Navy's Most Controversial Commander*. New York: Palgrave Macmillan, 2010.

Zinnemann, Fred, dir. *A Man for all Seasons*. 1966. Culver City, CA: Sony Pictures Home Entertainment, 2007, DVD.

Discography

Please Please Me, Parlophone, 1963.
With The Beatles, Parlophone, 1963.
A Hard Day's Night, Parlophone, 1964.
Beatles for Sale, Parlophone, 1964.
Help!, Parlophone, 1965.
Rubber Soul, Parlophone, 1965.
Rubber Soul, Capitol, 1965.
Pet Sounds, Capitol, 1966.
Revolver, Parlophone, 1966.
Sgt. Pepper's Lonely Hearts Club Band, Parlophone, 1967.
Smiley Smile, Capitol, 1967.
Magical Mystery Tour, Capitol, 1967.
The Beatles, Apple, 1968.
Abbey Road, Apple, 1969.
McCartney, Apple, 1970.
Let It Be, Apple, 1970.
John Lennon/Plastic Ono Band, Apple, 1970.
Yoko Ono/Plastic Ono Band, Apple, 1970.
Ram, Apple, 1971.
Imagine, Apple, 1971.
Fly, Apple, 1971.
Wild Life, Apple, 1971.
Some Time in New York City, Apple, 1972.
Approximately Infinite Universe, Apple, 1973.
Red Rose Speedway, Apple, 1973.
Goodbye Yellow Brick Road, DJM, 1973.
Mind Games, Apple, 1973.
Feeling the Space, Apple, 1973.
Band on the Run, Apple, 1973.
Caribou, DJM, 1974.
Walls and Bridges, Apple, 1974.
Rock and Roll, Apple, 1975.
Venus and Mars, Apple, 1975.
Shaved Fish, Apple, 1975.
Wings at the Speed of Sound, Capitol, 1976.
Hejira, Asylum, 1976.
Thrillington, Capitol, 1977.
London Town, Parlophone, 1978.
Wings' Greatest, Parlophone, 1978.
Back to the Egg, Columbia, 1979.

McCartney II, Columbia, 1980.
Double Fantasy, Geffen, 1980.
Season of Glass, Geffen, 1981.
Tug of War, Parlophone, 1982.
It's Alright (I See Rainbows), Polygram, 1982.
Pipes of Peace, Parlophone, 1983.
Milk and Honey, Geffen, 1984.
Give My Regards to Broad Street, Parlophone/EMI, 1984.
Press to Play, Parlophone, 1986.
Снова в СССР, Melodiya (Мелодия), 1988.
Flowers in the Dirt, Parlophone, 1989.
Paul McCartney's Liverpool Oratorio, EMI Classics, 1991.
Off the Ground, Parlophone, 1993.
Strawberries Oceans Ships Forest, Parlophone, 1993.
The Beatles Anthology 1, Apple, 1995.
The Beatles Anthology 2, Apple, 1996.
The Beatles Anthology 3, Apple, 1996.
The Ballad of the Skeletons, Mercury, 1997.
Flaming Pie, Parlophone, 1997.
Standing Stone, EMI Classics, 1997.
Rushes, Hydra/EMI, 1998.
Wide Prairie, Parlophone, 1998.
Chaos and Creation in the Backyard, Parlophone, 2005.
Egypt Station, Capitol, 2018.
McCartney III, Capitol, 2020.

INDEX

Beyond the Fringe 11, 26
'Big Barn Bed' 93
'Bip Bop' 88–89
'Bip Bop Link' 89
Bishop, Dave 158
'Blackbird' 53–54, 89, 114, 117, 175
Black Dyke Mills Band, The 123
Blake, Peter 46
Bluesology 109
Bobrowski, Russell Joseph 114
Bowlly, Al 14
Bradley, John 152
Branch, John K. 114
Brett, Adrian 142, 155
Britton, Geoff 113
'Broadcast, The' 124–125
Brown, Alan 54
Brown, Jason 30, 38n29
Browning, Robert 143
Buckmaster, Paul 109
'Bus Stop' 18
Butler, Gerry 148

Cage, John 52, 99
'Calico Skies' 169, 177
'Can't Buy Me Love' 18–19, 158
Capitol Records 49–50
Caribou 110
Carroll, Lewis 17, 40, 43, 48, 77
Casey, Howie 116, 123
Cavett, Dick 96
Ceiling Painting (YES Painting) 52
Celtic Eloquence 170
Chamberlain, Simon 152
Channel, Bruce 11
Chaos and Creation at Abbey Road 174
Chaos and Creation in the Backyard 174
Снова СССР 157
'Circus Animals' Desertion, The' 65
Clark, Tony 87, 88
Clarke, Stanley 140
Clements, Vassar 170
Cliff, Jimmy 111
Cloud Nine 164
'Cloud Piece' (poem) 79–80, 81, 112
C Minor 171, 172
Cobra movement 7
Cochran, Eddie 157
Cocker, Jarvis 176
'Cold Turkey' 70, 115
Collins, Phil 151
Coltrane, John 28
'Come Back Baby' 109
'Come Together' 57, 112

'Coming Up' 134–135, 136, 137
'Confirmation' 28
Connolly, Ray 91
Conversations with McCartney 124
Cook, Peter 26, 41
Cooke, Sam 157
Cooper, Michael 46
Cooper, Ray 93, 152
Corneille, Pierre 7
Costello, Elvis 109, 156, 157–158, 158–159, 163
Coward, Noël 11, 159
Creme, Lol 108, 124
Crocker, Terri Blom 142–143
'Cuff Link' 120

Danto, Arthur C. 44, 164
Davies, Ray 156
Davis, Carl 162–163
Davis, Chris 158, 159
Davis, Jesse Ed 111
'Day Tripper' 44
'Deaf Ted, Danoota, and Me' 26
Dean, John 148
'Dear Friend' 90, 171
'Dear Yoko' 136–137
de Kooning, Willem 154–155, 170
Del-Vikings 8
DeSalvo, Donna 44–45
Destro, Ron 166
Devlin, Keith 30–31
'Dialogue Room' 91
Dick James Music 109
Diddley, Bo 157
Diptych 44
'Distractions' 159–160
Domino, Fats 157
'Don't Let It Bring You Down' 150
'Don't Let the Sun Go Down on Me' 110
Dorsey, Tony 113, 114, 115, 116, 123
Double Fantasy 131, 136, 137, 138, 143
Dougal, Robert 108
'Dougal bits' 108
'Do You Want to Know a Secret?' 18
'Drive My Car' 33
Dudgeon, Gus 109
Du Noyer, Paul 66, 90, 132, 135
Dwight, Reginald Kenneth 109
Dylan, Bob 26–27, 55, 156

'Eat at Home' 77–78, 94
Echoes 163
Ed Davis, Jesse 110
Edwards, Gordon 97, 98